Infants, Toddlers, and Caregivers

FIFTH EDITION

Janet Gonzalez-Mena
Napa Valley College

Dianne Widmeyer Eyer
Cañada College

D0025559

Mayfield Publishing Company
Mountain View, California
London • Toronto

To Magda Gerber

Library of Congress Cataloging-in Publication Data

Gonzalez-Mena, Janet.
     Infants, toddlers and caregivers / Janet Gonzalez-Mena, Dianne Widmeyer Eyer. — 5th ed.
          p.   cm.
     Includes bibliographical references and index.
     ISBN 0-7674-1684-8 (alk. paper)
     1. Child care—United States.   2. Child development—United States.   3. Education, Preschool—Activity programs—United States.
I. Eyer, Dianne Widmeyer.   II. Title.
HQ778.7.U6G66   2000
362.71'2—dc20   00-02355

Manufactured in the United States of America

10   9   8   7   6   5   4   3   2

Mayfield Publishing Company
1280 Villa Street
Mountain View, CA 94041

Sponsoring editor, Franklin C. Graham; production editor, Windy Johnson; copyeditor, Mary Ray Worley; design manager, Glenda King; art manager, Rennie Evans; cover designer, Joan Greenfield; cover photograph, Rich Shulman; manufacturing manager, Randy Hurst. The text was set in 10/12 New Baskerville Roman by TBH Typecast, Inc., and printed on 50# French Opaque by R. R. Donnelley & Sons Company.

Acknowedgments and copyrights continue at the back of the book on page 299, which constitutes an extension of the copyright page.

 This book is printed on acid-free paper.

Contents

Part 3   Focus on the Program

Preface

The field of early education is constantly changing. Consider, for example, the sleeping positions of newborns. For years, pediatricians have told parents to put babies to sleep on their stomachs. The theory was that if babies were placed on their backs they might vomit and choke. Recent research has changed that view, however. It has been shown that laying babies on their stomachs increases their risk of Sudden Infant Death Syndrome (SIDS or crib death). Medical experts now say that babies should sleep on their backs or sides. Luckily, this book was one step ahead of medical research in this area.

The philosophy behind this text is based on the philosophy of Magda Gerber, an expert in infant care, who is originally from Hungary but now resides in Los Angeles. Gerber has always advocated putting babies down on their backs. We didn't highlight that fact in the first three editions of this book because it went against the official advice of the American Pediatric Association. However, we didn't support the advice to put babies on their stomachs either, so we just quietly left it out.

An important feature of any textbook is to stay current with the issues. Through regular updating, this book has managed to keep current without diluting its main philosophy, which is to record recent research but also to maintain a focus on practical application.

Perhaps the most important feature of the book is the consistency with which it outlines well-established practices designed to promote children's total well-being, including physical growth and development, mental health, emotional stability, and human relationships. Research on brain development in animals once again threatens to push the field in the direction of simplistic prepackaged training programs that focus on infant stimulation. This book is designed to counterbalance one-sided treatments that do not consider all facets of a child's development. To that end, we wove implications of the latest brain research into every chapter!

Also, we continue to focus on several issues raised by the Child and Family Studies training team at the Far West Laboratory for Educational Research (particularly Dr. J. Ronald Lally, Dr. Peter Mangione, and Sheila Signer, as well as two experts in infant care at the California Department of Education: Janet Poole and Mary Smithberger). They have drawn attention to the importance that sensitive care and proper program planning have on the identity formation in infants and toddlers. The factors that influence identity formation include culturally sensitive caregiving, continuity of care, group size, and primary caregiving systems.

As before, we are concerned about the inclusion of infants and toddlers with special needs in child care and early education programs. Caregivers need to understand how to care for children with all kinds of needs, because children with disabilities and atypical development are entering child care at a greater rate than ever before. The goal is to place all children in "natural environments," which mean that those with special needs will be in the same environments as their typically developing peers. So this book's focus on inclusion is timely and useful. The skills and sensitivity emphasized here can help caregivers make a difference in the development of all children, including those with special needs.

Responding to diversity is a necessity, and we've focused more on cultural differences in this edition, even though we still present a cohesive philosophy without confusing it with multiple views on each and every subject.

This book has always been about curriculum in infant-toddler programs, even though that word isn't in the title. Today as more and more people in the field are looking for clear and easy answers, they are turning to books that have the word curriculum in the title. We've tried to explain even more strongly that this book is a curriculum—it's a respectful and responsive curriculum based on relationships.

Gender equity is mentioned frequently in this book. We point out the pitfalls of gender role stereotyping and ask the reader to consider what subtle messages adults give that narrow rather than expand children's views of appropriate gender behavior.

Bilingualism is promoted in the text. An important part of caregiver training is learning to understand, acknowledge, and respond to language and cultural differences. Knowing how to promote home language is also important.

A unique feature of this book is the focus on the reader's personal experience. Regularly throughout the book, questions are asked that require self-examination. Only through understanding ourselves can we understand infants and toddlers. Sensitivity is an important qualification for anyone who works with very young children, because the children are still mostly in the preverbal state. Self-examination on the part of the adult is an important key to increased sensitivity.

The book is divided into three parts and is organized in a unique way. Instead of starting with standard child development information and its practical application, part 1 focuses on the caregiver's actions and relationships with the children. By starting with the *interactive* aspect of caregiving, we highlight the philosophy from the beginning pages of the book. Part 1 is an explanation of how the caregivers' actions and interactions with the children make up the curriculum in infant-toddler programs, both center based and in family day care.

Part 2 presents basic child development information along with the curriculum implications of that information. Part 2 reflects the basic philosophy found throughout the book.

Part 3 looks at additional infant-toddler child-care components and includes environments as well as adult-adult relationships. These are examined from a programmatic point of view in both center and family child care settings.

Appendix A is a checklist for determining quality in infant-toddler programs. Appendix B includes an environmental chart that combines the information from all three parts into one concise but comprehensive chart designed for practical use in program design and implementation. The chart tells you what to do when, and with what, based on infants' and toddlers' specific stage-related developmental needs. Appendix C contains a short paper that explains the issue of curriculum and lesson plans. Written by Dr. J. Ronald Lally of WestEd's Program for Infant Toddler Caregivers, this paper can relieve the minds of caregivers who are mandated to write lesson plans. Appendix D gives a sample set of guiding principles for working in partnership with parents. The principles used as examples are from the Parent Services Project (P.S.P.), headed by Lisa Lee and Ethel Seiderman.

Although designed for preservice training of child care workers and family child-care providers who work with children under three years of age, the book has also been useful for other purposes, such as parent education and in-service training.

The book has been used as a text for students in the classroom as well as an on-the-job training tool by community college and four-year college teachers, public health nurses, social workers, counselors, program directors, training coordinators, parent educators, high school child development teachers, and teachers in teen parent programs.

The overall goal of the book is to help readers gain knowledge and be able to apply that knowledge while exploring and understanding their own experience as it relates to the subject matter. As readers gain understanding, they also develop a perspective that helps them find their own unique ways of relating to the children they will care for. This approach increases the reader's confidence in his or her ability to relate to very young children in whole and healthy ways.

We wish to thank those who reviewed the manuscript: Cheryl Dreska, Kishwaukee College; Rebecca Marine, Cerritos College; Tisha Rivera, California State University, Los Angeles; Linda H. Ruhmann, San Antonio College; and Sandra Tucker, Palomar College.

Introduction

This new edition of *Infants, Toddlers, and Caregivers* comes at a time when interest in infants is booming. New information from brain research is drawing everybody's attention to the early years: parents, scientists, educators, policy makers, even entertainers like Rob Reiner, who put on a national campaign to draw attention to the importance of a good start in infancy. In addition, with welfare reform in full swing, infants are coming into child care in far greater numbers than ever before. Early Head Start is making a difference too. Across the United States programs are coming into being with the goal of strengthening families' abilities to relate to and care for their infants. Never before in the experience of the two authors has there been such a widespread interest in babies. It's as if a whole nation has opened its eyes and discovered that babies are not just cute little blobs but full human beings with lots of capabilities and needs. We're trying hard not to say "We told you so!"

The challenge now is to create programs that are good for infants and toddlers and to train caregivers to work in such programs. Poor-quality care harms children. We must ensure that every child in this nation has good-quality care. That means increased attention and resources! It also means awareness of the need to improve salary and status issues for caregivers. The turnover rate is high, so if infants and toddlers are to make connections and feel at home and comfortable in child care, we have to work hard as a society to find ways to keep caregivers happy in their jobs so they won't leave.

This book is part of the picture of improving child care in that it can support the skill development and knowledge acquisition that caregivers need to work successfully and sensitively in the field.

ABOUT THE AUTHORS

The authors of this text became concerned with some of the questions relating to the quality and training in the mid-1970s while teaching child and infant development at Cañada College in Redwood City, California. Janet Gonzalez-Mena became an intern in Magda Gerber and Dr. Tom Forrest's program, the Demonstration Infant Program (now called Resources for Infant Educarers—R.I.E.), where she learned the philosophy on which this book is based.[1] Dianne Widmeyer Eyer completed a second master's degree in special education and developed curriculum in early childhood special education, with a sensitivity toward quality intervention for young children with disabilities.

A few years later both authors became more involved with family child care. As Director of Child Care Services for Family Service Agency in San Mateo County, California, Janet supervised a network of family child-care homes that served infants and toddlers (as well as preschoolers). Under her direction, the agency opened a new infant center and also created a pilot program of therapeutic child care for abused and neglected infants and toddlers. Dianne worked with the Child Care Coordinating Council of San Mateo County to develop a Certificate Training Program for Family Child Care Providers at Cañada College. This curriculum also models the Gerber philosophy of respect and responsiveness for infant-toddler care. Janet went on to teach at Napa Valley College until she retired from there in 1998. Today Janet continues to educate and train infant-toddler caregivers in a variety of settings. She is currently a visiting faculty member for Pacific Oaks College in northern California and also works with WestEd's Program for Infant Toddler Caregivers training trainers. She also continues to write articles and books. Dianne continues to be very involved in her role as the Early Childhood–Child Development Program Coordinator at Cañada College. She recently completed a new curriculum specialization in Family Support, working in collaboration with Ethel Seiderman, the director of Parent Services Project, Inc. This specialization is the first of its kind in California. Dianne is also a Professional Growth Adviser for the California Child Development Permit.

SPECIAL FEATURES OF THE NEW EDITION

The new brain research and its implications for infant-toddler care are to be found in nearly every chapter. We didn't avoid the controversy either, which is just beginning to brew as we finish up this revision. We point out myths that are a natural consequence of any scientific breakthrough. We also point out the pitfalls of misinterpreting the implications for infants and toddlers.

Special needs have always been a concern of ours, and they become even more important in this edition as many more infant-toddler programs will be taking in children who formerly might have been rejected from child care. Too often in the past someone decided arbitrarily it would be too hard to meet the special needs of some children. The amendments to the Individuals with Disabilities Education Act (IDEA), which took effect in 1998, make it illegal to exclude children with disabilities from child care unless there is proof that the child's needs cannot be met.

Sensitivity to parents and to diversity continues to be an interest of ours. We've expanded our attention to cultural differences, even though we still haven't gone all the way to fully incorporate diversity in this text. Because we are trying to present a cohesive philosophy, we don't want to distract the reader with widely varying views. The more we understand about cultural differences, the more we appreciate the numbers of areas of disagreement about infants and toddlers—who they are and what they need. Those arguments and disagreements are beyond the scope of this book, but they can be found in Janet's *Multicultural Issues in Child Care,* a suggested companion text for this one.

If caregivers work in programs in which parents sign up because of the particular philosophy of the program, it's important that the program stick to the philosophy as advertised. But many times parents have little choice about where to place their infant or toddler in child care. They find themselves in a program in which the philosophy is different from what they believe in and want for their children. In that case it is important to be sensitive to the needs and goals of those parents. The program doesn't have to give up its philosophy, but it must recognize and respond to differing perspectives. When dissonance occurs, communication skills are called for, along with some time and attention to solving the problems that can arise. When caregivers put themselves in the parents' shoes, they are better caregivers for that family's children.

We listened to reviewers who worried we might have focused too much on center-based care and not enough on family child care. We revised with that in mind, looking at where we might have neglected family child care providers. In the physical environment chapter we added a section on working with infants and toddlers as part of a mixed age group in a family child care home.

Curriculum and lesson plans are a major issue for some caregivers who are being asked to put things in writing. We tried even harder to explain our all-inclusive concept of curriculum that centers on connections and relationships. To put it briefly, curriculum has to do with respecting and responding to each child's needs in warm and sensitive ways that promote attachment and development. We also included in the appendix a short paper, written by Dr. J. Ronald Lally of WestEd's Program for Infant Toddler Caregivers, which explains the issue of curriculum. Many directors and caregivers struggle with what it means to "educate" a child under three. The new brain research has made this an even bigger question. Too many people are still looking to school-type models and creating adult-directed "cognitive" games and activities. Even child-directed activities, often the major focus of adult attention, can be a disservice to infants and toddlers. When adults put a good deal of effort into planning for and implementing "activities," they take attention away from the real prime times for learning. Instead of focusing on relationships, they focus on gathering materials, setting up, and cleaning up. The important learning comes in one-to-one interactions with infants and toddlers that occur during caregiving times and between the planned activities. To the uninitiated, very little that naturally occurs in an infant center or even a toddler program looks educational. One of the purposes of this book is to help the reader better articulate to the uninitiated how infant-toddler care is much more than just custodial care but is truly educational as well.

THEORY VERSUS PRACTICE AND THE PROBLEM OF ANALYSIS PARALYSIS

Knowing *about* is different from knowing *how to*. Knowing about means learning theory. Knowing how to puts theory into action. We purposely organized this book to emphasize action because we know that even people with considerable understanding of infants and toddlers have trouble acting on that understanding unless they have also learned to *apply* theory. Knowledge does not necessarily build skill.

Caregivers who have knowledge but lack confidence in their ability to use it may suffer from "analysis paralysis," which prevents caregivers from making quick decisions, from stating their feelings clearly, and from taking needed action.[2] A common pattern when analysis paralysis strikes is inaction, then indecision, then overemotional or otherwise inappropriate reaction, followed by more inaction. Take for example an inexperienced caregiver in an infant-toddler center who stands by, watching a toddler throwing sand in the air, unsure whether the child's obvious enjoyment of this new accomplishment is more important than the possibility of getting sand in her (or someone else's) eyes. The caregiver may hang back, doing nothing for a time, then hesitantly suggest that the child stop, but do nothing when the child continues. She may say or do nothing until the conflict within grows strong enough to cause another reaction. This time she may laugh and play with the child, enjoying with her the pleasure of her new discovery, until sand gets in someone's eyes, at which time the caregiver may angrily remind the child that she told her to stop a long time ago.

When adults have analysis paralysis and either cannot react or react inconsistently, infants cannot learn to predict what will happen as the result of their own actions. This learning to predict what effect they have on the world is the primary accomplishment of infants in early life. Depriving them of this learning affects their development.

Because of internal conflicts, adults may put up with behavior that bothers them. Infants and toddlers can sense adult conflicts. They then continue with behavior that adults disapprove of—testing to see what will happen. They get no clear message about the approved way to behave or about the effects of their behavior.

A PHILOSOPHY OF RESPECT

As in the first edition, *Infancy and Caregiving*, respect is the foundation of the philosophy on which this book is built. Is respect different from kindness and warmth? The answer is yes. What does it mean to "respect" infants and toddlers? The answer to that question lies in the ten principles on which the book is based:

1. Involve infants and toddlers in things that concern them. Don't work around them or distract them to get the job done faster.
2. Invest in quality time, when you are totally available to individual infants and toddlers. Don't settle for supervising groups without focusing (more than just briefly) on individual children.
3. Learn each child's unique ways of communicating (cries, words, movements, gestures, facial expressions, body positions), and teach them yours. Don't underestimate children's ability to communicate even though their verbal language skills may be nonexistent or minimal.
4. Invest time and energy to build a total person (concentrate on the "whole child"). Don't focus on cognitive development alone or look at it as separate from total development.
5. Respect infants and toddlers as worthy people. Don't treat them as objects or cute little empty-headed people to be manipulated.
6. Be honest about your feelings around infants and toddlers. Don't pretend to feel something that you don't or not to feel something that you do.
7. Model the behavior you want to teach. Don't preach.
8. Recognize problems as learning opportunities, and let infants and toddlers try to solve their own. Don't rescue them, constantly make life easy for them, or try to protect them from all problems.
9. Build security by teaching trust. Don't teach distrust by being undependable or often inconsistent.
10. Be concerned about the *quality* of development in each stage. Don't rush infants and toddlers to reach developmental milestones.

These principles are shown in action throughout the book, especially in part 1. They are supported by the information on infant and toddler development in part 2. They underlie the information on programs in part 3.

TERMINOLOGY

In this book the youngest children—those from newborn to walking—are called infants. The children who are walking (from about a year old) to two years are called young toddlers. Children from two to three are called older toddlers. Children from three to five are called preschoolers.

What to call the adults in this book was a concern. Adults in the teacher/caregiver role go by different titles, depending on where they work. Magda Gerber coined the term "educarers," which she uses to call the people she trains to work with children under three. We decided to call the adults in this book "caregivers" to simplify matters and to emphasize the importance of "caring" in programs for the youngest children. The caregiver role incorporates that of teacher, educator, child rearer, and surrogate parent.

The message of this book is that infants and toddlers need attention to their physical and psychological needs; a relationship with someone they can trust; respect; a safe, healthy, and developmentally appropriate environment; chances to interact with other infants and toddlers; and freedom to explore using all their senses. The purpose of this book is to show, in as visual a way as possible, just how all those elements fit together in a child care program.

Notes

1. The original ideas and research for the philosophy came from Emmi Pikler, M.D., who has been known for her work not only in her native Hungary but also all over Europe and the United States.
2. As far as we know, the expression "analysis paralysis" was first used by Lilian Katz, professor of early childhood education at the University of Illinois.

CHAPTER 1

Principles of Caregiving

This book emphasizes relationships—those between caregivers and very young children. Relationships don't just spring into being—they grow. They grow from a number of interactions. So this book is also about interactions—not just any kind of interactions, but those that are **respectful, responsive,** and **reciprocal.** Here is an example of a "three-r" interaction.

A five-month-old is lying on the floor with several toys scattered within reach. She is contentedly surveying the six other infants and toddlers who are in the room with her. Reaching now and then, she caresses a toy first with her eyes, then with her hands. As we look more closely, we can see that some suspicious moisture has crept onto the infant's outer clothes in the area of her bottom. We are seeing a very contented, but a very wet, young person. A step is heard, and the infant's eyes travel in the direction of the sound. Then we see a pair of legs and feet traveling along in the direction of the infant. A voice says, "Caitlin, I'm wondering how you're getting along."

The legs move over close to the blanket, and the rest of the person appears. A kindly face comes close. Caitlin smiles and makes a cooing noise. The caregiver responds, then notices the dampness of the clothing. "Oh, Caitlin, you need a change," she says. Caitlin responds by smiling and cooing.

Reaching out her hands, the caregiver says, "I'm going to pick you up now." Caitlin responds to the gesture and words with an ever-so-slight body movement. She continues to smile and coo. The caregiver picks her up. As they walk across the room, Caitlin reaches for a toy lying just out of reach on a shelf.

"I know you want that toy, but you have to wait a few minutes," says the caregiver with understanding. "First I am going to change your diaper," she adds with gentle firmness. She lays Caitlin on the changing table.

Caitlin's attention wanders around the room. The caregiver talks to her, bringing her gaze back to her own face.

"Look Caitlin, I'm taking off the wet diaper." She shows her the diaper. Caitlin watches, but then starts to squirm, fussing a little.

"See where the diaper goes?" The caregiver once again retrieves her attention by making a production of disposing of the wet diaper.

"Now the dry diaper, Caitlin . . ." The caregiver shows her the fresh diaper. Caitlin reaches for it. "Yes, you can touch, it," responds the caregiver.

"Lift up," says the caregiver, patting her bottom. Caitlin is distracted by a noise in another part of the room. The caregiver waits. Then when she has her attention again, she repeats, "Lift up, please." She raises Caitlin's bottom as she says this, and slips the dry diaper under.

"Susan, look—I fixed it!" says a young voice.

The caregiver keeps her attention focused on Caitlin. "I can't come right now, Greg. I'm changing Caitlin. I'll be with you when I'm finished."

Caitlin has begun to squirm. She tries to roll over. "We're almost finished now." The caregiver pats her, bringing her back to the task. "Look, I'm fastening it now."

Caitlin squirms to look. "I like the way you're paying attention." The caregiver smiles.

"Okay, that's it; we're finished. Want to come up now?" She reaches out for her.

Caitlin stretches out her arms, making bubbling noises at the same time. The caregiver imitates her sounds. Both laugh. Then the caregiver picks Caitlin up in her arms and gives her a hug.

Notice the chain reaction as the caregiver responded to Caitlin, who responded to her, who in turn responded to Caitlin's response. This scene illustrates a responsive interaction chain that is the basis of effective caregiving. A number of interactions such as this kind of diaper changing build a partnership. This feeling of being part of a team instead of an object to be manipulated is vital to wholesome development. Reciprocal interactions like these promote attachment between caregiver and child. This scene illustrates principle 1.

PRINCIPLE 1: INVOLVE INFANTS AND TODDLERS IN THINGS THAT CONCERN THEM

Caitlin isn't just the recipient of her caregiver's actions; she's a participant in what happens to her. She and her caregiver do things together. If the caregiver had given Caitlin a toy to play with to keep her occupied while she changed her diapers, the whole tone of the scene would have been different. The partnership would have vanished, and in its place would have been a distracted child and a caregiver dealing with a damp bottom and a wet diaper instead of a whole child. Or if she had distracted her with other sorts of entertainment, the caregiver still would have had Caitlin's attention, but focus would have been on fun and games rather than on the task at hand.

The caregiver's primary goal in this scene was to keep Caitlin involved in the interaction as well as focused on her own body and on what was happening to it. Diapering then became an "educational experience," through which Caitlin increased attention span, body awareness, and cooperation. A number of experiences like these give Caitlin an education in human relations from which she can build her whole outlook toward life and people.

Why should diapering be the first example in this book? Diapering involves one-to-one interactions, and it occurs regularly. Imagine the amount of time spent in diapering each child each day. That time adds up. If the time spent together is quality time—that is, time when both partners are fully present, focused on the same task at hand—diapering can provide a lot of educational time.

There is a rumor that infants and toddlers have short attention spans. They can't pay attention to anything for very long, some people say. You can test that rumor for yourself. Watch an infant or toddler who is actually involved in something that concerns and interests him. Clock the amount of time he spends on the task or event. You may be surprised at what a long attention span infants and toddlers have when they are interested because they are involved. Consider how long Caitlin paid attention to her diapering because she was involved in the task.

Think about a time in your own life when you were involved in a respectful, responsive, reciprocal interaction. You don't have to be an infant to experience the focused attention of someone else. This can happen when someone is teaching you something. Or it can happen when you are in the doctor's office. Can you use your own experience to help you understand the benefits that babies derive from being involved in the things that concern them?

PRINCIPLE 2: INVEST IN QUALITY TIME

The scene between Caitlin and her caregiver is a good example of one kind of quality time. The caregiver was fully present. That is, she was attending to what was going on; her thoughts were not somewhere else. How often caregiving tasks are done routinely, with neither caregiver nor infant present any way but physically! This caregiver was quite conscious of quality time, as is evident by the way she handled Greg's interruption. How much more efficient it would have been to deal with him at the same time she was changing the baby. Obviously it is easy to diaper and talk to someone else at the same time. Yet she valued the time together with Caitlin and apparently had taught Greg about its value. He was probably so willing to leave her alone and wait his turn only because he had experienced quality time himself. Otherwise he might well have continued to try for her attention. He perhaps knew that when she finished with Caitlin, then he might have some minutes of quality time himself.

Magda Gerber calls the kind of quality time illustrated by the diapering scene "wants something" quality time. The adult and child are involved in a task the caregiver has set up. Diapering, feeding, bathing, and dressing fit into this category of quality time. If the caregiver pays attention to the child, and asks in return that the child pay attention, the amount of "wants something" quality time mounts up. In child care programs this can provide the one-to-one interactions that may be difficult to attain in a group setting. "Wants something" quality time is educational.

Another kind of equally important quality time is what Magda Gerber calls "wants nothing" quality time. This happens when caregivers make themselves available without directing the action, for instance, just sitting near babies, fully available and responsive but not in charge. Just being with toddlers while they play, responding rather than initiating, describes this type of quality time.

The Child-Family Study Center at the University of California at Davis uses "floor time" in their toddler program. "Floor time" is a concept they credit to Stanley Greenspan's work.

When a toddler is exhibiting difficult behavior, instead of putting the child in "time out" and trying to ignore her, they do the opposite. They don't withdraw attention; they give more. The child is given a half hour of one-on-one time with an adult whose sole goal is to be **responsive** to that child and that child alone. The adult sits on the floor, available to the child. The environment is conducive to play, as there are interesting toys within reach. The adult has no plan or expectation but just waits to see what the child will do and then responds. This is the opposite of the common approach in programs where teachers and caregivers become even more directive rather than less in the face of difficult behavior.

The adults at the Child-Family Study Center are directive only when they remove the child from the classroom. They explain where they are going, but use no shame and no punishing overtones. Floor time may seem like being sent to the principal's office, but it's more like play therapy. However, the staff aren't therapists, and floor time isn't therapy. It's merely "wants nothing" quality time. For a half hour the child is given total attention.

Does the child become "spoiled" with such lavish attention? No. According to reports, this approach works miracles. Its effectiveness seems to lie in the fact that it meets the child's needs.

Many psychotherapists attest to the benefits of being fully present to another person without being directive; yet most of us seldom get this kind of attention from the people in our lives. Think for a moment of the delight of having someone's whole attention at your command for more than a moment or so.

This kind of quality time is easy to give, but often not understood or valued. Caregivers just sitting on the floor where babies and toddlers are playing sometimes feel as though they are not doing their job. They want to play the role of teachers, which they interpret as "teaching something." It is very hard for most adults to be around small children and not be directive. Being receptive and responsive is a skill most adults need to learn; it doesn't seem to just come naturally. Try it yourself. Choose a time when you will not initiate, only respond. See how long you can keep in the receptive, responsive mode.

Another kind of quality time, perhaps the most commonly understood, is shared activity. The initiating mode moves back and forth between adult and child during playtimes as the two enjoy each other's company. These times are often rewarding for the caregiver in ways that the other two kinds of quality time are not.

An interesting aspect of quality time is that a little goes a long way. No one wants (or can stand) intense interaction all the time—even when it is fun and games. Children (and adults) need to be private as well. Although privacy is not an issue with all families; for some it is a strong cultural value. In infant-toddler programs and in family day care, time alone is hard to attain. Some children manage to be alone only by sleeping. Others can focus inwardly and ignore what's going on around them. The adult can help young children gain private time by providing small spaces. (See chapter 12, Physical Environment.)

When people never have time alone, they get it by drifting off, by not paying attention, by being elsewhere mentally if not physically. This attitude becomes a habit, so that time spent constantly together tends to become time when the person is "only half there." "Half-there" time, even lots of it, never equals "all-there time."

Being able to "turn off" is an issue for caregivers as well as infants and toddlers. No adult can be expected to be completely present and responsive to others all day every day. Provision must be made for both adults' and babies' needs in programs if the adults are to be effective caregivers.

Of course every person's life is filled with time that is neither quality time nor private time. Children have to learn to live in a busy world of people. They are bound to get ignored, moved from place to place, or worked around sometimes. The point is that there is a difference between quality time and other kinds of time and that all children deserve and need some quality time in their lives.

Quality time is built into the daily routine when diapering, dressing, and feeding become occasions for close one-to-one interactions. In group care in which a caregiver is responsible for several babies or a small group of toddlers, paying attention to just one child may be difficult unless caregivers free each other up by taking turns supervising the rest of the children. It is up to the director to ensure that each caregiver be freed at times from responsibility for children other than the one she is changing or feeding. That means that it must be permissible, even encouraged, for a caregiver to focus on just one child.

In family day care where there is no other adult, the caregiver has no one else to turn to when she feeds or diapers a baby. But caregivers can still focus on just one child by setting up a safe environment and encouraging the rest of the children to play on their own. Of course the caregiver must still keep a watchful eye on the group—a skill that can be developed with practice. It's amazing to watch an experienced caregiver give full attention to one child but still manage to catch a dangerous or forbidden action going on in another part of the room.

PRINCIPLE 3: LEARN EACH CHILD'S UNIQUE WAYS OF COMMUNICATING AND TEACH THEM YOURS

Notice how the communication between Caitlin and her caregiver worked. The caregiver talked directly to Caitlin about what she was going to do, using body movements that matched her words. Caitlin used her body, facial expressions, and voice to communicate her responses. The caregiver responded to her responses by interpreting, answering, and discussing. The caregiver did not carry on endless chatter. She said little, but what she said carried a lot of meaning, backed up by action. She is teaching Caitlin to listen, not tune out. She is teaching that talking is communication, not distraction. She is teaching words and language in context, by talking naturally, not repeating words over and over, or using baby talk. She also communicated with her body and with sounds other than words—and she responded to Caitlin's communication (sounds, facial expressions, and body movements). The communication between Caitlin and her caregiver went way beyond words.

Think about someone you know very well. Can you remember some ways that person communicates with you without using words? Facial expressions are obvious ways, but each person has certain little gestures or actions that give hints about what he or she is feeling. If you make a list of the nonverbal means of communication of someone you know well, you'll see how each of us has a unique system. No one knows a baby's or toddler's system as well as those people to whom he or she is attached. For that reason (and others) programs for infants and toddlers should encourage attachment between the children and the caregivers.

It's also important to note here that each of us uses a system of body language that is particular to our culture, and within the culture specific to gender, and perhaps social class as well. Just one example is in the difference in how men and women in white, European-derived, North American culture cross their legs. Another example is the contrasting walk between the African-American man and the African-American woman. These are unconscious positions and movements, but members of the culture know them well. Children learn the rudiments of culturally based nonverbal communication from adults in their lives, as well as creating their own body language that is specific to them.

Eventually babies come to depend more on words to express themselves in addition to other means of communication. They learn to express needs, wants, ideas, and feelings more and more clearly. They also learn to enjoy language for itself—to play with words, phrases, and sounds. Adult reactions and encouragement to use language facilitate their development. By late toddlerhood most children can express themselves in words, though, of course, they continue to use nonverbal communication throughout their lives.

It is important to recognize that some cultures value and depend on verbal exchanges more than others. European-Americans tend to use direct communication. Because babies can't talk (in fact the word origin of "infant" can be traced back through Middle English to Old French where it is a combination of "in" [not] and "fans" [speaking]) researchers at the University of California at Davis have found a way around that problem. They discovered that they can introduce direct communication to babies by teaching a gesturing system.[1] Caregivers from highly verbal cultures need to be extra sensitive to children who use a good deal of nonverbal communication instead of words.[2]

Young children should see adults using words that match their nonverbal communication. If the face and body movements say one thing and the words say something else, children are receiving double messages, which get in the way of true communication. They not only have problems deciding which to believe, but they model after the adult and thus learn to give double messages themselves. Clear communication is important.

PRINCIPLE 4: INVEST TIME AND ENERGY TO BUILD A TOTAL PERSON

The implications of the new brain research support the goal of building a total person instead of concentrating on cognitive development alone. An article written by J. Ronald Lally for *Exchange* magazine, "Brain Research, Infant Learning, and Child Care Curriculum" (May 1998), explains the connections. Because some parents realize that the early years are important ones in intellectual growth, whether or not they have heard about the brain research, they may expect to see some evidence that caregivers are providing "cognitive activities." Their concept of cognitive activities may be based on what they know about preschool. They may expect caregivers to teach such concepts as colors, shapes, even numbers and letters through an activity approach.

On the other side, caregivers, also concerned with intellectual development, may think that the way to promote it is through specialized equipment, exercises, or activities. Books and programs are readily available for a price to, as they say, "stimulate cognitive development." Catalogs and stores are full of toys, equipment, and gadgets advertised as making babies smarter. Of course providing a rich environment with interesting things to do is desirable. And yes, you can promote cognitive development. But be careful about falling into the trap of thinking that you can stimulate cognitive development without working on physical, social, and emotional development at the same time. It isn't the clever little toys that you provide or activities you do with the children that make a difference. It's the day-to-day living, the relationships, the experiences, the diaperings, the feedings, the toilet training, and the playing that contribute to intellectual development. And those same experiences help the child grow physically, socially, and emotionally as well.

Think of how rich the experience of diapering was for Caitlin. She was immersed in sensory input—visual, auditory, tactile, olfactory. How often are caregivers and parents told to hang a mobile over the changing table so that the diapering can be an "educational experience." How limited an experience a mobile provides compared with what Caitlin was enjoying.

Also consider that some cultures are not as concerned about cognitive development as others. Some have a different set of priorities—just keeping the baby healthy may be the primary concern. Those families spend little time worrying about how early experiences in infancy contribute to later academic success.

PRINCIPLE 5: RESPECT INFANTS AND TODDLERS AS WORTHY PEOPLE

Respect is not a word usually used with very young children. Magda Gerber introduced this concept in relation to infants and toddlers. Usually worries about respect go the other way, as adults demand (or wish for) children to respect them. There is no better way to gain respect for yourself than to model it for children.

What does it mean to respect a child? The diapering scene provides an example. Before the caregiver did anything to Caitlin, she explained what would happen. Just as a respectful nurse warns you before putting a cold instrument on your skin, so Caitlin's caregiver prepared her for what was to come. Until you realize the difference, the natural tendency is to pick up a child without saying anything. Babies are often carried around like objects—even when they are old enough to walk and talk. Adults often pick a child up and put him or her in a chair or stroller without a word. That kind of action is not respectful.

To clarify the concept of respecting an infant, try imagining how a nurse would move a fairly helpless patient from a bed to a wheelchair. Then just change the players and imagine one is a caregiver and one is an infant. Except for the size and weight involved, if the adult is treating the infant with respect, the scene should look much the same.

To better understand the concept of respecting a toddler, try this. Imagine you have just seen a man fall off a ladder. Think how you would respond. Even if you are strong enough, you would probably not rush over and set him back on his feet. You'd start talking first, asking if he was hurt or needed help. You'd probably extend a hand if he indicated he was all right and started getting up. You'd comfort him if that was called for. Most people have no trouble responding respectfully to an adult.

Why then do adults rush over and pick up a fallen toddler without a moment's pause? Why not see first what it is the toddler needs? Maybe all that is required is some reassurance—not physical help. Perhaps the child is angry or embarrassed and needs an adult who can accept those feelings and allow expression of them. Perhaps the toddler needs nothing, and without adult interference will get up and go about his business on his own. More aspects of respect come out in the next scene.

Twelve-month-old Brian is sitting at a low table with several other children eating a piece of banana. He is obviously enjoying the experience in more ways than one. He has squashed the banana in his hand, crammed it in his mouth, and it is now oozing out between his teeth. He is relishing it. He reaches for his mouth with the very last piece and, plop, it falls on the ground. He stretches out a hand for it, but the caregiver is quicker. "I'm sorry Brian, but the banana is dirty now. I can't let you eat it." Brian's eyes open wide, his mouth drops open, and a sorrowful wail comes forth. "That's all the banana we have," the caregiver adds as Brian reaches out to her for more. She sits back down at the table after having disposed of the dropped piece. She offers him a cracker, saying, "We're out of bananas, but you can have a cracker instead." Brian rejects the offered cracker. Aware now that he will get no more, he begins to scream.

"I see how unhappy you are," says the caregiver calmly but with genuine compassion. "I wish I had more banana to give you," she adds.

Brian's screams become more piercing, and he begins to kick his feet. The caregiver remains silent, looking at him as if she really cares about his feelings.

The other children at the table are having various reactions to this scene. The caregiver turns to them and explains, "Brian lost his banana, and he didn't like it." She turns back to Brian. He continues to cry. The caregiver waits. Sobbing, he gets off his chair, toddles over to her, and buries his head in her lap. She touches him on the back, stroking him soothingly. When he has quieted down, she says, "You need to wash your hands now." He doesn't move. She waits. Then gently she repeats, "You need to wash your hands, Brian. I'll come with you," she adds. Turning the table over to another caregiver, she gets up and walks slowly across the floor with Brian. Brian is licking globs of banana from his fingers. A last sob escapes from his lips as he reaches the sink.

The caregiver respected Brian's right to have feelings and to express them.[3] She offered support without gushing sympathy. Because she did not distract him with great amounts of warmth or entertainment, he was able to pay attention to what was going on inside himself. He was learning that it was all right to respond honestly to the situation.

Sometimes adult attention is so rewarding that children associate anger, frustration, or sorrow with attention. They use their feelings to manipulate. We would all be better off to ask directly for what we need than to use emotional displays to get hugs and touching. That's why the caregiver remained available but let Brian indicate what he needed. She did not pick him up but let him come to her. When he was ready for comfort, she was there to give it to him, but it didn't come so early that he was not able to express himself.

Following are some examples of less respectful ways to respond to Brian.

> "Stop that screaming—that's nothing to get so upset about—you were almost finished anyway."
>
> "Poor little Brian, let's go play with the doggie that you like so much—look, Brian—see him bark—bow-wow!"

PRINCIPLE 6: BE HONEST ABOUT YOUR FEELINGS

In the last scene the child was encouraged to recognize his feelings. He was angry, and he was not asked to pretend to be something else. What about adults? Is it all right for caregivers to express their anger to young children? Yes. Children in day care need to be around real people—not warm empty role-players. Part of being a real person is getting angry, scared, upset, and nervous now and then. Here is a scene showing a caregiver expressing anger:

> A caregiver has just separated two children who were coming to blows over a toy. "I can't let you hurt Amber," she says to Shawn, who is eighteen months old. She has him firmly but gently by the arm when he turns to her and spits in her face. Her expression changes from calm to anger, and she takes his other arm as well. Looking him right in the eyes, she says clearly, but with emotion in her voice, "I don't like that, Shawn. I don't want you to spit at me." She lets go, stands up, turns her back, and walks away. When she is a few steps away, she gives a quick glance back to see what he is doing. He hasn't moved, so she walks to the sink and washes her face. She keeps an eye out to make sure he doesn't return to hitting Amber. By the time she comes back, she is calm. Shawn is climbing up the slide, and things have returned to normal.

This caregiver was saying honestly what effect Shawn's action had on her. Notice how she expressed her feelings. She didn't put on such a show as to hook him on doing it again for his own entertainment, a problem that can occur when displays of adult anger are dramatic and lengthy. She didn't blame, accuse, judge, or belittle Shawn. She merely verbalized her feelings and connected them clearly to the situation. She let Shawn know what made her angry and stopped him from continuing the action. Having expressed herself, she left the scene. In short, she neither masked her feelings nor blew up.

And expressing her feelings seemed to have been enough to let Shawn know that this behavior was unacceptable. She didn't have to do anything further about it—this time, at least. If it occurs again, she might have to do something more than just tell Shawn how she felt.

Compare the reaction of this caregiver with the times you've seen people angry with a child, yet smiling and talking in a honeyed voice. Imagine the difficulty a child has in reconciling the two sets of messages he gets at the same time.

PRINCIPLE 7: MODEL THE BEHAVIOR YOU WANT TO TEACH

All the caregivers in the previous scenes have been modeling behavior that is acceptable for children as well as adults. You've seen examples of cooperation, respect, honest feelings, and communication. Take a look at how this principle works in a more difficult situation—when aggression is involved.

Shawn and Amber are struggling over a rag doll again. A caregiver starts to move over near them. Before he reaches the pair, Shawn reaches out and gives Amber a slap on the arm. She lets out a wail. The caregiver kneels on the floor before the two children. His face is calm; his movements are slow and careful. He reaches out and touches Shawn, rubbing his arm on the same spot where he hit Amber. "Gently, Shawn, gently." At the same time he strokes Amber. Shawn remains silent. Amber continues to wail. The caregiver touches her again. "You got hit, didn't you, Amber? It hurt!" Amber stops crying and looks at him. All three are silent for a moment. The caregiver waits. Shawn clutches the doll and starts to walk away with it. Amber grabs it. The caregiver remains silent until Shawn raises his arm to hit again. "I can't let you hurt Amber," he says, catching the arm midair. He touches him softly. "Gently, gently." Amber suddenly jerks the doll and Shawn lets go unexpectedly. Taking the doll in triumph, she starts across the room. Shawn looks sad, but remains in the same spot. The caregiver stays near. "She has the doll," he observes. Amber sees a ball at her feet, drops the doll, and picks up the ball. She throws it and runs after it giggling. Shawn moves quickly over to the doll, picks it up, holds it tenderly, and coos to it. The scene ends with both children playing contentedly, and the caregiver is no longer needed.

Notice how this caregiver modeled gentleness—the behavior he wished to teach. A more common approach when an adult arrives on the scene of a dispute is to treat the children with even more aggression than they have been displaying themselves. "I'll teach you to play rough," growls the adult, jerking the child by the arm and shaking him. This approach models the very behavior the adult is trying to eliminate. (And shaking a young child is dangerous because the weight of the head whipping around on a young neck can cause damage.)

The caregiver in the Shawn versus Amber scene knew that both children needed assurance that control would be provided when needed. It is frightening to both aggressor and victim when there is no protecting adult around to stop the violent action. The aggressor needs to be dealt with gently and nonjudgmentally. The victim needs to be dealt with empathetically but not sympathetically (that is, acknowledging her distress without feeling sorry for her). Sympathy and a good deal of attention may reward victims. In that way they learn that being victimized pays off in adult love and attention. How sad that some children actually learn to become victims.

PRINCIPLE 8: RECOGNIZE PROBLEMS AS LEARNING OPPORTUNITIES AND LET INFANTS AND TODDLERS TRY TO SOLVE THEIR OWN

The same scene also illustrates this principle: let children, even babies, handle their own problems to the extent that they can. The caregiver could have stepped in and taken care of this tugging situation by creating a solution for the conflict. He didn't, however. He let the toddlers make a decision themselves. (Though he did, of course, keep them from hurting each other further.) Very young children can solve more problems than many people give them credit for. The caregiver's role is to give them time and freedom to work on the problems. That means not responding to every frustration immediately. Sometimes a bit of facilitating will move a child forward when he or she gets stuck on a problem, but the facilitating should be the least help necessary, leaving the child free to work toward his own solution.

In a movie called *On Their Own with Our Help*,[4] Magda Gerber illustrates this principle beautifully. A baby crawls under a low table, then tries to sit up. When he discovers he can't, he starts crying. He doesn't know how to crawl out again, and he looks very fearful. Instead of rescuing him (it would have been easy to just lift the table up), Magda guides him out—reassuring and directing him with both her words and her hands.

Magda is using an approach called "scaffolding." This term comes from Jerome Bruner and fits with the theory of Lev Vygotsky.

To scaffold, adults keep a constant eye out for a child who is in a situation in which there is a potential for learning. The adult sensitively structures that situation so that problem solving is encouraged and supported. Sometimes scaffolding requires a little assist; sometimes the adult presence is all the scaffold an infant or toddler needs.[5]

Problems can be valuable learning opportunities. Another of Gerber's videos, *See How They Move,* illustrates this principle. The viewer is treated to scene after scene of children doing gross-motor problem solving all by themselves. The adults stay back and let the children work without interference. The only scaffold provided is the adult presence, which is enough to allow the children to freely experience their own ways of moving and exploring.[6]

Can you remember a time when you were working on some problem that was quite challenging to you? How would you have felt if someone had come along and said "Here, let me do that for you" and taken the problem out of your hands? Can you see a parallel between your situation and that of infants who get rescued from most of their problems by well-meaning adults who want to save them frustration?

PRINCIPLE 9: BUILD SECURITY BY TEACHING TRUST

For infants to learn to trust, they need dependable adults. They need to know that they will get their needs met in a reasonable amount of time. The examples have shown dependable adults who met needs as well as offered strength and support. They didn't trick the children.

One of the times adults are most tempted to deceive children is during good-bye times. When everyone knows that a child is going to suffer loudly with protests and wails when the parent leaves, some are willing to trick the child to avoid a scene. However, it is much better when the parent leaves a child by saying good-bye outright, and the caregiver accepts protests and wails. While providing security, support, and empathy, he or she can express acceptance of the baby's right to be unhappy. The baby learns that he can predict when his mother will go, rather than worrying constantly that she has sneaked away when he was occupied. He knows that as long as she hasn't said good-bye, she is still around. He comes to depend on his knowledge that the adults around him don't lie to him or trick him. Learning to predict what will happen is an important part of building trust. Always being happy isn't.

PRINCIPLE 10: BE CONCERNED ABOUT THE QUALITY OF DEVELOPMENT IN EACH STAGE

We live in the period of the hurried child (a term coined by David Elkind in his book by the same title). The pressure starts at birth as many parents anxiously await the time their child reaches each milestone, comparing his or her progress with that of other children or with developmental charts. The message is everywhere—"Fast is better." Books advertise "Teach your baby to read." Institutes promise miracles. Children are pushed, pushed, pushed. When adults have this hurry-up attitude, babies are propped up before they can sit on their own, walked around by the hand before they can even stand by themselves, taught to ride a tricycle when they can barely walk.

Caregivers feel the pressure from every side—from parents, sometimes even from directors as they are urged to speed up development. Yet development cannot be hurried. Each child has a built-in timetable that dictates just when he or she will crawl, sit up, and start to walk. The way caregivers can help development is to encourage each baby to do thoroughly whatever it is that he or she is doing. Learning is what counts—not teaching. The important learnings come when the baby is ready—not when the adults decide it's time.

Some programs write objectives for each child. A hurry-up program will write objectives that focus solely on the next step. However, it is possible to write objectives that help broaden the child's experience in the stage where he or she is. Doing something very thoroughly is the best preparation for moving forward.

Take crawling as an example. Instead of standing the child up and continually encouraging him or her to walk, it is better to celebrate the crawling. The only time in his life that he'll ever be so conveniently close to things on the floor is the same time in his life when he is so very curious about everything that is within reach and just beyond it. Caregivers can provide experiences and opportunities for him to develop not only his crawling but his curiosity.

If you are to help counteract the pushy approach, you need to sell parents on the idea that perfecting skills is more important than pushing children to develop new ones. The new ones will come when the child has thoroughly practiced the old ones. The age at which a child first walks in no way correlates with whether or not he or she will become an Olympic runner.

The ten principles for respectful adult-infant interactions carry with them regard for the individual: the very young child, even the new infant, is treated as the full human being that he or she is. A good adult-infant relationship is built on a series of respectful, responsive, reciprocal interactions over a period of time. Such a relationship is the basis of good caregiving. It is also the basis of infant-toddler education, which is the subject of the next chapter.

Thought/Activity Questions

1. When were you involved in a respectful, responsive, and reciprocal interaction? Describe what that was like. Then contrast that description with an experience you've had with a disrespectful, unresponsive, nonreciprocal interaction. What are the implications of your experiences for working with infants?
2. Think about the benefits of quality time for an infant. Can you remember a time when someone was fully available to you without being directive? What was that like for you? Can you understand from your own experience how that might benefit an infant?

3. Think about someone you know very well. Can you picture some ways that person communicates with you without using words?
4. Have you ever been rescued from a problem in a way that frustrated you? Have you ever seen an infant in the same situation? How did you feel? How did the infant feel?
5. What are your reactions to the phrase "Faster is better" as it relates to infant and toddler development?

Notes

1. Linda Acredolo and Susan Goodwyn, *How to Talk with Your Babies before They Can Talk* (Lincolnwood, Ill.: Contemporary Books, 1996).
2. See further explanation in Gonzalez-Mena, *Multicultural Issues in Child Care* (Mountain View, Calif.: Mayfield, 2001).
3. Although expression of anger has been used as an example of relating in a respectful way to infants and toddlers, it is important to note that this particular example is culture bound. Not all cultures believe in the individual's right to express feelings unless that expression somehow serves the group.
4. Bradley Wright Films, 1 Oak Hill Drive, San Anselmo, California 94960.
5. Jerome S. Bruner, "The Organization of Action and the Nature of Adult-Infant Transaction," in *The Analysis of Action,* edited by M. von Cranach and R. Harre (Cambridge: Cambridge University Press, 1982).
6. This hands-off approach is a cultural issue. In some cultures children are taught that graciously receiving help is a skill to be learned and is more important than standing on their own two feet. See further explanation in Gonzalez-Mena, *Multicultural Issues in Child Care* (Mountain View, Calif.: Mayfield, 2001).

For Further Reading

Laura Davis and Janis Keyser, *Becoming the Parent You Want to Be* (New York: Broadway Books, 1997).

Polly Ferraro, "Supporting Competence in Children," *Educaring* 8(2), Spring 1993, pp. 1–3.

Magda Gerber, *Dear Parent: Caring for Infants with Respect* (Los Angeles: Resources for Infant Educarers, 1998).

Magda Gerber, *Resources for Infant Educarers* (Los Angeles: Resources for Infant Educarers, 1991).

Magda Gerber and Allison Johnson, *Your Self-Confident Baby* (New York: John Wiley & Sons, 1998), p. 23.

Alice Sterling Honig, "Quality Infant/Toddler Caregiving: Are There Magic Recipes?" *Young Children,* May 1989, pp. 4–10.

Tuan Dinh Nguyen, "Honey, the Baby Is Wet!" *Educaring* 16(2), Winter-Spring 1995, pp. 10–12.

Carol Pinto, "Is Faster Better?" *Educaring* 16(2), Winter-Spring 1995, pp. 4–6.

Aletha Solter, "Listening to Infants," *Educaring* 15(1), Winter 1994, pp. 1–4.

Lev S. Vygotsky, *Mind in Society: The Development of Higher Psychological Processes* (Cambridge: Harvard University Press, 1978).

CHAPTER 2

Infant-Toddler Education

Day care programs for infants and toddlers are necessarily educational, whether or not that is their primary purpose. There is no way to keep children for a number of hours every day without educating them. You can leave your car in a parking garage in the morning and expect to find it in the same condition that night when you pick it up again. But children aren't cars. Children are changed as the result of their day care experiences. How they are changed and what they learn can come without thought or planning, or the changes can be planned for in a systematic way. This chapter looks at a philosophy of education appropriate for infants and toddlers in day care. Chapters 3 and 4 look at how you plan for that education.

WHAT INFANT-TODDLER EDUCATION IS *NOT*

Infant Stimulation

The word "stimulation" has become synonymous with the word "education" in the minds of many when talking about infants. Although infant stimulation is more of a special education concept, used for the infant with special needs or the at-risk infant, many group care programs feel pressure to incorporate it in their own approach. No one has ever proved that a program of carefully designed stimulation has a particularly beneficial effect on the development of a normal child. It has been proved that if you shock rats, they run mazes better, which is some of the research on which the infant stimulation approach is based.

In this book the word "education" does not mean "stimulation." Of course stimulation is important—the right amount—for all of us, but even more so for babies. But if you look at stimulation as something you do *to* babies, rather than something that happens because of a relationship and because of the way you meet a variety of needs, you might as well be raising rats to run mazes.

If you are primarily concerned with stimulating, with doing something *to* the baby, you ignore a vital requirement for learning and development: babies need to discover that they can influence the people and things around them. Yes, they need stimulation, which they get from objects and, more important, from people. But they need to perceive their own involvement in these stimulating experiences. Their involvement comes when they are able to have some effect on—that is, interact with—the people and things that are part of the experiences. When stimulation is provided without regard to the baby's response, the baby is being treated as an object.

The attention on infant stimulation came partly in response to some crib-bound, institutionalized babies who failed to thrive. Being left alone, without much sensory input, but more important without attachment, they naturally failed to thrive. But adding mobiles, music boxes, or fish tanks to the crib isn't the answer. Getting somebody to meet the baby's needs is what is called for—not merely providing stimulation.

In group care for infants the problem is usually overstimulation rather than the opposite, as sights and sounds bombard the infants. So in order to meet individual needs, infant education for some may be cutting down the stimulation—the sensory input—rather than adding to what's already present in the environment.

Preschool

Education for toddlers in day care is often built on the model of part-time preschools, where the children come in for a few hours in the morning and engage in a variety of activities set up especially for their learning. Often these activities are more appropriate to older children, so when they are offered to toddlers, the adults are disappointed with the results. When presented with a preschool curriculum, toddlers often look fairly incompetent because they don't conform to the expectations of the adults. They draw on themselves instead of on the paper; they put beans in their mouths instead of gluing them down into the puddles they've produced with glue bottles on paper; they cut their clothes instead of paper; they explore toys and materials in ways that no one ever thought of before. Rather than find a more appropriate approach, or at least activities, some programs dedicated to this model seem to wait for the toddlers to grow up a bit, and just tolerate them in the meantime. But while they're waiting, they spend a lot of time restricting children and teaching them to do these standard preschool activities. (By the time you finish this book, you'll have lots of ideas of what kinds of activities *are* appropriate for the toddler age group.)

Programs that regard toddlers as immature preschoolers have more problems than just with their education-as-activities approach. If the programs see prime time for education as the activity period—usually around 9 to 11 A.M. and perhaps after nap time—they get frustrated with all the noneducational time. Caregiving routines and transition times seem to extend endlessly and take incredible amounts of energy.

There's much more to toddler education than setting up activities, even very appropriate ones. As it does with infants, education happens during caregiving routines as well as during free playtime. Activities are just a small part of toddler education.

EDUCATION AS FACILITATING PROBLEM SOLVING

This book proposes a way of looking at infant-toddler education that differs from either the stimulation or the activity-centered point of view. The educational approach in this book is based on a *problem-solving approach* in which babies and toddlers learn how to make things happen in their world. Sensory input, of course, is an important part of this approach, but it comes about mostly as a result of the children's actions. The children are in charge. The adults are facilitators rather than *stimulators*. Age-appropriate activities are also part of this approach, but only one small part, not the whole curriculum.

What kinds of problems do infants and toddlers face? Watch an infant or toddler for just one hour, and you will go a long way toward answering that question. You will note that infants and toddlers deal with a variety of kinds of problems, including physical ones, such as hunger or discomfort; manipulative ones, such as how to get a toy from one hand to the other or how to get one block to balance on top of another; and social and emotional problems, such as coping with separation from parent or caregiver or trying to interact with a peer who is not interested in interacting. Some problems are specific to particular levels of development and will eventually be solved. Others are specific to the situation and may or may not be solved. Still others are ones the child will be dealing with, in one form or another, throughout his or her lifetime. Education for children under three lies in learning to deal with this enormous variety of problems, learning various ways to approach them, and learning when they can be solved and when to give up. As babies continually experience the problems that come from everyday living, the problems they encounter in play as well as in being fed, changed, dressed, bathed, and put to sleep, they eventually become toddlers who come to see themselves as problem solvers. If they come to see themselves as good problem solvers, and indeed they are, they will have been, by the definition of this book, well educated.

THE ROLE OF THE ADULT

The primary function of the adult in infant-toddler education is to facilitate learning rather than to teach or train. Start by appreciating the problems the babies encounter. Allow them to work on solving those problems themselves. Also, you, as caregiver, will present problems to the babies while you provide for their needs and set up the environment for their play. You facilitate infant education by the way you direct and respond to the problem-solving baby during "wants something" and "wants nothing" quality time.

The two kinds of quality time relate to two ways of being with an infant or toddler in an educational way, which we'll call "caregiver presence." To get an idea of these two ways of being, try this exercise. Find someone who is willing to be your mirror. Stand facing that person, and ask the person to copy each of your movements. Then using your body, facial expressions, and hands, do something for the "mirror" to copy. You may want to move around. After you have experienced being the doer, try being the mirror. When you finish, discuss the experience with your partner. What role did you prefer—doing or mirroring (leading or following)? What was hard about each one? What are the advantages and disadvantages of each?

This mirroring exercise shows the kind of reciprocal interactions that constitute the responsive relationship first discussed in chapter 1. It also illustrates the two kinds of caregiver presence—active and receptive. Perhaps you prefer the active mode—being a leader, directing what is going on. Or perhaps you prefer the receptive mode—following the child's lead, being responsive. To be a good infant-toddler educator, you need to develop both modes, no matter what your preference. Knowing which you prefer can help you concentrate on improving the other.

Notice in the following scene how the adult's being receptive or active works when the child has a problem to solve.

> Jason toddles in crying loudly and holds his fingers out in front of him.
>
> "Oh, Jason, something happened to you," says the caregiver.
>
> Jason continues to cry and holds his fingers up for inspection. The caregiver touches his fingers gently. "It looks like you hurt your fingers," he says in a calm but understanding voice.
>
> Jason pulls his fingers away and tugs at the caregiver's pants, indicating he wants to show him something.
>
> "You want me to come," he verbalizes Jason's desire and follows him to an area behind a partition where another adult and several children are on the floor. Jason, sobbing, leads him directly to a cupboard with the door standing ajar. His cries change slightly as he nears the scene of the accident.
>
> "You pinched your fingers in the door?" guesses the caregiver.
>
> Jason, angry now, picks up a wooden block and gets ready to throw it at the cupboard door.

"I see you're mad, but I won't let you throw the block. You might hurt something," says the caregiver firmly, holding Jason's arm.

Jason seems to reconsider. He puts down the block and goes to the cupboard. Still crying, he closes the door and opens it again. He is very careful in his actions.

"Yes, you can do it now without pinching." The caregiver puts Jason's actions into words.

Jason ignores the words and continues to open and close the door. The angry cries subside and pained whimpering takes their place. He sits down by the cupboard and remains there crying.

"Let's go put some cold water on your fingers," says the caregiver, bending over to him with his arms out.

This scene showed both active and receptive presence, with an emphasis on receptive. Only twice did the caregiver take the lead. Notice that the caregiver was calm and not overemotional, though he was able to empathize with Jason (to feel his hurt). Because he did not get drawn into the situation and could provide support to Jason in his pain, he facilitated Jason's problem-solving abilities. The scene might have been very different if the caregiver had given Jason advice or "taught him a lesson." The scene might also have been very different if the caregiver had offered sympathy. Imagine if he had picked up Jason and murmured phrases like, "Oh, poor Jason, you got hurt, poor, poor little boy." But the caregiver gave neither advice nor sympathy. Instead he gave his full calm attention, both receptive and active, thereby giving Jason the support, strength, and acceptance he needed to pursue the problem he had encountered. This scene shows infant-toddler education at work.

The adult role of directing and responding to infant-toddler problem solving is made up of four skills. The adult must be able to ascertain the optimum level of stress for the child faced with a problem, provide appropriately for the child's need for attention, give feedback, and model desired behavior. These roles are summarized in box 2.1.

Determining Optimum Stress Levels

One way the adult facilitates learning is by being sensitive to the stress levels of babies and toddlers. This sensitivity is important in scaffolding learning. When a young child faced with a problem is going beyond a tolerable frustration level, a little nudge from the adult can reduce the frustration enough so the child can continue to work to solve the problem.

When a sensitive adult scaffolds as part of the infant-toddler education, he or she provides the smallest bit of help possible, not to get rid of frustration but to keep the child working on the problem. This type of help improves attention span and teaches children that they are capable problem solvers.

The problem is that most adults want to shield their charges from uncomfortable feelings. They don't realize that stress and frustration are an

---

BOX 2.1

Four Roles of the Adult in Infant-Toddler Education

1. **Determining optimum stress levels:** observing and deciding how much stress is too much, too little, and just right.

2. **Providing attention:** meeting children's needs for attention without manipulative motives.

3. **Providing feedback:** giving clear feedback so that infants and toddlers learn the consequences of their actions.

4. **Modeling:** setting a good example for infants and toddlers.

---

important part of infant-toddler education. They come naturally with problem solving. In order to develop physically, emotionally, and intellectually, children occasionally need something to fight against, to pit their will and strength against. In this way they can discover that they are competent problem solvers. With no stress, no frustrations, and no problems, children have no way to try themselves against the world. Consequently, their education is severely limited. A young parent, thinking about stress as a part of infant education, wrote the following:

> I was watering my garden the other day and I found out more about stress and development. I'd been watering every day for some time and found that some of my seedlings weren't growing deep roots. As I thought about it—if a plant doesn't have some stress factors so that it has to look for food and water, its roots won't grow as deep, therefore it won't be as stable in the world. Its foundation will be too shallow.[1]

The right amount of stress—not too much, not too little—promotes development. The optimum level of stress depends entirely on the individual. The caregiver must decide what *optimum* means for any particular child and then try to allow for it—opportunities will arise naturally in daily life.

How can you decide what is enough stress? You can decide the optimum level of stress by watching the child's actions. Children under too much stress are not able to solve problems effectively; they may become greatly emotional, or they may withdraw.

You can also decide what is enough stress by being empathetic (imagining what a child is actually feeling) and by remaining calm and not being swayed by either the child's emotions or your own. Being calm gives a perspective that facilitates good decision making.

What should you do if children are either overstressed or understressed? Take a look at the problems each child faces. Perhaps there are too many of them, in which case some changes need to be made to cut down on the number. They may be too hard to solve, in which case he or she may need more help.

If children are understressed, they may not be encountering enough problems in their lives—perhaps not enough is happening, the environment is lacking in variety or interest, or someone else is solving the children's problems.

Providing Attention

The way an adult responds to a child's actions is an important part of infant-toddler education. The adult response has a lot of power because infants and toddlers essentially live on attention from others, especially the others who are important to them. For each individual there is an optimum amount of attention—optimum again, not maximum. If the person gets enough, satisfaction results. If the individual doesn't get enough, he or she will seek it in a variety of ways.

Some typical ways that people get attention are by being attractive to look at, by being kind and sweet, by being smart, by misbehaving, by being loud, by talking a lot or very little, by being outgoing or shy, by being sick or helpless. Are you aware that girls are more likely to be noticed for what they wear or how they look, but boys are more likely to be noticed for what they can do—their capabilities? How long do you think it takes for children to fall into patterns where they tend to get attention by taking on confining sex roles?

If babies find that smiling, cooing, and being peaceful are not enough, or toddlers find that playing and keeping a low profile does not bring them attention, they will try other behaviors. Children seriously in need of attention will find out how to "push the buttons" of the important people around them. Adults must recognize when children are trying to get attention by upsetting them and when children are directly communicating their real needs. It is not always easy to tell the difference. Take a look at the following scene:

A caregiver is sitting in a comfortable chair feeding a six-month-old a bottle. A seventeen-month-old, Mike, at her feet, keeps tugging at her arm and trying to reach the bottle. Another adult removes Mike and tries to engage him in play while explaining that his caregiver is busy right now. When she turns her back to settle a dispute in another part of the room, Mike walks over to another child and grabs the toy he is playing with. Both caregivers admonish Mike, who glows with the attention. As soon as they turn back to their various occupations, Mike goes to the doorway separating the playroom from the kitchen. He hangs on the gate across the opening and fusses.

"You just ate!" responds his caregiver from her chair. "It's hard to believe that you're still hungry, but I'll get you a snack when I finish feeding Becky," she tells him, then settles her gaze back on the baby she is feeding. Mike walks over immediately and pulls all the toys off the shelf and stamps on them. Both caregivers admonish him. Again he glows with the attention. But when both withdraw it, he starts throwing toys over the gate across the open kitchen door. Again he has two adults' full attention. The free adult helps him retrieve the toys and put them back on the shelf while his caregiver in the chair watches and comments from time to time. When order is restored, she puts her attention back to the feeding while the other caregiver starts to change a diaper. The scene ends as Mike walks over and slaps a child who has been playing quietly in the corner all this time.

In this scene Mike continually got attention for undesirable behavior. It's easy to see that he knows how to get attention when he needs it, even when both caregivers are busy. There is no easy answer to this problem. However, if both caregivers are aware that he needs attention, they can concentrate on giving it to him when he is not misbehaving. Perhaps he'll have less need for adult attention when it's difficult to give it to him. The adults can also put into words what it is that he needs by saying things like "I know you need my attention right now, Mike."

If you are generous with your attention during caregiving times, most children can go on about their business during playtimes when you can't respond to them in playful ways. They won't hunger for adult attention. But if a child has learned that misbehavior is satisfying in terms of the reward it brings, you must change your approach.

Start by ignoring undesirable behavior that is designed to attract your attention (without disregarding needs or safety, of course). At the same time, pay lots of attention to behavior that is desirable. Be specific when you talk about the behavior—don't just throw out nonspecific global judgments like "good boy." Instead say things like "I really like the way you're playing with that toy, Mike. You put the toy back when you're finished, good for you, Mike. You're letting me feed Becky without interrupting. You're doing a good job of waiting. You're being gentle with Jason."

When behavior needs changing, positive reinforcement can be quite effective, especially when you are changing a learned behavior, that is, one that has been rewarded in the past, such as Mike's bids for attention.

But don't go overboard in using positive reinforcement. Attention and praise work and are powerful motivators. However, they can be addictive. Many activities are rewarding for their own sake. They lose that reward when adults add external rewards to the intrinsic ones. So when a toddler is playing and an adult constantly interrupts to praise her, the message is that the activity itself is not that great, so the child needs motivation. Eventually that comes to be the case as the child gets the message. It's easy to spot a child who is used to a lot of praise while playing. She is the one who constantly looks to the adult after each little accomplishment while playing. She seems to constantly need someone to say "Wonderful! You stacked that block on the other one." The accomplishment itself is empty without the adult praise.

When children are overpraised, they may lose touch with their own feelings and motives. They look around after every act to see if they did it right. They seek approval for everything they do. Activities and accomplishments are pleasing only for the rewards they bring from the outside. In short, these children cease to get pleasure and satisfaction from the activities themselves.

In *Toward a Psychology of Being* Abraham Maslow states that when a child is faced with a conflict between inner delight at his own accomplishment and the rewards offered by others, he "must generally choose approval from others, and then handle his delight by repression or letting it die, or not noticing it or controlling it by will power. In general, along with this will develop a disapproval of the delight experience, or shame and embarrassment and secretiveness about it, with finally, the inability even to experience it."[2]

Maslow is giving a powerful message about the use of praise in infant-toddler education. His message is quite different from the common practice of many caregivers, who lavish praise on children so they will feel good about themselves. Children generally feel better about themselves when adults limit their praise and respond to successes with words like "You must feel good about finally getting that shoe off," thus acknowledging the child's own inner delight.

Providing Feedback

Closely related to the subject of praise and attention is feedback. Part of infant-toddler education depends on the child getting clear feedback, that is, responses. Feedback comes both from the environment and from people. Children need to learn what effect their actions have on the world and on others. If they drop a glass of milk, it spills. That's feedback about the qualities of liquids. The child needs no further feedback about milk. Now what's needed is a response about how to remedy the situation. "The milk spilled. You need a cloth to sop it up" is a good response.

Some things children do result in caregivers expressing pain or anger. That expression is also feedback. For example, the child who scratches the caregiver can be told "It hurts when you scratch me. I don't like it." The message should be clear if the feedback is to be useful to the child. If the caregiver responds to a scratch in a honeyed voice, smiling all the while but holding the child tightly as if angry, the child gets a mixed message rather than clear feedback.

Adults can also help provide feedback about the environment, as well as verbalizing the reaction they see in the child. In this way children learn to give themselves clear feedback. Here is an example of that principle:

> Jamal is playing with several other toddlers when his caregiver comes in the door. As Jamal rushes over, he slams his elbow into a table. He approaches his caregiver crying.

His caregiver says, "Oh, Jamal, I saw that. You bumped your elbow on the table." Jamal confirms his caregiver's statement by holding his elbow up.

"Me!" he exclaims.

"Yes," replies his caregiver. "Right here is where you bumped it." He touches the spot gently.

Jamal goes back to the table that he bumped. "Table!" he explains.

"Yes," confirms his caregiver. "Right there—you bumped your elbow right there on the table." He knocks on the table. "It's hard."

Jamal touches the table. "It hurt when you hit your elbow on it," continues his caregiver.

"Hard," repeats Jamal. He cries less now. He concentrates on his elbow, then the table, then his elbow again.

Jamal's caregiver helped him focus on what just happened, and Jamal learned something about cause and effect. Jamal was shown what hurt him and gained some understanding of the relationship of the pain to the source. His caregiver helped Jamal understand the full experience, rather than letting him get lost in the pain; yet he didn't deny his pain or distract him from it.

Modeling

Practice, don't preach! Model the behavior you want from the child. What you do speaks louder than what you say. For instance, if you want to teach the child to share, you need to *be* a sharing person yourself. You need to share your own possessions with others if that's what you expect a child to do. You can teach children to perform the actions of sharing by using rewards and punishments, or you can *make* them share by using your size and power. But neither of these approaches will make children sharing people. They will become sharing people (with lots of modeling) only after they gain the concept of possession. Gaining this concept is one of the tasks of toddlers (hence all the "Me!" and "Mine!" statements you hear when you work with this age group).

Children model after other qualities of their caregivers as well—qualities such as gentleness. Children who are treated gently are more likely to treat other children gently. Respect is another example. Children who are treated with respect are more likely to be respectful to others than children who are not.

Another example of modeling behavior is expression of anger. If you work all day, every day in an infant-toddler center, your own anger is bound to be an emotion you'll deal with at least occasionally. The children pick up on how you cope. If you smile and sing and deny that you're feeling furious, they learn to hide their feelings too. (And they learn to give the same mixed messages you are giving.) But if you use the energy to confront the source and problem solve, they learn that way of dealing with conflicts. Or if confrontation is not appropriate, they can learn your coping mechanisms, such as working out the feelings through talking about them, through redirection into physical exercise or expression, or through soothing activities. (For some adults washing dishes is as soothing as water play is to children.)

In short, modeling behavior is more effective than "teaching" it. Just think of the habits, mannerisms, attitudes, gestures, and expressions you use that came straight from your parent(s). We "pick up" behaviors and mannerisms without even being aware of it, and without being taught. As a caregiver, you must be conscious of the behavior you model, so that what you do and what you say are in accordance with one another.

Obviously, no one can be a model all the time. Everyone acts in ways they would rather not have children imitate. If you expect to be a perfect model, you set yourself up for disappointment. However, as you respond to your own weaknesses, your own imperfections, and your humanness, you are modeling. For example, when you make a mistake, you can show the children that mistakes can be forgiven by forgiving yourself. When you're feeling needy, you can tune in on your needs, modeling for the children that responding to needs is important. When you bring modeling to the conscious level of awareness, you can make decisions about it. Modeling is a powerful tool and can work either for you or against you. Because caregiving is already a difficult task, you might as well have all your tools working for you.

In summary, the adult role in infant-toddler education involves allowing for an appropriate degree of stress when a child is trying to solve a problem, responding appropriately to demands for attention, providing feedback, and modeling desirable behavior. The role of the infant-toddler educator can be carried out at any time—during caregiving tasks or when children are playing without direction.

The hardest part of infant-toddler education is trying to explain it to people who think learning comes only from school-like activities. A good task to prepare yourself to be an infant-toddler caregiver is to prepare an answer to the question "Do children learn anything in your program, or do they just play?" You're bound to be asked that question at some point in your career, or perhaps "Is your program educational or just baby sitting?" A short convincing answer should be right at your fingertips.

AN EXAMPLE OF INFANT EDUCATION

The focus of this chapter has been on the adult role in facilitating infant-toddler education. Kahlil Gibran has summed up the kind of relationship between the "educator" and the child that has been presented here: "If he is indeed wise he does not bid you to enter the house of his wisdom, but rather leads you to the threshold of your own mind."[3] The following scene both illustrates and sums up this approach to infant education. Notice how the principles introduced in chapter 1 are handled here in practice.

You're moving through a door in your mother's arms. You find yourself in a familiar room when a quiet voice says your name. You look into the eyes of your caregiver. At the same time you see and hear her, you notice her special smell, which is pleasantly familiar to you. You hold out your arms. She takes you briefly, then puts you on the floor.

Now you're aware of a smooth, cool floor. You're staring at your mother's shins. Up you get on all fours, and without giving much thought to where you are going, you take off. You leave the voices of your mother and caregiver behind. You notice a change under your knees. The smooth hard feeling has become soft and spongy. You stop for a moment to stick your fingers into the nap of the rug, then keep right on going past a ball and a brightly colored scarf. You're headed for a shelf of toys you can see ahead of you. Whoops, what is that? A face comes into view. You stop to investigate. You regard this face quietly and at the same time feel a big presence come up close beside you. You ignore this adult and reach for the face. You touch the smooth skin, and the eyes come to rest on you. You feel good. You pat the soft hair, then have an urge to know what the hair will feel like on your lips. You reach down and touch your lips to the hair.

You sense the pleasure of the adult sitting by you. You look up for a moment, but this big face isn't as appealing or as reachable as the small face on the floor by you. You move back to your examination of the face. Then you begin to get more energetic about your explorations. You feel a big hand stroking your small one, and you hear a voice saying, "Gently, gently." You go back to your original soft stroking. Suddenly a small hand comes up and attaches itself to your hair. You move back, startled.

This movement puts you in a new position, and from this place you can see a big, bright ball. You move over to it. You reach out and touch it—it rolls away from you. You feel excited about this and crawl after it. You try to hold it, but it keeps getting away from you.

You stop for a moment and take your bearings. You're far from the rug now, and the toy shelf you were originally after has disappeared completely. You find that the ball has rolled to a small bed with a doll on it. You reach for the doll, pick it up by one foot, and drop it. You take the blankets off the bed one by one, comparing their textures. When you get down to the hard bare wood, you figure you've seen enough and move on. As you pass by the doll, you give a little attention to its face. You glance back to the small person on the rug, and a fleeting glimpse of that face crosses your mind. It's different from this one. You compare the two.

Suddenly you remember your mother. You have a tight feeling inside. Where is she? You sit straight up and look around. Not far away is a familiar pair of shoes, feet, and legs. You look up and up until you get to her face. Her familiar voice says, "Yes, I'm still here." You crawl over and touch her leg. Then you take off again.

You are aware now and then that there are other voices in the room. You don't pay much attention to them. You are busy trying on the hats that are in a box on the floor in front of you. You're very busy when you see your mother's legs again, then look up into her face. You hear her voice say, "I have to leave now. Good-bye." She leans over and kisses you on the forehead.

You sit up straight and still, wondering. You watch as your mother's feet move slowly away from you. A feeling of distress comes over you, but you remain stunned. You want to do something to stop her, but you can't. Her feet disappear out the door, and you can't see them anymore.

You feel a tenseness in your face and a pounding in your ears. You hear a loud noise and feel something come out of your throat. You're all alone in the world. You have just time to fully react to this feeling when a hand touches you and a voice says, "Your mother had to go to work." You stop for a moment to consider what that means. But your mother doesn't come back, so you get the same feeling again, and your cries come pouring forth. The warm, familiar voice says, "You miss her." You don't really understand these words, but the tone of the voice captures your attention, and you feel understood. You crawl into the arms of your caregiver, who is sitting on the floor near you. You sob briefly; then you feel better.

Just beyond her you see a big, soft, floppy ball. It's a beach ball only half blown up. You reach out for it and grab it in your hand. Just as you are about to enjoy it, you find it in the hands of someone else. You are surprised and disappointed at the same time. You reach for it—but the person moves away. You follow and reach again. You just get your fingertips on it when it suddenly is yanked away again. You sit back in tears. A hand touches you and a voice says, "You don't like it when Kevin takes the ball." Such understanding is conveyed by that voice that your feeling changes. You cry a few more sobs, look at the face, and crawl away.

You find yourself at a small table with a puzzle on it. Kevin is just removing two pieces. You push the puzzle with your hand, and it falls on the floor with a great big delightful noise. Kevin looks at the puzzle, then at you. You take the piece he has in his hand. He looks surprised. You pick up a piece on the floor and begin to bang the two together. Then you shove the puzzle under the table and crawl under after it. You turn on your back and contemplate the textures of the unpainted side of the table. A feeling of peace comes over you as you lie there.

You crawl out and over to a low platform. You want very much to get up on it, but you don't know how. You make several attempts to crawl up, but it is just a little bit too high. You are just about to give up when a voice says, "Maybe a cushion will make it easier for you." A flat, firm cushion appears between you and the platform. You sit back to think this over—but only for a minute. You climb up on the cushion, and from there you can easily get onto the platform.

What a great feeling to be up there! You take only a moment to let it sink in, and then crawl back down. You want to try to get up there again. You manage the climb the second time and get the same feeling. You repeat this sequence a number of times until the pleasure of it begins to wear off.

You notice a caregiver is bringing out something new in another part of the room. Curious, you head over to see what it is. You forget you were on the little platform. You miss the cushion and find yourself sprawled on the floor. You're surprised and upset. You let out a loud series of cries. You have your eyes closed, so you don't see your caregiver come to your side. You hear a voice say, "You fell down." You lie there a moment, gathering your scattered feelings before you attempt to pick yourself up. The adult waits. You wait. The adult says, "Do you need some help?" You respond by getting up by yourself.

An image of your mother flashes across your mind, and you think you might need her very much in the next instant. But the toys the other caregiver is getting out are appealing, and you continue to crawl to the other side of the room. You are vaguely aware of a little sensation in your leg that wasn't there before, as well as a slight throbbing in one cheek. By the time you reach the toys, these sensations are no longer important—all you can think of is exploring these new objects in front of you.

Notice that this infant encountered some problems that could be solved alone and some that required help. The adults were both active and receptive. The infant felt some stress, but never so much that it prevented problem solving. Needs for attention (which were never very great in this scene) were satisfied in ways that did nothing to encourage undesirable behavior. The infant received feedback—both from actions on the objects in the environment and from the adults present. And the adults consistently modeled the behavior they wanted to teach.

Look now at a scene where a toddler is experiencing an educational situation.

You are two years old, and you have just said good-bye to your father. You watch out the window as he gets into his car and drives off. Tears roll down your cheeks, even though you know he will be back. You've been through this often enough now not to be terrified, but you still feel sad about the departure. You feel a warm hand in yours, and you and a caregiver stand side-by-side by the window even after the car has disappeared. Then you are offered a tissue from a box, which you take and use to wipe your nose. You are about to throw the tissue on the floor when you are directed gently to a wastebasket, where you deposit the used tissue. "Want to hear a story?" asks the adult, motioning to a cozy corner of the room where another adult sits with several children snuggled into soft cushions. You join the group, plopping down on the caregiver's lap. She moves the book so all can see, including you, and continues on with the story she was in the middle of. Before she has finished, you get off her lap and wander to the bookshelf and select another book. "Here," you say, as you thrust it into her face.

She moves your book, looks into your eyes, and explains, "I'll read that one when I finish this one." You sit beside her, turning the pages of the book until she has finished reading. Then she reaches for your book.

"Me!" you tell her, holding it away from her.

"Oh, you want to read it to us?" she asks. She sits back and waits. You open the book and begin pointing to objects, naming them. She is interested in what you are saying. She adds a few words for objects you don't know the names of. One child, who can't see the pictures, leaves the group. Two others move in closer. One climbs on the adult's lap.

"No!" you shout, shoving the child. You're stopped firmly. The caregiver looks into your eyes and says, "I can see that you don't want Roberto on my lap." You feel understood, but Roberto is still there, and that frustrates you. But while you are worried about that, another child takes the book you had been reading and trots off with it. You run after her saying "my book" emphatically. She drops it. You pick it up, return, sit down, and begin "reading," glad to have the book back. You're still concerned that Roberto has taken your place, but you continue turning pages and naming objects. When you get to the beginning (you've been reading it backward), the caregiver says to you, "It's time to wash your hands for breakfast."

You jump up right away. Hand washing is your favorite activity. You find a crowd at the sinks, but by pushing slightly you manage to get close to one. You're vaguely aware that you're supposed to wait, not push, but no one really noticed. You remember another time when you pushed hard and you were taken away and were told not to push. You've learned to avoid that situation.

The water feels oh so good on your hands. You reach for the soap and lather all the way up your arms. You stand for a long time rubbing the soap in your hands and arms. Then you rinse and soap up again. By now the sinks are nearly empty. You rinse and soap up once more.

"Time to rinse off and dry," says the caregiver who was reading to you. She stands near you with a towel. You rinse off your hands reluctantly, leaving soap on your arms.

"How about your arms?" she suggests.

You put your arms under the running water. She hands you the towel and then turns to help another child. While her back is turned, you run water over the towel and start wiping out the sink. Then you push the end of the towel into the indentation of the drain and turn the water on harder. You're watching delightedly as the sink begins to fill with water. Right before it runs over onto the floor and your shoes, the caregiver gets back to you. She quietly corrects the problem, hands you a dry towel, and directs you to the breakfast table.

You settle down at the table with a feeling of satisfaction, and very clean arms and hands. You grab a cup from the child next to you and begin pounding it on the table, looking toward the caregiver who is offering cups to seated children. The child next to you grabs his cup back, and you are about to scream when the caregiver says, "If you want my attention, just say my name." You say her name and are offered the choice of a red or blue cup. You take the blue one and show it to the child next to you, who has the same color. The caregiver smiles at you and says "Yes, they're the same, aren't they?" You return the smile and sit back in your chair ready to enjoy the breakfast you can smell in the kitchen.

This child encountered some problems and created some. The adults were both active and receptive in facilitating the child's problem solving. Needs for attention were met in ways that didn't encourage undesirable behavior. The child received feedback from both the environment and the people in it. Although nothing in this scene looked like a school-type activity, the child was, nevertheless, receiving an education, as he or she dealt with a variety of problems, problems that belong to the physical, social, emotional, and intellectual realms.

This chapter has focused on problem solving as an approach to infant-toddler education. It has examined the adult role in facilitating problem solving in very young children, including determining optimum individual stress level, adult attention, feedback, and modeling. The two chapters that follow examine how the educational approach explained in this chapter can become a curriculum, that is, a plan for learning, in a program.

Thought/Activity Questions

1. Perhaps you can think of a time in your own life when stress was good for you. Can you relate your experience to that of an infant or toddler in group care? How good are you at telling the difference between optimum stress and too much stress in your own life? Does this ability relate to how you can tell when a child is having too much or too little stress?
2. Think about how you satisfy your own needs for attention. How aware are you of the ways you get people to pay attention to you? List some ways you get attention from

other people. Are you satisfied with the ways you get attention? Would you want infants and toddlers to get attention in the same ways?

3. Think of a time in your own life when feedback was useful to you in a problem-solving situation. Can you apply your own experience to that of an infant or toddler?

4. Think of an answer to a parent when he or she asks, "Do children learn anything in your program, or do they just play?" How can you explain that your program is educational, not "just babysitting"?

Notes

1. Personal letter from Patti Wade, October 1978.
2. Abraham H. Maslow, *Toward a Psychology of Being,* 2nd ed. (New York: Van Nostrand, 1968), p. 51.
3. Kahlil Gibran, *The Prophet* (New York: Alfred A. Knopf, 1965), p. 56.

For Further Reading

Lorraine DeJong and Barbara Hansen Cottrell, "Designing Infant Child Care Programs to Meet the Needs of Children Born to Teenage Parents." *Young Children* 54(1), January 1999, pp. 37–45.

Amy Laura Dombro, Laura J. Colker, and Diane Trister Dodge, *Creative Curriculum for Infants and Toddlers* (Washington, D.C.: Teaching Strategies, 1997).

Lyn Fasoli and Janet Gonzalez-Mena, "Let's Be Real: Authenticity in Child Care," *Exchange,* March 1997.

Jill Flyer, "Profound, I Say!" *Educaring* 15(2), Spring 1994, pp. 1–3.

Magda Gerber, *Dear Parent: Caring for Infants with Respect* (Los Angeles: Resources for Infant Educarers, 1998).

Magda Gerber, *"Conflict Resolution with Infants," Educaring* 4(4), Fall 1983, p. 3.

Stacie G. Goffin, with Claudia Q. Tull, "Problem Solving: Encouraging Active Learning," *Young Children* 40(3), March 1985, pp. 28–32.

Janet Gonzalez-Mena, "Praise with a Purpose Is Sneaky and Manipulative," *Educaring* 14(4), Fall 1993, pp. 1–4.

Janet Gonzalez-Mena, "Toddlers, What to Expect," *Young Children* 42(1), November 1986, pp. 47–51.

Polly Greenberg, "Do You Take Care of Toddlers?" *Young Children* 46(2), January 1991, pp. 52–53.

Jim Greenman and Anne Stonehouse, *Prime Times* (St. Paul: Redleaf, 1996).

Kathleen Grey, "Not in Praise of Praise," *Child Care Information Exchange* 104, July/August 1995, pp. 56–59.

Fran Hast and Ann Hollyfield, *Infant and Toddler Experiences* (St. Paul: Redleaf, 1999).

Seymore Levine, "Stimulation in Infancy," *Scientific American,* May 1960, pp. 436, 624.

Howard P. Paretteo Jr., Nancy S. Dunn, and Debra Reichert Hoge, "Low-Cost Communication Devices for Children with Disabilities and Their Family Members," *Young Children* 50(6), September 1995, pp. 75–81.

Judy Reinsberg, "Reflections on Quality Infant Care," *Young Children* 50(6), September 1995, pp. 23–25.

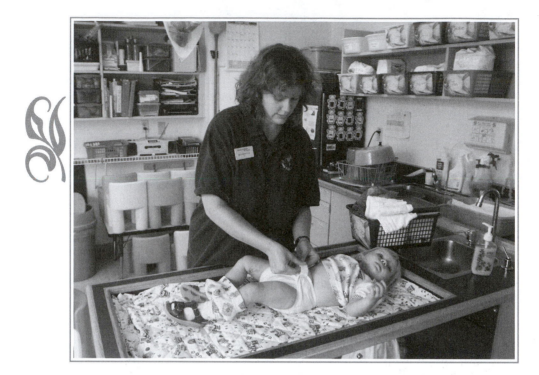

CHAPTER 3

Caregiving as Curriculum

Curriculum is a major issue because we now know that infants and toddlers are competent learners and that the early years are an important foundation for learning in the later ones. Gone are the days when child care was merely custodial, without concern for each child's development. *Education* must be a primary concern, and if you are to educate, you must have a *curriculum,* that is, a plan for learning.

The problem is that curriculum doesn't look the same in infant-toddler programs as it does in educational programs for older children. One difference is that you can't just educate the mind because there is no way to separate intellectual needs from other needs at this beginning level. Therefore, curriculum modeled after school programs where intellectual needs are the main concern is inappropriate for the very young.

Another problem is that the curriculum is so broad in infant-toddler programs that it is very difficult to define. Curriculum is really everything that happens in the program; therefore, this whole book is about curriculum. To try to talk about curriculum in just two chapters is difficult. Yet we need to learn how to talk specifics in order to educate parents and policy makers about infant-toddler programs. Those who don't already know must be made to understand that infant-toddler programs are educational when they are designed to meet the children's needs—all their needs. They need to understand that there is a plan for learning, though the adults are not primarily teachers. This chapter and the next, as well as the environmental chart in appendix B, provide those specifics.

In a paper written for the Program for Infant Toddler Caregivers, J. Ronald Lally says that in the United States we have practiced curriculum extremes in infant-toddler programs. One extreme says that all that infants and toddlers need is tender loving care in a safe environment. Intellectual stimulation is not necessary. The other extreme says that infants and toddlers need intellectual stimulation in the form of adult-directed activities appropriate for their stage of development. Lally has a different idea. He and his colleagues at WestEd and in the California Department of Education who run the Program for Infant Toddler Caregivers, which trains trainers across the United States, advocate good, loving care in a safe environment *and individualized child-directed learning.* They teach caregivers to understand how to use each child's natural interests, curiosity, and motivation to guide them in planning for learning for each individual child. They also stress the learning context and the planning of settings that allow the child to learn, each in his or her own unique way. Lally's paper is included as appendix C.[1]

If you approach infant-toddler education as facilitating problem solving, then the curriculum occurs naturally during the two main activities of the day: caregiving and free play. In the course of these activities children encounter and solve problems. The basis of the curriculum is interaction—with people (adults and peers) and with objects. This chapter concentrates on interactions with adults as they occur during caregiving times.

The importance of the adult's attitude toward caregiving has been emphasized in previous chapters. Because caregiving activities provide regular times when each child has full adult attention on an individual basis, the adult needs to be fully present, providing "wants something" quality time.

One important component of the curriculum as it occurs during both caregiving and free playtimes is attachment. Learning and attachment are related. Through caregiving interactions, attachment grows. When caregiving times are quality times, much learning takes place. Diapering, for example, becomes not just a chore but a vital part of the curriculum. Lifelong learnings and attitudes can be initiated on the diapering table. Likewise, feeding is a vital part of the curriculum. Not only does it promote attachment between infant and caregiver; it provides a variety of sensory experiences, much pleasure and satisfaction, and an opportunity to learn social and self-help skills. Dressing, grooming, and washing are other opportunities for providing sensory experiences and developing self-help skills, as well as promoting attachment. We will discuss the implications of new research on brain development in more detail in part 2. But here we want to just mention that the interactions with caregivers actually build structures in the brain that have long-lasting cognitive effects, supporting our position that caregiving is curriculum. Attachment is also part of curriculum as it enhances and enriches interactions.

Young children need attachment, a tie to a special person, who in turn gives them a feeling that they are important—that they matter. Although most infants and toddlers in day care are attached to their parent(s), if they are to spend long hours a day away from them, attachment to caregivers is additionally beneficial. Both caregivers and children gain from attachment because communication is enhanced and needs are understood. The caregiver is rewarded by the child's feeling for him or her, and the child gains a feeling of importance. Through attachment the child knows that he or she is being cared *about* as well as *for.*

Attachment is promoted by assigning one caregiver to several infants and young toddlers in what is called a "primary caregiver system." The idea behind this is that, if caregivers see three or four children as their own special charges, they can promote a stronger attachment than might happen if attachment were left to chance.

When some people hear about a primary caregiving system, they worry that the children will become too attached to the primary caregiver and then suffer when they go on vacation or are sick. These are legitimate concerns. That's why it's important to create a system of teams so that there's always a familiar adult present even if the primary caregiver is absent. In a smoothly working primary caregiver system, caregivers interact with children other than their special charges.[2]

Naturally, shifts change and caregivers move on. A primary caregiving system doesn't solve all attachment issues, but it makes a big step toward addressing them. It's important that the attachment needs of infants and toddlers in child care be recognized and provided for. (More on this subject in chapter 5.)

Older toddlers are more likely to become attached if they are grouped with a consistent caregiver who pays special attention to them. With children over two, the groups can be larger than just the three or four appropriate to younger children.

In the following scene with eight infants and young toddlers and two caregivers, consistent feeding by one caregiver, who is released from other duties to give his full attention to the baby he is feeding, promotes attachment. Notice in this scene not only how the caregiver builds attachment but also how the children use their attachment to the *other* caregiver. When a threatening situation arises (when a stranger walks into the room), the children head for the person to whom they are attached.

A slender middle-aged woman is sitting low on the floor on a large cushion. On her lap is a baby who has climbed there to pat her cheek. Clinging to her shoulder is a toddler who is also trying to climb on her lap. The baby pushes gently at the toddler to try to keep him off. "No," says the toddler, who continues to hang on tight. A short distance away, two toddlers are banging wooden spoons on empty margarine cartons. A third child sits looking on, quietly opening and closing a small cardboard box that has a big plastic bead inside. Just beyond the seated woman is a large pen that fences off one corner of the room. In it two very young infants are lying on their backs, waving their arms and looking at each other and at the scattering of toys close to them. In another area of the room, a man is seated in a comfortable chair, quietly giving a baby his bottle. The man's full attention is on the baby he is feeding while the woman is obviously taking charge of all the rest of the children in the room. She focuses on the two children interacting with her, but she also manages to spread her awareness to the other children.

A large bearded man in a uniform walks into the room. The child who was opening and closing the cardboard box starts to cry. All action immediately stops except the arm waving in the one corner and the feeding in the other. The climbers and the bangers sit with their eyes on the stranger. The crying child starts creeping backward toward the woman in the beanbag chair, never taking her eyes off the man's face. When she reaches the comfort and safety of the familiar lap, she climbs on, clutching at her caregiver's blouse. The woman puts her arm reassuringly around the child and speaks first to her and then to the man. "That's Christopher's father, Laila," she says matter-of-factly. Then to the man, "Hello, David. You're early today. Christopher is still in the nap room, but he is probably just about starting to wake up. Oh, by the way, be sure to check his log—he didn't eat much lunch today—see what's written down. He may be ready for something to eat when he gets home. Also, as I recall, he was tired this morning, but couldn't sleep. He's been grumpy all day, but had a long nap this afternoon."

The man thanks her and leaves the room to get his son. The action starts up again. Laila crawls down and goes back to her cardboard box, taking the plastic bead out, then putting it back in and closing the box. In the corner pen both infants have started whimpering, and one occasionally breaks into a loud cry. The woman gets up, telling the children around her that she is going to do so beforehand. She goes into the pen to talk to the two needy babies. "Yes, I know, Nathan," she says to the one crying loudest. "You need to eat. I'm going to feed you just as soon as Raheem finishes and can take over for me." And then turning to the other child, who has settled down a bit with her presence, "And then it's your turn to eat. I don't think you're too hungry yet, are you?" Turning back to the first infant, she says, "It's hard to wait, I know."

Notice that this scene showed examples of how attachment can work in an infant-toddler center. Notice, too, that in this center caregivers kept daily logs on "their" children so that parents can receive a comprehensive and detailed report when they arrive to pick them up. This record keeping also serves to make the caregivers pay special attention to "their" children.

Determining children's needs is the first step in performing caregiving tasks. This is easy when the child is old enough to tell you. But those who are too young to express themselves beyond squirming and crying can cause you some real anguish. It is easier when you are attached to the children or know them well enough to understand their unique ways of communicating.

Whenever a child communicates a need to you, either directly or indirectly, ask yourself, "What is it this child really needs?" This is a much easier question to ask than it is to answer, especially in the urgency of the moment, when a young baby is already screaming.

The best approach, if the need is not immediately obvious, is to ask the child. If the child is a toddler and has learned to express his or her needs directly, it is easy. But with a young infant, you may have to work hard to figure out what the need is. Nevertheless, asking directly is a good approach. Ask aloud. Talk to the infant, expressing your desire to understand what he or she needs. Listen, look, and feel for the answer. If you're beginning to learn his or her system of communication (the third principle in chapter 1), you may get your answer directly from the child. By taking this approach, you're beginning to set up a two-way communication pattern that will serve the child well for the rest of his or her life. Children (even the youngest) who are encouraged to express their needs can become quite skilled at doing just that.

Adults sometimes develop a singular approach to responding to a child's crying. "Oh, he's tired" may be one caregiver's standard response. "He needs a nap." Another caregiver may wish to feed all cranky children. A problem arises when a baby with one need has an already satisfied one met. For example, when a child is uncomfortable, restless, sleepy, or irritable and food is given, the child's ability to identify the real need may be impaired. This is more apt to happen with infants than with toddlers because comforting with a bottle is so easy for many babies. Food becomes a substitute for cuddling, attention, or rest. How many adults reach automatically for food when they have some kind of need? This behavior is learned in the early years.

Some needs cannot be met by caregivers. For example, some infants cannot go to sleep without crying, which seems to release tension and relax them. In those cases the best approach, when you're sure these infants need sleep, is to put them in a crib; let them know you understand if they are unhappy about being put there. By accepting the crying, you don't have to make yourself responsible for stopping it.[3]

In infant-toddler care it sometimes happens that an adult's or the group's needs conflict with individual needs. A child must be awakened from a nap because it is time to go home or be fed early for some reason. Or an infant must wait to be fed because several others are simultaneously making demands. Once again the best approach is to let children know that their needs have been recognized and then accept the fact that they may cry until it is their turn for attention. If you can think of the crying as good—as a sign that the children are communicating their needs—it is sometimes easier to accept. When it is the crying child's turn, you will, of course, give him or her your full attention.

Children are resilient, and they can cope with their individual needs being put second sometimes. However, it can be harmful to children when needs other than their own are *usually* put first. To avoid the effects of institutionalization, caregivers must be very careful to make sure that individual needs are taken into consideration. Infants and toddlers must not be put on a rigid schedule that meets program needs rather than their own.

This institutionalization effect can be a danger when toddlers are mixed with older children who have learned to subordinate their individual needs to the dictates of a daily schedule. For most of us, our first away-from-home experience was school, where we subordinated our wide range of needs to more narrow educational goals, to the group, and to the schedule. *School must not be the model for programs for very young children.*

The key to effective caregiving is a good relationship. Anne Morrow Lindbergh in *Gift from the Sea* says this:

> A good relationship has a pattern like a dance and is built on some of the same rules. The partners do not need to hold on tightly, because they move confidently in the same pattern, intricate but gay and swift and free, like a country dance of Mozart's. To touch heavily would be to arrest the pattern and freeze the moment, to check the endlessly changing beauty of its unfolding . . . now arm in arm, now face to face, now back to back—it does not matter which. Because they know they are partners moving to the same rhythm, creating a pattern together and being visibly nourished by it.
>
> The joy of such a pattern is not only the joy of creating or the joy of participating, it is also the joy of living in the moment. Lightness of touch and living in the moment are intertwined. One can't dance well unless one is completely in time with the music, not leaning back to the last step or pressing forward to the next one, but poised directly on the present step as it comes.[4]

Take a look now at an example of a good relationship in one of the primary caregiving tasks—feeding an infant. Imagine yourself in a small body with a bib around your neck.

> Hear a familiar voice say to you, "Here's some applesauce for you." Look around and see a spoon, a hand, and beyond it a small dish of applesauce. Take time to really perceive all this. Feel the coziness as well as the anticipation. Hear the same voice say, "Are you ready?" See the spoon come up to your face. There is plenty of time for you to open your mouth for the bite. You feel the applesauce in your mouth. You taste it. You notice the texture and the temperature. You thoroughly explore this bite before you swallow. Some goes down your throat; some runs down your chin. You look up to find the familiar face. Seeing the face adds to your pleasure. You open your mouth again. You feel a scraping on your chin. The next bite comes into your mouth. You explore it. You compare it to the first bite. You take your time and get the most out of this bite before you swallow it. When you swallow, you get an excited feeling—an anticipation of the next bite. You look at the face again. You reach out, and your fingers touch something soft and smooth. All of these feelings are present as you open your mouth for the next bite.

Come back now from your imagining. Reflect on this experience for a moment. Now compare that imaginary experience with this one:

> You feel yourself plopped into a high chair without a word. A strap is put around your middle, and you are left alone with an empty tray. You look around and see a number of other babies. You pound on the tray. It's cold and hard, as is the back of the chair. You feel impatient. It

seems like forever that you are sitting there. You squirm and twist. Suddenly there is a spoon in between your lips forcing them open. You look toward the source of the spoon, at the same time tasting applesauce. You wiggle your tongue around, swallowing down the bite. The spoon again comes between your lips, and your teeth are forced open. You take another mouthful while looking into an expressionless face of a person who seems to have her mind somewhere else. You enjoy the taste and feeling of the applesauce—pushing it around in your mouth and out between your teeth—down your chin. You feel metal scraping your chin. More applesauce comes into your mouth. You are about to swallow this mouthful when the spoon arrives again. You take a second mouthful into the first, which you haven't swallowed yet. You work on swallowing while you feel scrape, scrape on your chin as the spoon gathers up what is running down. More applesauce arrives in your mouth. You swallow a little of the big load, and you get ready to swallow more. Before you can, the spoon finds its way in between your teeth again. Now your mouth is fuller than before. You sense a bit of urgency to get this down before the next load. You try to hurry, which only slows you down. More applesauce squishes out and runs down your chin. You feel the spoon—scrape, scrape, scrape—and more applesauce comes into your mouth. Hold onto that feeling now and stop imagining.

Just think what the long-term effects of a number of feedings like the second one might be! How much better it is to be fed sensitively, by a caring person.

Notice how the first experience encompassed the ten principles of caregiving. The infant was involved in how the task progressed. The infant and caregiver were sharing quality time—that is, both were paying full attention to each other and the task at hand. They were interacting responsively. They were communicating. The infant was being respected. It's not easy always to feed every infant in day care in the manner of the first feeding, but it is certainly a goal worth striving for.

FEEDING

Programs for infants and toddlers, both centers and family day care, should make every provision possible for nursing mothers. Both mothers and infants benefit, even though it may be less convenient for caregivers. Help the mother feel welcome, and provide a place for her and her infant to be quiet and comfortable.

Bottle-fed infants deserve the same kind of one-to-one attention and physical closeness that breast-fed infants receive. A well-organized center will find ways to release a caregiver to sit and feed an infant while holding him or her, without requiring that the caregiver jump up and down to take care of the needs of other children. In family child care this "release time" is harder to come by, but caregivers who make it a priority to hold each baby while feeding can find ways to work it out.

Feeding time should be quality time. One reason is that, during feeding, attachments are formed between caregivers and the children they feed. For this reason, the same caregiver should feed the same babies daily insofar as possible.

When infants begin to feed themselves, the mess level rises dramatically. Most caregivers are willing to put up with the mess because they value independence. They want children in their care to learn self-help skills. Accepted practice in this country is to let or even encourage children to take over their own feeding as soon as they are able. Usually when a baby grabs the spoon, he or she is given one and allowed to try getting it to the mouth.

Here are some hints to help children learn to become self-feeders.

1. Use child-size unbreakable utensils.
2. Provide finger food. Chunks of soft food that can be picked up in the hands, such as banana, can be a welcome treat to the child who is just learning to use utensils.
3. Give only small amounts of food. Better to let the child ask for more than to discourage him or her with too large a portion. Also it's easier to clean up a smaller amount.
4. Allow time for play and experimentation, but be aware of your own limits. End the meal for the child before the play begins to bother you. A tension-free setting promotes self-feeding skills.

Eating is an emotional process. The adults bring to a feeding situation feelings, ideas, and traditions that have nothing to do with the immediate experience but come from their own personal history and culture. People have strong feelings about what should or should not go on at the table. For some, the taboos about what cannot be done are deeply ingrained and very important. The way they eat seems to define who they are. For others, the resentment of the taboos is equally strong. The point is that eating is connected with strong feelings, and these feelings affect the way an adult approaches or reacts to children eating.

It is also important to recognize that not all cultures view early independence, self-feeding, and big messes in the same way. Although you may not wish to do it yourself, you should respect the fact that a parent may continue spoon-feeding a child long past the age you approve of.

Understanding each child's signals, giving some choices, defining limits clearly, reacting honestly, and interacting responsively are all keys to pleasant feeding experiences. Ending a meal for children when their hunger has been satisfied is important. Children cannot be expected to restrain from playing with their food if they are full and it is still in front of them.

The following scene shows some of the principles mentioned here in action:

Four toddlers are seated at a low table intently watching a caregiver who has several plastic cups in his hand. He turns to the child on his right and holds out two cups. "Do you want this one, Aiesha, or this one?"

The cups are different colors and shapes. One has a handle. Aiesha reaches for one of the cups. The caregiver puts the other one on a table behind him and brings a pitcher around in front of him.

"Now everyone has a cup," he says, looking around at the expectant children. "Here is the juice." He smells it. "It smells like apple juice to me."

He pours a small amount of juice in a pitcher and hands it to Xian, who is sitting to his left. Xian grabs the pitcher and pours with great excitement, missing his cup.

The caregiver hands him a cloth. "Here's a cloth for the spill," he says calmly. Xian pays little attention, but the cloth is close enough to the spill that the liquid runs into it and becomes absorbed. Xian looks carefully at the juice left in the pitcher and then with precise movements pours the small amount into his cup. He abandons the pitcher and concentrates then on the cup, with a satisfied look on his face.

"Your turn, Nicole," says the caregiver, refilling the pitcher and passing it to her. She takes the pitcher, pours some juice, then shoves the pitcher toward the next child, who receives it gratefully.

The child next to him bangs his cup, yelling, "Me!"

"You want your juice, Yei Hoon," says the caregiver.

"No!" says Yei Hoon, emphatically.

"Maybe you're ready for some cereal," speculates the caregiver, reaching for a bowl with dry cereal in it.

"No!" repeats Yei Hoon.

"Well!" says the caregiver, stumped. In the meantime he refills the small pitcher, which is still going around the table.

Yei Hoon points at the counter behind them. On it a box of raisins is in full view.

"Oh," says the caregiver. "You want raisins, right?"

"Raisins!" repeats Yei Hoon carefully. When he receives a handful, he crams a number into his mouth and sits contentedly chewing and sucking on the raisins without removing his fingers.

This caregiver was able to give the children some choices without setting out a whole smorgasbord. He communicated with each child and read signals. He was sensitive and responsive. He set limits.

Perhaps you have not seen toddlers eating at a table instead of in high chairs. Seating them together provides a more social experience than seating them in rows in high chairs. And they have more choice about leaving when finished. They don't have to wait for an adult to take them down. If independence is a value, this simple technique goes a long way toward promoting it.

DIAPERING

Did you think the diapering episode in chapter 1 was too idealistic? The following scene doesn't go so smoothly, but it is based on the same principles as the first one.

The scene is a small center. The room is set up for the toddlers who are now occupying it. One is a small boy playing contentedly with an empty can and a wooden spoon. He sees a pair of feet and legs approach. The child looks up as a voice reaches him. "Justin, I smell something! I think you need changing," says a caregiver.

"No!" responds Justin.

"Justin, you need a clean diaper," says the caregiver, holding out her hands. Justin ignores her. "I can see you don't want to be changed, but I'm going to do it anyway. Do you want to walk, or shall I carry you?"

Justin gets up and walks in the other direction. "Okay, I'll carry you," says the caregiver firmly, picking him up. He struggles in her arms. "Would you rather walk to the changing table?" she says, putting him down. He reluctantly moves toward a corner of the room. When he reaches the changing table, he turns and tries to run off in the other direction.

"I'm sorry, but you just have to put up with this," says the caregiver, holding him firmly and lifting him to the table. "First we have to get your jeans off," she says, struggling with suspenders. Justin squirms under her grasp.

"I know—you really don't like this." She continues undressing him, then unfastens the diaper. He tries to stand up. She holds him down firmly. "I know you want to stand up, but you have to wait just a minute. See, I'm putting the diaper here." She shows him where she disposes of the diaper. He twists to look, finally showing some interest in what is going on.

"Look, I'm going to wipe your bottom with this." She takes advantage of his momentary interest. He squirms as he feels wetness on his bottom. He struggles to sit up. "Almost finished," the caregiver is obviously hurrying. She puts the clean diaper in place. He lifts his bottom as she slides it under him. "I like the way you help me, Justin." She smiles at him. "There, all done—let me just pull your pants up again." He willingly puts his arms into the suspenders.

"Get down!" he demands.

"Yes, I'll put you down now," says the caregiver, holding out her arms as he sits up. She puts him on the floor. He runs immediately to the can and wooden spoon he was playing with before. He looks relaxed and happy—giving no hint that he just went through some kind of ordeal.

Notice that the caregiver did not give up. She tried to involve Justin in the task, even though it wasn't easy. She acknowledged his feelings and verbalized them for him. She respected his feeling annoyed and wanting to be active. She worked quickly with as little fuss as she could manage. In short, she treated Justin as a human being—never as an object. She treated him with respect.

All children go through periods of being uncooperative, as Justin did in the preceding scene. It is important that they do so, even though it is hard on the caregivers. Resisting is a sign of growth; by resisting, children assert their individuality. They learn something about the push toward independence that will one day make them individuals who no longer need the kind of care they now receive.

TOILET LEARNING

Part of the job of toddler caregivers who work with children over two years of age is to help them use the toilet. Toilet learning happens as a part of normal development because children want to be like the other children they see using the bathroom. The key to ease in toileting is readiness. Children must be physically ready, which means they can hold on and let go at will. In addition children must be mentally ready, which means they know what is expected. And finally, children must be emotionally ready, which means they are willing. When these three conditions are present, toilet learning occurs naturally as the caregiver asks for cooperation just as he or she does in all caregiving routines.

Most programs are concerned about cooperating with the parent when it comes to toileting. In many programs the policy is not to initiate toileting until the parent suggests it; then the staff is assured that the child will find consistency at home and at the center. Consistency may be more difficult if the parent is from a culture that views toilet learning as a first-year task. Although staff may not be willing to try to "catch" children and put them on the potty before they consider them really ready, it is important to respect a different view.

Here are some hints for making toilet learning easier.

1. Help children feel physically secure by providing potties (if licensing allows) or very low toilets, if possible. The easier it is for children to get on and off by themselves, the more independence is promoted.
2. If appropriate, ask parents to dress children in loose, simple clothing they can remove themselves (elastic waistbands rather than overalls, for example).
3. Be gentle and understanding about accidents.
4. Avoid power struggles. You can't win them, and children can be left with long-lasting effects if toilet learning has been a highly emotional affair.

A note about cultural sensitivity. Although what has been stated here about toilet *learning* is developmentally appropriate and is the accepted practice of the experts in the United States and other Western countries, this approach is not universal. Around the world and among subcultures and immigrants in this country, toilet *training* is the norm and takes on a whole different character. We won't explain it here, but want to acknowledge that differences exist; we urge caregivers to respect diversity in perceptions, timing, and styles of toileting.[5]

WASHING AND BATHING

Most programs leave bathing up to parents except under very special circumstances. Some parents become insulted if their children are sent home cleaner than they arrived. Cleanliness can be a great point of conflict between parents and caregivers if they have different standards. Parents may be angry if a child with hard-to-wash hair comes home with a head full of sand. Cultural issues can give people different perspectives on the subject of cleanliness, so respect ideas that differ from your own.

Hand washing before meals is not such a touchy issue as bathing. Hand washing is popular with most children and can even be the highlight of the day for some toddlers. Short attention spans lengthen appreciably when toddlers are sent off to wash. Hand washing can be the most pleasant self-help skill to learn if low sinks are available and toddlers are allowed to use them at leisure. In fact, hand washing can become a major activity because toddlers greatly enjoy the sensory properties of soap and water.

DRESSING

Caregivers can promote autonomy by setting up tasks in such a way that the child makes maximum contributions.[6] You can easily see examples of this principle in dressing activities. For instance, when taking off the socks or booties of even a very young baby, you can pull them half off and ask the child to finish the job. It takes little coordination when the task is set up like this. Even young babies get real pleasure and satisfaction from helping out. The idea is to simplify the task just the right amount so that the child gets practice in the dressing and undressing process. At first it takes longer to work cooperatively, but as child and caregiver come to see themselves as a team, the earlier patience pays off. By toddlerhood, children who were encouraged to help dress and undress themselves have become proficient, needing very little help except with such things as buttons and starting zippers.

Here is a scene that shows how it would be if the caregiver did not aim for teamwork.

Imagine yourself a young toddler. You are about to be taken outside for a walk. Without anything being said to you, you feel your arm being grabbed. You're thrown off balance. Then you find yourself being hauled over to a coatrack. Your arm is held tight and then thrust into a sleeve. Your thumb gets stuck and stretches back as the sleeve comes up your arm. Then you feel yourself being swung around. You feel annoyed. When the other sleeve comes up your other arm, you stick your thumb out on purpose. Then you become all floppy. You feel a tighter grip on you, and some tension transfers from the hands holding you. You become even floppier. Finally a face comes down near yours, but the eyes look only at the zipper, which is resisting getting on the track. You feel the hands struggle with the piece of metal; then suddenly the zipper moves upward. It stops only when it touches your neck and feels cold, uncomfortable, and tight. The face disappears, and you're left standing alone while the child next to you is readied in the same impersonal way.

Not a very enjoyable experience, was it? This child was being treated more like an object than a person. Can you remember a time in your own life when you were treated as an object? If you can, then you know why it is important not to treat a child (of any age) that way.

NAPPING

It is important that infants be allowed to rest according to their individual needs rather than according to someone else's schedule. Infants' sleep patterns change—sometimes from day to day as well as over a period of time. No one napping schedule will fit all babies in a program, and each baby's personal schedule changes from time to time.

Not all babies express their need for rest in the same way. Experienced, sensitive caregivers learn to read each child's signals, which may range from slowing down and yawning to increased activity and low frustration threshold.

Parents are the best source of information about their baby's sleep patterns and needs. Experienced caregivers are aware how useful it is to know that the baby woke up extra early that morning or got less sleep than usual over the weekend. They understand fussy behavior in a different light if they know the reason for it.

Babies should be put down for a nap in the way most familiar to them. However, it's also important that every caregiver know the results of recent research regarding the relationship between sleeping position and Sudden Infant Death Syndrome (SIDS, or crib death). SIDS is the label given to unexplained deaths, usually, but not always, occurring when a baby is sleeping. SIDS is not the same as smothering, choking, or dying from a disease. Infant deaths are labeled SIDS only when no cause can be found. For years, North American pediatricians have told parents and caregivers to put babies to sleep on their stomachs. New research shows that *back sleeping* is associated with lower risk of SIDS. The evidence is compelling.[7]

Each baby should have a personal crib that is located in the same spot every day. That kind of consistency and security may help the baby feel at home faster. Decisions about when to put a baby in the crib and how long to leave him or her there depend on the adult's perception of the particular child's needs. Some children need to be confined for some time before they can fall asleep, even when they are very tired. They may play or cry before sleeping. Other children fall asleep immediately. The waking up period also takes some adult judgment. Does the child wake up energetic, active, and ready to play, or is there a long transition period between sleeping and waking during which the child may need to remain in the crib? Reading a young child's signals about rest needs is not always easy. Again, the parent is a good source of information. Find out what kind of self-calming behaviors a child has and encourage them. Some children stroke a blanket; others twist their hair. The most common self-calming behavior is thumb sucking. Ask how the child naps at home. Can you use some of the same devices or rituals the parent uses? Perhaps a favorite toy or blanket provides comfort.

Once again, cultural factors may enter into attitudes about sleeping. Some cultures see being alone in a dark room as the way to promote independence. Others feel that babies should not sleep alone. You may not agree with an attitude that is different from your own, but be sure to respect it. If you can't do what the parent wants, talk about it with him or her. Negotiate, discuss, exchange viewpoints. Don't just ignore a parent's wishes and do what you think is best.

As children move through toddlerhood and nap only once a day, they can learn to rest according to a group schedule. However, individual needs are still important, and provision should be made for the toddler who needs a quiet time earlier in the day, if not an actual nap.

Toddlers who feel nervous, scared, or lacking in trust may have sleep problems that consistency would help alleviate. A favorite toy or blanket may also provide needed security. Sometimes a caregiver can do nothing at the moment to promote security, but must acknowledge the child's insecure feelings and wait until he or she eventually learns that it's a safe place. In some programs, the children who need it have a back rub to help them go to sleep. Here are some further hints about how to help toddlers get to sleep.

1. Provide visual privacy for those children who need it. Some toddlers are too stimulated by being near another child to go to sleep.
2. Provide a quiet, peaceful atmosphere. Some programs use soft music to help. Start winding down before nap time.
3. Make sure all children get plenty of fresh air and exercise. Being tired is the best motivator for napping.
4. Don't let children get overtired. Some children have a hard time settling down to sleep when they are exhausted.

Caregiver Lynne sees the importance of creating a ritual around going to sleep. The toddlers she cares for are old enough to have an established group nap time. So after lunch she starts the ritual of first transforming the room so it suggests sleeping instead of play. The toys are hidden away, lights are turned down, windows shaded, and there's a quiet story time for children who settle down that way. The atmosphere is subdued and hushed so that children feel the transition. As stimulation is lowered and the environment gives the message about what's expected, the children's activity level goes down and rest comes easier than when the transition is abrupt and children don't ease in to the nap time.

If adults regard caregiving tasks as vital learning experiences, they are more likely to approach them with patience and attention. In group care, even when the adult-child ratio is good, an infant's main opportunity to enjoy a long period of one-to-one interaction is during caregiving times like feeding, diapering, and dressing. If those times are used well, babies require far less adult attention during the other periods of their day. Babies can go about their play (interacting with the environment and with the other babies) with no more than general supervision from an adult who may be watching a number of babies.

As toddlers develop self-help skills, this built-in one-to-one time disappears. Therefore, caregivers must provide it some other way even to the oldest toddlers. The fact that required ratios of adults to children may change when the children are about two adds to the difficulty of giving the kind of individual attention each child needs. Some get it by being charming and appealing to adults. Others get it by exhibiting unacceptable behaviors. Some don't get it at all. One way to ensure that all children are getting individual attention, once the caregiving tasks are no longer such a focus during the day-care day, is to keep brief anecdotal records. If during nap time you write a single sentence about each child in your care that day, you'll soon see the patterns. You'll see that some children stand out because of their behaviors. Some children are practically invisible, and it's hard to think of anything to write about these youngsters. Once you see these patterns, you can make better conscious decisions about how to make sure that all children get individual attention each day.

When infants and toddlers are treated with respect and caregiving is done with a teamwork approach, relationships grow—relationships that help children learn about themselves and the world. They come to anticipate what will happen to them and realize the world has some predictability. They learn they have some power to influence the world and the people in it. They begin to make sense out of life. When used to their fullest, these times can become focuses in children's days—something they look forward to—their chance to "dance" with their partner!

This chapter has examined the role of attachment in determining needs as well as the importance of a relationship in order to make caregiving activities a viable part of the curriculum. But caregiving is only half the story. The next chapter explores the role of free play in making up the other half of the curriculum.

Thought/Activity Questions

1. Think for a minute about how you determine your own needs and get them met. Can you remember a time when you needed something that you could not get by yourself? How did you communicate this need? Were you direct about it? Was your

message received? Did you get the results you wanted? Perhaps you can relate your own experience to that of infants and toddlers in day care.

2. Can you remember a time when you were treated as an object? How did that feel? Do you know why it is important not to treat a child that way?

3. Think of ways that you can make a caregiving routine into a "shared experience." Discuss how the kinds of one-to-one interactions like you described become the curriculum in an infant program.

4. What do you know about cultural differences in caregiving routines? How does what you know differ from what's shown in this chapter? What would you do if you were told to "follow the book" and you didn't believe in it? What would you do if a parent's beliefs about carrying out a particular routine differed from yours?

Notes

1. J. Ronald Lally, *Curriculum and Lesson Planning: A Responsive Approach* (Sausalito, Calif.: Program for Infant Toddler Caregivers, 1997).

2. J. Ronald Lally, "The Impact of Child Care Policies and Practices on Infant/Toddler Identity Formation," *Young Children* 51(1), November 1995, pp. 58–67. In this article, Lally makes a compelling case for the importance of such practices as primary caregiving systems.

3. This paragraph is written from a European-American view. Many parents would never put their babies down to sleep if they were crying. Many parents never use cribs for their babies. It's important to recognize cultural differences and talk about them with parents. For more information about cultural differences in child care settings, see Gonzalez-Mena, *Multicultural Issues in Child Care* (Mountain View, Calif.: Mayfield, 2001).

4. Anne Morrow Lindbergh, *Gift from the Sea* (New York: Pantheon, 1955), p. 104.

5. Navaz Bhavnagri and Janet Gonzalez-Mena, "The Cultural Context of Caregiving," *Childhood Education* 74(1), Fall 1997, pp. 2–8.

6. The suggestions in this chapter fit the overall philosophy of the book, which is based on a value of independence and individuality. It's important to note that not all cultures have these values. Therefore these approaches to caregiving should be discussed with the families, and some agreement should be reached. See Gonzalez-Mena, *Multicultural Issues in Child Care* for more information about how to communicate with parents regarding cultural issues. Also see the video on the subject: *Early Childhood Training Series: Diversity,* Magna Systems, 1995.

7. S. M. Beal and C. F. Finch, "An Overview of Retrospective Case Control Slides Investigating the Relationship between Prone Sleep Positions and SIDS," *Journal of Pediatrics and Child Health* 27, 1993, pp. 334–339.

For Further Reading

Navaz Bhavnagri and Janet Gonzalez-Mena, "The Cultural Context of Caregiving," *Childhood Education* 74(1), Fall 1997, pp. 2–8.

Amy Laura Dombro, Laura J. Colker, and Diane Trister Dodge, *Creative Curriculum for Infants and Toddlers.* Washington, D.C.: Teaching Strategies, 1997.

Magda Gerber, "Respecting Infants: The Loczy Model of Infant Care," in *Supporting the Growth of Infants, Toddlers, and Parents,* edited by Elizabeth Jones (Pasadena, Calif.: Pacific Oaks, 1991).

Magda Gerber, *Resources for Infant Educarers* (Los Angeles: Resources for Infant Educarers, 1991).

Magda Gerber and Allison Johnson, *Your Self-Confident Baby,* New York: John Wiley & Sons, 1998.

Janet Gonzalez-Mena, *Infant-Toddler Caregiving: A Guide to Routines* (Sacramento, Calif.: Far West Laboratory and California Department of Education, 2000).

Janet Gonzalez-Mena, *Multicultural Issues in Child Care* (Mountain View, Calif.: Mayfield, 2001).

Janet Gonzalez-Mena, "Understanding the Parent's Perspective: Independence or Interdependence?" *Exchange,* September 1997.

Janet Gonzalez-Mena, "Dialogue to Understanding across Cultures," *Exchange,* July 1999, pp. 6–8.

Janet Gonzalez-Mena and Judith K. Bernhard, "Out-of-Home Care of Infants and Toddlers: A Call for Cultural and Linguistic Continuity," *Interaction* 12(2), Summer 1998.

Janet Gonzalez-Mena and Navaz Bhavnagri, "Diversity and Infant/Toddler Caregiving," *Young Children,* in press.

Janet Gonzalez-Mena and Anne Stonehouse, "In the Child's Best Interests," *Child Care Information Exchange,* November/December 1995, pp. 17–20.

Jim Greenman and Anne Stonehouse, *Prime Times* (St. Paul: Redleaf, 1996).

Zina Josephs, "Reducing the Risk of SIDS," *Educaring* 14(4), Fall 1993, p. 5.

Marjory Keenan, "Making the Transition from Preschool to Infant/Toddler Teacher," *Young Children* 53(2), March 1998, pp. 5–11.

Beverly A. Kovach and Denise A. Da Ros, "Respectful, Individual, and Responsive Caregiving for Infants: The Key to Successful Care in Group Settings," *Young Children* 53(3), May 1998, pp. 61–64.

J. Ronald Lally, "The Impact of Child Care Policies and Practices on Infant/Toddler Identity Formation," *Young Children* 51(1), November 1995, pp. 58–67.

Robin Leavitt, *Power and Emotion in Infant-Toddler Day Care* (New York: State University of New York Press, 1994).

Peter Mangione, ed., *Infant-Toddler Caregiving: A Guide to Culturally Sensitive Care* (Sacramento, Calif.: Far West Laboratory and California Department of Education, 1995).

Karen Miller, "Caring for Little Ones," *Exchange,* July 1995, pp. 75–76.

Carol Brunson Phillips and Renatta M. Cooper, "Cultural Dimensions of Feeding Relationships," *Zero to Three* 7(5), June 1992, pp. 10–13.

Sally Provence, "Feeding Problem," *Zero to Three* 7(5), June 1992, pp. 18–19.

Helen Raikes, "A Secure Base for Babies: Applying Attachment Concepts to the Infant Care Setting," *Young Children,* July 1996, pp. 59–67.

Judy Reinsberg, "Understanding Young Children's Behavior," *Young Children* 54(4), July 1999, pp. 54–57.

Ellyn Satter, "The Feeding Relationship," *Zero to Three* 7(5), June 1992, pp. 1–9.

CHAPTER 4

Play as Curriculum

A main ingredient of any infant or toddler program should be play. Early childhood educators have long recognized play as vital to growth and learning. It is natural to young children and should be regarded as an *important* use of their time, not as something secondary or optional.

The benefits of play are enormous and go far beyond the kinds of things we talk about so easily, like developing skills and learning concepts. Play offers children opportunities that come from nowhere else. Through play, children get involved in open-ended exploration. They are not confined by rules, procedures, or outcomes. Children at play have self-direction. They have power. Through total absorption during play, they make discoveries they might otherwise never make, they work on problems, they make choices, and they find out what interests them.

In the foreword to *Mindstorms,* Seymour Papert talks about a play theme that started when he was a toddler, continued throughout his childhood, and has been an important influence throughout his whole life. Here is what he says about "The Gears of My Childhood":

> Before I was two years old I had developed an intense involvement with automobiles. The names of the car parts made up a very substantial portion of my vocabulary: I was particularly proud of knowing about the parts of the transmission system, the gearbox, and most especially the differential. It was, of course, many years later before I understood how gears work; but once I did, playing with gears was my favorite pastime. I loved rotating circular objects against one another in gearlike motions, and, naturally, my first "erector set" project was a crude gear system.
>
> I became adept at turning wheels in my head and at making chains of cause and effect: This one turns this way so that must turn that way so . . .[1]

61

He went on to use his model for learning mathematics. He feels that "working with differentials (gears) did more for my mathematical development than anything I was taught in elementary school." From his own experience he formulated what he still considers the fundamental fact about learning: "Anything is easy if you can assimilate it to your collection of models. If you can't, anything can be painfully difficult. . . . What an individual can learn, and how he learns it, depends on what models he has available."[2]

Children collect models through play. Papert talks about how children learn through models: "You can *be* the gear, you can understand how it turns by projecting yourself into its place and turning with it. It is this double relationship—both abstract and sensory—that gives the gear the power to carry powerful mathematics into the mind." He goes on to explain that no one told him to learn about gears. It was his own idea—indeed, a passion. "I remember that there was a FEELING, LOVE, as well as understanding in my relationship with gears."[3]

What are the implications of Papert's story for caregivers? Should all children be encouraged to play with gear sets? He says, "To hope that every child might have the experience I had would be to miss the essence of the story. I FELL IN LOVE WITH THE GEARS . . . something very personal happened and one cannot assume that it would be repeated for other children in exactly the same form."[4]

Papert's story has great implications for promoting free play, with the adult in the facilitator role. Papert obviously had someone who capitalized on his early interest and helped him in his pursuit. He or she probably provided further materials. But the important point is that *Papert* was the one who made the choices. Papert's interest, his initiative, provided the push. And what he gained was a set of models that served him throughout his academic career in learning the abstractions of mathematics. Early play in Papert's life (as in all children's lives) provided an important foundation for later learnings and understandings.

The way we respond to infants and toddlers at play by giving them freedom, by helping them pursue their special interests, and by providing resources may result in children gaining lifelong models such as Papert's gears.

Elena Bodrova and Deborah Leong discuss how play influences development in their book *Tools of the Mind: The Vygotskian Approach to Early Childhood Education.*[5] They explain that Vygotsky had an integrated view of play when he wrote about its contribution to cognitive, emotional, and social development. He saw play as a tool of the mind with its roots in the manipulation and exploration of infancy and toddlerhood.

Letting free play remain free is difficult for some adults once they recognize how important play is for infants and toddlers. They want to set up objectives and plan for, indeed, control, outcomes. This is especially true for programs for low-income children because of the urgency to prepare them for elementary school.

Some visitors to an infant-toddler program arrived in the morning to see the children playing freely with a variety of toys. They were impressed with how involved and interested the children were. But then the director arrived breathless, apologized that things were late in starting that morning, and proceeded to organize groups, get out "activities," and herd toddlers into chairs around tables. Here they were drilled on names of objects in pictures, told to match shapes, and shown how to make circles and squares out of play dough. The teachers who had earlier been playing a background role, except when there was a call to be responsive, suddenly took charge of everything. The focus became very objective oriented. When the visitors later had a look at individual education plans, they discovered that cognitive objectives were defined very narrowly (for example, "shown pictures of a dog, a horse, and a cat, child will identify two out of three"). No wonder "playtime" was so objective oriented.

One reason adults sometimes want to control toddler play is that they don't understand it. Preschool play they understand because it looks involved and productive, and it fits into categories such as "dramatic play" or "art" or "block play." But toddler play may not look like much. Toddlers may not look involved. They dabble at things, wander around, often carrying objects with them. But if you watch carefully, you see they are not uninvolved, nor are they in transition. They are walking and carrying. They are making choices. In addition, perhaps they are enjoying the sensory changes as they move around. Sometimes they are keeping in contact with the person they are most attached to (touching home base).

Toddlers are easy to satisfy as long as they have room to move and things to examine and manipulate. They may seem to have short attention spans because of their gross motor focus and this need to change location. However, they can also get very involved, especially in problem solving or a self-chosen sensory activity. Toddlers at a sink with soap, water, and paper towels can spend up to half an hour messing around. (That's not a short attention span.)

THE ADULT ROLE IN PLAY

Children learn from other children. By interacting with their peers, infants and toddlers learn much about the world, their power in it, and their effect on others. Through the kinds of problem-solving situations that present themselves in child-child interactions, youngsters come to learn such valuable skills as how to resolve conflicts. The adult's role in these child-child interactions is to encourage them, then step back until needed. Sensitive caregivers know when to intervene. Timing is crucial. If you step in too soon, valuable learning is lost. But if you step in too late, children can hurt each other. Timing and selective intervention are important skills for caregivers to acquire in order to facilitate infant-toddler social play.

Adults promote free play by providing time, space, and materials. The adult should remain available while infants and toddlers are playing, giving "wants nothing quality time." They should restrain from interrupting the child who is really absorbed in play. Absorption is a quality we should value.

Adults can be part of the play, but they must remain in a playful mode, open to what happens, without setting up goals or playing for particular results, or the play ceases to be play and becomes an adult-directed "activity." You'll see examples throughout this book of adults in a "wants nothing" mode, playing with children.

Adults can also engage in mutual play with children for their own enjoyment. But be careful about becoming a child's major entertainment device. Some children get hooked on adults playing with them and are unable to play with other children or on their own when the adult steps back.

Adults also provide safety. Without safety, there is no free play. Children can feel comfortable only when they know no one will let them get hurt.

Adults support problem solving. It takes sensitivity by the caregiver to recognize the intellectual value of the many problems that arise during free play. Maria can't get the ring on the stick; Blake's block stack keeps falling over; Jamal can't reach the toy just beyond his grasp. The frustrations from these kinds of problems seem to interrupt free play, and it's tempting to just solve the problem for the child. But rescuing a child takes away a potentially valuable learning experience.

Adults provide scaffolding for children's problem solving (see box 4.1). It takes skill to know when to help. Often, adults do too much and interfere with the child's ability to solve the problem. They deprive the child of discovering his or her own approach. The key to scaffolding effectively is to determine the point at which the child is about to give up. A small assist at just the right time will keep the child working on the problem. If it's too early or too late, the child loses interest. It's not that caregivers have to "motivate" chil-

---

BOX 4.1

Magda Gerber Gives Some Advice about Scaffolding

"Allow children to learn on their own, without interference. If you wait, you will find out that many things get resolved on their own; even though you thought you had to help, the child didn't really need your help. We are child-loving people—too eager, so we think, 'Oh, poor baby would like to get that toy but can't reach it,' so we push it nearer. But the message we give is, 'You need us. We are all-knowing giants and you are a helpless little creature.' That's not the message I would like to give. I wait until the child really lets me know, 'I cannot handle it any more.'"[6]

BOX 4.2

Adult Roles in Infant-Toddler Play

1. Encouraging interactions and then stepping back

2. Practicing selective intervention

3. Providing time, space, and materials

4. Remaining available but not interrupting

5. Providing safety

6. Supporting problem solving

7. Providing scaffolding

8. Observing

---

dren. Rather, the assist is the type of support that helps children stay with something long enough to finally gain a sense of satisfaction. Satisfaction is the kind of reward that lingers and is remembered the next time a problem arises. Box 4.2 provides a quick look at eight adult roles in infant-toddler play.

The adults in a child care program that stresses free play sometimes look as though they aren't doing anything. Some people think that adults in a "wants nothing" mode—available but not directive—look too passive. Read the following scene, which shows adults facilitating free play, and decide for yourself if the adults are too passive.

The play area is set up for older toddlers, who are busily exploring what has been put out for them. Two adults are sitting on the floor on opposite ends of the play area, and a third adult is sitting on a low chair by a table set up with play dough. In one end of the room a group of children are carrying around large plastic blocks. One seems to have a plan in mind; two seem to be just interested in the transporting activity, without regard to where they are going. A fourth child has built a four-block enclosure and is sitting in the middle of it. A fifth child is walking across the blocks that are lying flat on the rug. A tussle starts as the child in the enclosure defends his structure from one of the transporters, who is determined to take one of his blocks. The adult moves calmly close to the action. When the tussle continues, she says quietly, "Christopher doesn't want you to take his block."

The other child ignores her and keeps pulling on the block that Christopher is now sitting on. "How about this one?" says the adult, offering the child a similar block. The child hesitates a moment, then moves toward the block the adult is holding. The conflict resolved, the teacher moves back to her original spot.

At the other end of the room, a group of children is playing in a housekeeping area. One has gathered an armload of dolls and is trying to climb the stairs to the low loft, where there are several doll beds. He can't manage the stairs with his arms so full and is beginning to look frustrated. The caregiver walks over to him and suggests it would help if he could see the stairs. He drops the doll in front of his face and starts to climb, but staggers slightly. The teacher holds his arm with one hand and with the other hand touches the stair rail, saying, "You need a hand here to help you." He immediately gets the idea and drops the dolls in one arm. He then grabs the rail and carries the other armload of dolls upstairs, returning quickly for the ones he dropped. The adult in the meantime has gone to sit on the floor and is drinking pretend coffee that another child offered her in a plastic cup.

The children at the play dough table are contentedly poking, prodding, and patting the play dough. They are ignoring the adult who is sitting there, and he sits quietly, not interrupting them.

Contrast that scene to this one:

This playroom has two main areas of activity at the moment. On a rug sits a group of toddlers with an adult directing a "circle time." She has been singing songs and doing finger plays, trying her best to get the toddlers to join in. None of them is singing. A couple of them are listening as they squirm around. Half the group is busy trying to escape to the toys in the other part of the room. Another adult is directing the escapees back to the circle time, saying, "Circle time isn't over yet." Then the caregiver in charge gets out a flannel board and begins to tell a story. She briefly captures most of the group's attention, but then one boy comes up and tries to take the figures off the flannel board. The others can't see, so they get squirmy, and two start wrestling.

In the meantime, in another area of the room, a third caregiver has a group of toddlers around a table. Each has a piece of paper with his or her name printed in bold letters. Each has a squeeze bottle of glue and a container of cutout shapes. The adult is explaining that they are going to "make a picture for their mothers." Before she has finished her explanation and given directions, one of the toddlers has begun sucking on the glue bottle while another has squeezed a huge puddle on his paper. A third drops the container on the floor and laughs as the papers fly out. While the adult is dealing with these mishaps, two other children leave to join the circle time, and the remaining children squeeze glue to their heart's content. One finger paints in it, then rubs his head with his gluey hands.

The adults in the second scene are *doing something*. It is more obvious what they are doing in this scene than in the first scene. They are being teachers. They are playing the role that most people expect them to play.

Which scene appealed most to you?

Did you notice that the toddlers in both scenes are making choices, as is appropriate in the play mode, but in the second scene choices weren't part of the plan? Did you notice how heavily taxed the adults were by being in charge?

Adults who are uninitiated to early childhood principles and practices can understand a program where children are engaged in adult-directed "learning activities" but may be critical of one where the adults just sit on the floor and respond. Parents may prefer that caregivers *teach* and look like they are in control of what is happening. They may not understand the role of facilitating learning through self-directed free play. Further, the caregivers themselves may feel like baby-sitters when in the "wants nothing" mode during free play time. They may resist this role. All these factors work against a curriculum in which free play is a main ingredient. Caregivers need to find ways to articulate what they are doing so they can counteract the pressure that comes from all sides to *teach* infants and toddlers rather than let them play. What the adult does do that is more important than teaching is to structure the environment so that it is conducive to play.

HOW THE ENVIRONMENT INFLUENCES PLAY

An important environmental factor is group size. Larger groups tend to be overstimulating, and quieter children get ignored. It's much harder for children to get truly absorbed in play in a large group than in a small one, even when the adult-to-child ratio is good.

Mixture of ages is another environmental factor. Adult preferences in age mixtures in groups vary. Some programs work well with a variety of ages; others work equally well with most of the children about the same age.

If you do mix ages, be aware of protecting the youngest children. In the case of infants mixed with toddlers, you must protect those who can't move around from those who can. One way to do this, if they are in the same room, is to fence off a portion of the room for the immobile children. Don't just keep them in playpens and cribs. They need floor space and room to stretch and move, as well as interactions that come from several infants and adults sharing floor space.

Sometimes the mixture is toddlers with preschoolers. In that case the toddlers need to be protected from equipment they aren't mature enough to use, as well as from conflicts they can't win. You can't just stand back and let the children solve their own problems if one is two and the other almost five. The two-year-old will probably need some help to hold his or her own.

Most programs and family day-care homes set up the environment so that it's clear what activities take place in it. Play space is usually separate from the rest of the areas. (See chapter 12 for more explanation of the other areas of the environment.)

Caregivers aren't providing structure by directing the play itself, but they structure the play environment. You can do away with most rules by setting up the environment so that a good deal of undesirable behavior is eliminated. For example, if the children aren't allowed to play in the kitchen, put a gate across the access.

Make sure that everything in the environment is touchable and even mouthable. You can expect older children not to put things in their mouths, but infants and toddlers learn through mouthing. Sanitize toys periodically rather than restricting children from their natural inclinations.

Provide for gross motor activity inside as well as outside. Toddlers run, climb, roll, jump all the time—not just when invited to. You should think of your toddler play area as a gym more than a classroom and set it up for active play.

Provide plenty of softness, both for the active play and for the quiet times. Cushions, pads, mattresses, and foam rubber blocks on the floor invite children to bounce, roll, flop down, as well as cuddle and snuggle with books or stuffed animals.

Provide hard surfaces as well. A vinyl floor provides a contrast to carpeting and is interesting to crawlers as well as beginning walkers. Hard surfaces also make cleanup easier when you set up such activities as cooking or perhaps water play. (A thick bath mat under a plastic dishpan gives toddlers a chance to play in water without making too big a mess.)

Make available toys that can be used in many ways—rather than toys meant to be used in only one way. Large foam blocks are an example. They can be hauled around, stacked, put together to make a structure, or sat upon. There is much more to do with large foam blocks than, say, a battery-operated or wind-up toy that puts the child in the role of a spectator.

Let children combine toys and materials as much as possible. If they want to haul stuffed animals into a block structure they have built, let them. If they take pots and pans out of the play stove to put the play dough in, let them.

Of course you can't let everything be combined. Play dough in the water play table makes a mess nobody wants to have to clean up and wrecks the play dough besides. If you don't want something combined, make a clear environmental limit. (For example, water play can take place only in the pan on the table. You can't carry water in cups to the rug area.)

Determine the right amount of toys to make available. Don't put out more than you can stand to pick up. Watch out for overstimulation. Excited toddlers who have too many choices are more apt to make themselves and everyone else unhappy than those who have just enough to do. On the other hand, bored toddlers in a nearly empty room create as many behavior problems as those in a room overstuffed with toys and people. Be aware of the optimum amount of things to do. You can judge the right amount by the children's behavior. The optimum amount changes with the day, the group, and even the time of year.

SETTING UP THE ENVIRONMENT TO SUPPORT PLAY

- Keep play space separate from caregiving areas.
- Make sure everything in the play space is touchable.
- Provide for both fine and gross motor activity.
- Provide both soft and hard materials and play surfaces.
- Let children find unique ways to combine toys and materials.
- Put out the right amount of toys.
- Provide the right amount of choices.

HAPPENINGS

Take advantage of happenings. For the infant or toddler, these happenings can be very simple and still be satisfying. Perhaps it is the leaf raking in the play yard. Let the children watch or help, then play in the pile of leaves afterward.

Set up some happenings. A favorite at Napa Valley College Lab School Infant Center is an ongoing collage. A large piece of contact paper put up on the wall (sticky side out) invites the children to stick various items on. The continual rearrangement of the elements of this collage shows clearly how much more important the process is than the product at this age.

Some happenings that toddlers enjoy are modified versions of preschool activities. For example, easel painting can be done with plain water on chalk boards or thick soapsuds (colored with food coloring) on plexiglass easels. Sponge painting can become squeezing sponges in trays with a little water covering the bottom.

One clever caregiver who knew how much infants and toddlers enjoy pulling tissues out of their box made a toy consisting of a tissue box filled with scarves tied together. Another simple happening the very young enjoy is crumpling tissue paper. (Use white so that if it gets wet, you don't have dye all over everything.)

Simple food preparation tasks (mashing bananas or peeling hard-boiled eggs) can delight toddlers. Even snapping spaghetti can be involving and satisfying for toddlers.

FREE CHOICE

The environment should be set up to provide choices. Free choice is an important ingredient of play. Here is a scene that shows a playroom set up to encourage free play with numerous choices.

One end of the room is fenced off. In it three infants are lying on their backs, waving their arms, and looking around. An adult sits near them, rearranging brightly colored scarves to be within the reach of each child. A floppy beach ball is also available. One of the infants grabs it, waves it in the air, and lets it go. It lands near another of the infants, who regards it briefly, then turns back to gaze at the red scarf standing puffed up near his face.

Beyond the small fenced-in area is a larger space where nine young toddlers are playing. Two are busily engaged in crawling in and out of the rungs of the ladder that is lying flat on the floor. One leaves to sit in an empty laundry basket nearby. He climbs out, turns it over, then crawls under it. He lifts it up to look out at two children who are trying on hats from a collection they have found in a box near a shelf of toys. One of these children puts three hats on his head, then picks up two in his hands and runs over to the fence and throws the hats, one by one, into the area where the infants are lying. He giggles delightedly at the reaction he gets from the surprised infants. The other hat player in the meantime has loaded several into the back of a small toddler trike and is riding around the room. He stops at a low table where several children are squeezing plastic zip top bags full of different substances. He looks at the caregiver sitting there when she says to one of the squeezers, "You really like the soft one, don't you?" He briefly pokes one of the bags. Finding it interesting, he abandons the hats and the trike and sits down at the table to explore the other bags.

In another area of the room, a girl is hauling large plastic-covered foam blocks from one corner and piling them on the couch, which is pulled out a few feet from the wall. Then she climbs up on the couch and proceeds to throw the cushions over the back until she has nearly filled the space. She gets down, walks around, and jumps on the pile she has made.

In another part of the room, a child is sitting with an adult on a large mattress (which actually is two sheets sewed together and filled with foam rubber scraps). The two are "reading" a book together. They are joined by one of the bag squeezers, who plops down on the adult's lap and takes the book away. It is quickly replaced by the other child, who has a stack of books next to her on the mattress.

In this scene the children have a number of choices. Free choice is an important ingredient of play as well as an important prerequisite to learning.

PROBLEM OF THE MATCH

J. McVicker Hunt talks about the relationship of learning to choice in terms of what he calls the "problem of the match." He says that learning occurs when the environment provides experiences just familiar enough that children can understand them with the mental ability they have already attained, but just new enough to offer interesting challenges.[7]

Learning occurs when there is optimum incongruity between what is already known and a new situation. If the situation is too new and different, children withdraw, become frightened, ignore it, or react in some way other than learning. If it is not novel enough, children ignore it. They won't pay attention to what has already become so much a part of them that it no longer "registers."

The question is, how can you set up an environment so that it has elements of "optimum incongruity"? How does anyone know exactly what a match is for each child in his or her care? The answer is to have some knowledge of ages and stages (see the environmental chart in appendix B). The developmental information in part 2 should help, too.

The other answer is by *observation*. When you watch the children, you have a good idea what kinds of things to put into the environment for your particular group. By providing a number of choices of appropriate toys, objects, and occurrences and letting the children play, you give them the opportunity to move to novel situations and novel uses of materials. No one is more creative than infants and toddlers when it comes to inventive uses of materials and objects. They have a need to learn, a desire to understand. Caregivers can capitalize on this need by letting them determine their own use of the environment (within reason of course). By directing children with either praise or pressure, we distract them from the inner delights mentioned by Abraham Maslow in chapter 2. Children get these inner delights from struggling with a problem that matches their learning level.

Sooner or later children in an interesting, challenging environment are bound to find a problem that they want to solve but can't. They "get stuck." If they can't figure out the next move, the adult can intervene by providing a tiny bit of help. Sometimes it's hard for adults to wait when they can solve a problem so easily. But if they wait, they provide children the best learning opportunities. Don't rescue children from problems; help them problem solve.

And don't push children. Here's another view of "getting stuck." Sometimes children get stuck by becoming satiated with something. They have had enough of some activity. *Adults* decide that children are bored, and they want to do something about it—quickly! Many adults have a great fear of boredom for infants as well as for themselves. This fear has perhaps been heightened by the trend for infant stimulation and pressures for academics before kindergarten. Yet boredom is educational and can be considered part of the learning plan of any program. As Maslow says,

> The single holistic principle that binds together the multiplicity of human motives is the tendency for a new and higher need to emerge as the lower need fulfills itself by being sufficiently gratified. The child who is fortunate enough to grow normally and well gets satiated and *bored* with the delights that he has savored sufficiently, and *eagerly* (without pushing) goes on to higher, more

complex, delights as they become available to him without danger or threat. . . . He doesn't have to be "kicked upstairs," or forced on to maturity as it is so often implied. He *chooses* to grow on to higher delights, to become bored with older ones.[8]

Children cannot push themselves on until they have done very thoroughly what it is they need to do. Until they have reached the state of boredom, they are still motivated by unfinished business and can't move on. Boredom, when they finally attain it, provides the push to move on—but the push comes from within, not from without. They can then leave behind the old level, the old needs, and deal with the new ones, giving them their full attention. When the push to move on comes from without—from the adult or the environment—children never quite satisfy themselves. They may move on to the next stage, task, or activity with leftover feelings from the previous one, perhaps unable to give full attention to the new.

This idea of children deciding for themselves when to move on is the basis of the play yard design of Jerry Ferguson, who is an architect as well as an early childhood educator.[9] Ferguson designs environments uniquely suited to allowing infants and young toddlers to decide when and whether they are old enough to leave each developmental area. For example, she designed a play yard for the Pacific Oaks Infant-Toddler Program in Pasadena, California, in which the very youngest infants were in a low-stimulation area in the middle yard but cut off from the rest by a variety of barriers. In this area was a grassy place, completely safe for tiny babies. Beyond the grass was a sandy place with a tunnel at the end connecting the sand to a still more challenging play yard. Between the grass and the sand there was also a low wooden walkway designed to present a sufficient barrier to infants who were not yet ready to cross it. Children who were just beginning to move around had to conquer the raised walkway before they would get to the sand. They could test the sand from the safety of the walk before deciding to go into it, and they did this, sometimes for a week at a time, before they were ready. By the time they chose to go into the sand, they were able to handle the risks it presented, and the sand then became a safe environment for them. The tunnel at the other end, though obviously open, presented a formidable barricade, and few children chose to go through it until they were nearly ready to walk.

Thus, by the time the infants were able to leave the safe inner yard (by their own choice), they were developmentally ready for the bigger challenges of the yard beyond. This yard was designed for the beginning walker and good crawler and was interesting and safe, yet challenging (that is, optimally risky). Beyond was the most challenging yard, with climbing equipment and wheel toys for the toddlers. Although all the children who left the inner yard could return to it, few did so except for occasional visits. They chose to play where the environment had more to offer them.

Jerry Ferguson stresses that her approach works only because the infants have learned to take some responsibility for their own well-being. They come to depend on their ability to make choices, which means they have had the opportunity to gain experience in making decisions.

Infants and toddlers learn a great deal by being in an environment that offers the freedom to explore and discover. The adult role is to set up that environment and to remain available but nondirective while the children play, intervening selectively to prevent children from hurting each other and to help them work at solving problems.

This chapter ends part 1, which focuses on the adult's role. Part 2 examines the progression of development in each of seven areas, starting with attachment.

Thought/Activity Questions

1. What are the models from your own childhood that you carry in your head today? Can you relate your own experience to Papert's "gears"?
2. Recall an early play experience of your own. Relive it, if you can. Think about what you got out of this experience. How can you use your own experience to understand the importance of free play for infants and toddlers?
3. Have you experienced a time when play was not playful? Discuss.
4. Where was your favorite place to play as a child? How can you use your own experience to design a play environment for infants and toddlers?

Notes

1. Seymour Papert, *Mindstorms: Children, Computers, and Powerful Ideas* (New York: Basic Books, 1980), p. vi.
2. Ibid., p. vii.
3. Ibid., p. viii.
4. Ibid., p. viii.
5. Elena Bodrova and Deborah Leong, *Tools of the Mind: The Vygotskian Approach to Early Childhood Education* (Columbus, Ohio: Merrill, 1996).
6. Magda Gerber, "From a Speech by Magda Gerber," *Educaring* 16(3), Summer 1995, p. 7.
7. J. McVicker Hunt, *Intelligence and Experience* (New York: Ronald Press, 1961), p. 267.
8. Abraham H. Maslow, *Toward a Psychology of Being,* 2nd ed. (New York: Van Nostrand, 1968), pp. 55–56.
9. Jerry Ferguson, "Creating Growth-Producing Environments for Infants and Toddlers," in *Supporting the Growth of Infants, Toddlers, and Parents,* edited by Elizabeth Jones (Pasadena, Calif.: Pacific Oaks, 1979).

For Further Reading

J. S. Bruner, "The Organization of Action and the Nature of Adult–Infant Transaction," in *The Analysis of Action,* edited by M. von Cranach and R. Harre (Cambridge: Cambridge University Press, 1982).

Amy Laura Dombro, Laura J. Colker, and Diane Trister Dodge, *Creative Curriculum for Infants and Toddlers* (Washington, D.C.: Teaching Strategies, 1997).

Magda Gerber, *Dear Parent: Caring for Infants with Respect* (Los Angeles: Resources for Infant Educarers, 1998).

Magda Gerber, "Good Play Objects for Babies," *Educaring* 7(3), Spring 1986, pp. 4–6.

Janet Gonzalez-Mena, "Toddlers: What to Expect," *Young Children,* November 1986, pp. 47–51.

Fergus P. Hughes, James Elicker, and Linn C. Veen, "A Program of Play for Infants and Their Caregivers," *Young Children,* January 1995, pp. 52–58.

Elizabeth Jones, "The Play's the Thing: Styles of Playfulness," *Child Care Information Exchange,* January/February 1993, pp. 29–31.

E. Jones and G. Reynolds, *The Play's the Thing: Teachers' Roles in Children's Play* (New York: Teachers College Press, 1992).

Lilian G. Katz, Demetra Evangelou, and Jeanette Allison Hartman, *The Case for Mixed-Age Grouping in Early Education* (Washington, D.C.: National Association for the Education of Young Children, 1990).

Patricia Monighan-Nourot, Barbara Scales, Judith Van Horn, and Milly Almy, *Looking at Children's Play: A Bridge between Theory and Practice* (New York: Teachers College Press, 1987).

Martha W. Pratt, "The Importance of Infant/Toddler Interactions," *Young Children* 54(4), July 1999, pp. 26–29.

Judy Reinsberg, "Understanding Young Children's Behavior," *Young Children* 54(4), July 1999, pp. 54–57.

Anna Tardos, "Facilitating the Play of Children at Loczy," *Educaring* 6(3), Summer 1985, pp. 1–7.

Mary Jane Tonge, "Hanging Out with Babies at Play: Vignettes from a Participant-Observer," in *Supporting the Growth of Infants, Toddlers, and Parents,* edited by Elizabeth Jones (Pasadena, Calif.: Pacific Oaks, 1991).

Judith Van Horn, Patricia Nourot, Barbara Scales, and Keith Alward, *Play at the Center of the Curriculum* (Columbus, Ohio: Merrill, 1993).

L. S. Vygotsky, *Mind in Society: Development of Higher Psychological Processes* (Cambridge: Harvard University Press, 1978).

Connie K. Williams and Constance Kamii, "How Do Children Learn by Handling Objects?" *Young Children,* November 1986, pp. 23–26.

CHAPTER 5

The Development of Attachment

Attachment is a complex, ongoing process. Its definitions may vary, but in essence it involves a *closeness* and a *responsiveness* to an infant. This chapter discusses this important two-way experience between an infant and an adult and the behaviors that indicate how it changes as the child grows. Also included are what can happen if a child cannot make an attachment and the special needs that result from such a breakdown. The chapter also examines some of the exciting new research related to brain development. It begins with an overview of early brain growth and goes on to examine just how significant such growth is to the formation of relationships and early attachments.

BRAIN RESEARCH

More has been learned in the last ten years about the human brain than in the last one hundred years! See table 5.1 for a summary of how our understanding of brain development has changed. Today new technologies in neuroscience that are noninvasive (they don't interfere with natural brain function) are making detailed exploration of the brain possible. Amazing new tools exist for mapping the brain and for understanding brain chemistry, as well as for appreciating the effect of environmental factors. This information has taught us many valuable lessons about how infants learn and why early experience is so vital to development. Looking at a brief overview of how the brain functions may help to foster an appreciation of just why particularly responsive, positive experiences are so important to an infant's early development.

TABLE 5.1
Rethinking the Brain

Old Thinking . . .	New Thinking . . .
How a brain develops depends on the *genes* you are born with.	How a brain develops hinges on a complex *interplay* between the *genes* you're born with and the *experiences* you have.
The *experiences* you have before age three have a *limited impact* on later development.	Early *experiences* have a *decisive impact* on the architecture of the brain, and on the nature and extent of adult capacities.
A *secure relationship* with a primary caregiver creates a favorable *context* for early development and learning.	*Early interactions* don't just create a context; they *directly affect* the way the brain is "*wired.*"
Brain development is *linear:* the brain's capacity to learn and change grows steadily as an infant progresses toward adulthood.	Brain development is *nonlinear:* there are prime times for acquiring different kinds of knowledge and skills.
A toddler's brain is much *less active* than the brain of a college student.	By the time children reach age three, their brains are *twice as active* as those of adults. Activity levels drop during adolescence.

Source: Rima Shore, *Rethinking the Brain: New Insights into Early Development.* Copyright © 1997, Families and Work Institute, 330 Seventh Avenue, New York, New York 10001. 212-465-2044. Web site: *http://www.familiesandwork.org.* All rights reserved.

The basic building blocks of the brain are specialized nerve cells called neurons. Each neuron has an axon, or output fiber, that sends energy, or impulses, to other neurons. Neurons also have many dendrites, which are input fibers that receive the impulses from other neurons. The dendrites grow and branch out forming "dendrite trees" that receive signals from other neurons. These connections, or synapses, are formed as an infant experiences the world. The connections used regularly in everyday life become reinforced, or protected, and become part of the brain's permanent "circuitry." The human brain at birth is still very immature, so these early experiences can have a dramatic effect over time on the growth and learning of an infant.[1]

In the early years, young brains produce almost twice as many synapses as they will need. The dendrite trees grow and become very dense. By age two, the number of synapses a toddler has is similar to that of an adult. By three the child has twice as many synapses as an adult. This large number is stable throughout the first ten years, but by adolescence about half of these synapses have been discarded or "pruned." The brain prunes, or selectively eliminates, unnecessary synapses.

Now the key question: how does the brain *know* which synapses, or connections, to keep and which ones to prune, or discard? Early experience seems to be much more critical than was first realized by many people. Experiences activate neural pathways, and information in the form of chemical signals gets stored along the pathways. Repeated experiences strengthen specific pathways. A particular pathway takes on a "protected" status; it is not pruned because it has been repeatedly used. These protected, strong pathways remain into adulthood. The "use it or lose it" saying applies to early brain development.

This text has emphasized numerous times the importance of quality experiences and responsive care for very young children. Now the brain development research indicates that these early experiences, if repeated, actually form stable neural pathways. The way we think and learn has everything to do with the extent and nature of these pathways. When a very young child experiences something new, or a "problem," brain activity increases. If neural pathways are strong, signals travel quickly and problems are easily solved.

Pause for a moment and think about a ten-month-old child whose mom is taking him to his child care provider as she goes off to work. He may experience a certain amount of stress (this is called "stranger anxiety" and will be discussed in more detail later in the chapter). However, when his caregiver is familiar with and can be responsive to his stress signals, he comes to *know* that he will be okay (the caregiver is a familiar friend and today his blanket is of particular comfort to cuddle and smell). His mother will return. In his brain connections have been formed that allow him to separate with relatively little effort. Through his experiences he has already developed efficient neural pathways. Responsive, positive experiences stabilize connections in his brain. These very early connections in the brain are related to attachment experiences.

Through attachment, two individuals come together and stay together. John Kennell defines attachment as "an affectionate bond between two individuals that endures through space and time and serves to join them emotionally."[2] The mother is usually the first and primary attachment the baby makes, but babies are becoming more and more strongly attached to their fathers, especially as issues involving working moms expand. When infants experience child care at a young age, these secondary attachments (people other than their parents) become very important.

Attachment to caregivers differs from that to parents in many ways. One obvious way is in duration. The long-term, even lifetime attachment one expects as a parent gives way to a much shorter period for caregivers. From day one, caregivers know that the children will leave their charge long before they grow up. The departure may come without warning because parents' lives and need for child care sometimes change suddenly. This expectation of permanence of the adult-child relationship is a big difference between being a parent and being a caregiver.

Parental attachment, this feeling of closeness, starts right at birth for some. In the ideal situation, where parents and alert newborn are allowed time together to get acquainted, what is called "bonding" may occur as they fall in love in a very short time. It might even be called "love at first sight." This love at first sight can occur between caregivers and children too, as an adult and child are drawn to each other at first meeting. More commonly, attachment grows slowly over time as individuals get to know each other and learn each other's special ways of communicating. These special ways grow and change as developmental milestones are reached. The brain research now available to parents and caregivers validates that warm, positive interactions stabilize connections in the brain. High-quality, responsive care must be provided for this critical process called *attachment* to thrive.

MILESTONES OF ATTACHMENT

Important milestones of attachment influence mental, social, and emotional development. A baby's crying, pulling away from strangers, and trying to follow a departing parent indicate how attachment changes. Looking at these behaviors in more detail clarifies how competent an infant is.

Babies are designed to promote their own attachment. Think for a moment about the variety of behaviors that attract adults to babies. Hearing the cry of a newborn elicits feelings in the people who hear it. It is hard to ignore. Crying becomes one of the infant's strongest signals to the people responsible for his or her care.

Another strong attachment behavior most babies have at birth is the ability to establish eye contact. When a newborn looks right into your eyes, most adults melt. And if you touch the little fingers, they are likely to curl around your big one. If you talk to alert newborns, they are likely to turn toward the sound of your voice. And if you move away from them slightly, their eyes will follow your face. All these behaviors promote attachment.

Studies indicate that babies react differently to the people they are attached to right from the beginning. Later this preferential response becomes obvious as babies cry when the object of attachment leaves the room. This is an important indication that trust is developing. They follow the person with whom they have the attachment, first with gaze alone, then, when they are mobile, by crawling after. Here is a scene showing some of the attachment behaviors we have mentioned.

A small baby is screaming, lying on the floor on a blanket in the family room of the home where he is cared for. A reassuring voice comes from the other room. "I know you're hungry! I'm coming!" The cries cease at the sound of the voice. Then when no one appears, they start again even louder.

The family day-care provider hustles into the room carrying a warm bottle. "I'm sorry you had to wait!" The screaming continues. "I know,

I know. I'm going to pick you up now so you can eat." She bends over with her arms outstretched. The screaming slows down. She lifts him gently and walks across the room to sit down in a soft chair.

As he is picked up, the baby's whole body shows his anticipation of what is to come. He stiffens and his arms wave in excitement. He looks intensely into his caregiver's face. Once settled into the chair, he begins to squirm frantically, his mouth searching for the nipple. As it comes into his mouth, he closes his eyes, clenches his fists, and sucks furiously. "There you are. That's better, isn't it?" coos the caregiver.

He begins to relax after a few minutes, and both adult and child settle back, moving around until comfortable. "You were really hungry, weren't you?" The baby continues to suck without stopping. Both begin to look more and more relaxed and contented.

The baby eases up a little. His fists unclench, and one hand reaches out, groping. The caregiver touches his hand with her finger. He wraps his fingers around her finger and holds on tight. The caregiver snuggles him a little closer and kisses the top of his head. He opens his eyes and looks up at her. She looks back, a warm smile on her lips. He stops sucking and lets go of the nipple. With his gaze fixed on his caregiver's eyes, his mouth breaks into a big grin. Then he snuggles in even closer and continues to suck contentedly, his little fist wrapped around her finger, his eyes looking into hers.

These two are a unit. Both feel that this is an intimate moment of a close relationship. This special form of communication—interactional synchrony— is like an "emotional dance." The caregiver and the baby send each other important signals. Both partners share emotions, especially positive ones.[3] The infant has the capacity to elicit delight from another; this in turn gives him pleasure. The example of the feeding experience illustrates some of the repertoire of behaviors involved in attachment. Through these mutually responsive behaviors, which include touching, fondling, and eye contact, as well as feeding, infants and adults form an extremely close relationship. Remember, too, that the new information on the brain indicates that these early behaviors begin to form pathways in the brain. These pathways form the *physical foundation* of trust. Positive experiences stabilize the brain connections. Infants need this relationship because they cannot physically attach themselves to people in order to get nourished and cared for. They are dependent. Attachment is nature's way of ensuring that someone will care (in the emotional sense) and provide care (in the physical sense).

Once babies can distinguish their mother or caregiver from other people, two new worries begin. First, at about eight to ten months of age, they begin to fear strangers. Second, now that they know who mother is, they worry about losing her. This latter fear usually appears by about ten to twelve months. Both of these fears indicate the infant's ability to discriminate and recognize difference and therefore are obvious signs of mental growth. Corresponding to this second developmental fear is the baby's inability to understand that objects gone from sight still exist. Jean Piaget called this "object permanence"; it will be discussed further in chapter 8. Infants' worry about losing their mother is understandable. They cannot foresee that a separation is only temporary. Knowing this, it is easier for caregivers to understand the desperation of the protest when a baby is left behind as a parent walks out the door.

It may be helpful to emphasize the interplay between dependency, mental development, and trust in this process of attachment. When an eighteen-month-old child is clinging to his mother and crying for her not to go (obvious dependent behavior), he is also saying I *know* I need you (a mental function). As his mental capacity grows, and his experiences teach him that he can trust his mother to return, from attachment comes trust as he learns that the world is basically a friendly place where he can get his needs met. From attachment also comes autonomy, or independence, as babies grow and begin to take over their caregiving by learning self-help skills. They also find it easier and easier to let go because they know that their parent will be back. This ability to trust a relationship is the foundation for independence—a focus of the toddler period.

This worry about leaving the parent or primary caregiver is called "separation anxiety." It is usually at its peak as the baby nears the end of the first year of life. If the child enters day care just at this time, the beginning can be very difficult. Children do better if they enter before or after the peak of separation anxiety.

In a quality infant-toddler day-care program, children gain courage to explore and participate (fostering mental and social skills) by using their parent or known caregiver as a home or trust base. Checking in periodically provides renewed energy to move out and continue exploration. It is important when the parent leaves that he or she not sneak away. By saying good-bye, the parent helps the child appreciate that the departure is predictable. Gradually a child learns that coming back is also part of saying good-bye. A sensitive caregiver can put into words what she perceives a potentially upset child to be feeling. Acceptance of these feelings, and not distraction from them, provides a young child with a secure base for emotional development.

The following suggestions may assist caregivers in helping parents with toddler separation:

1. Help the parent understand that once the good-byes are said, the departure should be immediate. Some parents have as much or more trouble than their toddlers separating. Help the parent know that you understand it is hard to leave, but it is easier on the child if departure is quick once the good-byes are said.
2. Allow the child his or her feelings, but don't get involved in them yourself. Separation feelings are hard for some adults because they trigger issues they may want to forget. One way caregivers respond to this situation is by trying to get rid of the child's feelings, through distraction or by minimizing them. ("Come on now—it's not that bad—she'll be back before you know it.")

3. Have an interesting, even enticing environment that calls out to children so that when they are ready, they can readily get involved in something.

Attachment is vital to infants' and toddlers' development and should be promoted in child care programs. At the same time, caregivers should realize that parents may fear their children may gain secondary attachments outside the home at the expense of their primary ones with parents. Caregivers can help ease parents' fears by letting them know they are unfounded. The secondary attachments are in addition to the primary ones—not replacements for them. Separation anxiety and all the feelings that go with being left in day care are also of concern to both parents and caregivers who have to help children cope until they feel comfortable. It may comfort parents to know that these feelings are a sign that attachment is strong and that it will hold. Children will learn to cope with separation, and this skill will serve them for a lifetime. The various attachment behaviors and coping skills that develop in children indicate they are establishing trust in others and, at the same time, becoming self-reliant.

What happens to the child who cannot get nurturing responses from people in her environment? And what about the child who seems indifferent to others or may even reject them? It is vital that the process of attachment be provided for, even if it takes a great deal of time and energy.

ATTACHMENT ISSUES

Not all babies enjoy an ideal relationship that fosters the attachment process; the infant and caregiver do not respond to each other in ways that bring mutual delight and the care necessary for the infant. What about a relationship that is less than ideal?

Sometimes infants are born without a strong set of attachment behaviors. They may not be responsive or attractive. Adults may find it neither rewarding nor satisfying to interact with such babies or to meet their needs. Not only may these infants lack a set of pleasing behaviors; they may even reject any advances. They may constantly stiffen when cuddled or cry when touched. Some babies are just not responsive. They may be too active to attend, or too passive. In these cases, it is up to adults to promote attachment.

Caregivers can promote attachment as a goal to develop a relationship. That means being persistent and not being put off by the baby. Sensitive caregivers find ways that cause less discomfort to hold the babies who reject them. They continue to touch and talk to these babies despite rejection. They use caregiving times to interact with and pay attention to the child at other times as well. Sometimes just observing such babies regularly and in depth will help caregivers develop a feeling for babies they are indifferent toward or even negative about. That feeling is part of the attachment process.

Caregivers also find ways to help too active and too passive babies attend. They discover ways to reduce stimulation or increase sensory input, depending on what is needed.

Center-based programs can provide for attachment needs through a primary caregiver system in which babies are assigned to a particular caregiver. Group size is important if babies are to be responded to consistently and sensitively in order to promote attachment. More than about twelve babies works against attachment.

Sometimes the attachment problems lie with the parents. The infant may be fully equipped with attachments behaviors, but the parent may fail to respond. Indifference, for whatever reason, can be devastating to an infant. The infant doesn't give up for a long time and may develop a set of behaviors that elicits a negative response from the adult, which is better than no response at all.

If the baby has no attachment or negative attachment, that is cause for alarm. Outside help is required. Child care workers may perceive the problem and refer the families, but it is beyond their realm of responsibility to solve it.

You may suspect this problem when a baby in your care does not thrive in the same way the other babies do. He or she may not be gaining weight or reaching milestones within a reasonable time. This failure to thrive may be related to a variety of other causes of an attachment problem. A clue that attachment is the problem is a lack of attachment or your having trouble getting attached. You may see that the baby is unresponsive to everybody. Or perhaps you see him or her responding exactly the same to everyone—parent, caregiver, and stranger.

What happens if there is no attachment? A significant answer came from Harry Harlow, who learned something about attachment without even setting out to study it. He was interested in isolating rhesus monkeys so they could live in a disease-free environment and not infect one another. He raised fifty-six newborn monkeys in separate cages, away from one another and their mothers. He was surprised to find that they grew to be very different adults from the rest of their species. They were more unsocial, indifferent, and aggressive than other rhesus monkeys, which are normally social and cooperative. None of the monkeys raised in isolation mated.[4]

Let's examine the implications for child rearing. Although virtually no one attempts to raise a child in total isolation, children are too frequently raised without enough human contact, without opportunities for interaction, and without consistent treatment. In such a situation, the problems are multiple. Though the infants have contact with adults who feed and change them, the adults may vary from day to day, and the infants may be unable to distinguish one from the other or may find that their attachment behavior brings no consistent response when they are being cared for. They find no one to call their own—no one whom they can influence. Eventually, such children give up and no longer try to influence anyone. Lacking not only attachment but adequate physical contact, these infants are deprived of the variety of sensory input that comes with a healthy relationship. They become passive and non-complaining, their development slows, and they may fail to thrive. Researchers believe it is important for babies to have established a consistent attachment to at least one person before four to six months of age.[5]

This consistent and sensitive care is emphasized in the brain development research mentioned earlier in this chapter. When infants experience these secure attachments, hormones called neurotransmitters are secreted, and they induce a sense of well-being. Positive, nurturing experiences seem to reinforce certain pathways in the brain. There is a dynamic relationship between the *care* an infant receives and his or her brain *growth*. Healthy attachment develops when caregivers are consistent and responsive; relationships are primary to development.[6]

Studies of children in institutions have kept many people from considering group care for infants. But infants in child care are different from infants in orphanages. They have parents (at least one). Most of them arrive in child care attached, and they remain attached. But we have learned from those sad orphanages of yesterday. We know now how vital attachment needs are. We know, too, that infants need ongoing, reciprocal, responsive interactions when they are outside their own home for significant periods during the day. We know that infants in child care retain their attachments to their parents.

Evidence of the effects of child care on the development of attachment in infancy is still sparse, though answers are beginning to come. The research shows that infant child care is not detrimental to development if the *quality* of care is exemplary. That means, among many things, that the caregivers are nurturing, responsive adults who meet each infant's individual needs. Quality care is vital. Infants not only deserve but *must have* fine care—not just good enough care.[7]

CHILDREN WITH SPECIAL NEEDS: INFANTS AFFECTED BY DRUGS

Some infants today have severe attachment problems because their mothers took drugs during their pregnancies. (The drugs vary, but cocaine or crack are among the most common types.) These babies usually have medical and behavioral problems. The following scene shows a typical profile of an infant exposed to substance abuse and suggests ways to care for such a baby. Special thanks to David Kaplan, pediatrician, for this information, for his specialized work with crack-addicted infants, and for his ongoing support to foster parents in San Mateo County, California.[8]

> Jenny is six months old. She is being undressed for her usual weekly medical exam in the doctor's office by Kathy, her foster mother. Jenny's mom took crack cocaine during her pregnancy with Jenny, and although she contacts Kathy regularly, she has seen Jenny only three

times and remains unable emotionally and physically to care for her baby. Jenny was born full-term but weighed only four and a half pounds. No other prenatal information was available to Kathy.

Kathy undresses Jenny slowly and speaks quietly to her. She tries to avoid unnecessary stimulation because Jenny is still prone to high-pitched, frantic crying. When the doctor comes in, he checks Jenny's color, reflexes, and weight. During the examination, Jenny does *not* make eye contact with the doctor. He, too, moves with gentle firmness in an effort to avoid overstimulating Jenny. His remaining assessment is done through conversation with Kathy. Jenny is placed on a soft flannel blanket in Kathy's lap in a sitting position with her shoulders and arms forward.

DOCTOR: Kathy, I see that Jenny has gained a little weight this week, although she remains below normal for her age. Has her feeding situation improved?

KATHY: Yes, I think so. I always try to feed her in a quiet place, and swaddling is no longer necessary. I think her sucking is stronger, and there is less spitting up. She still does not like to look at me, but generally she is more calm than a month ago.

DOCTOR: That's a very good sign. Remember to help the spitting up, feed her in a sitting or semireclining position. Feed slowly, burp frequently, and avoid overfeeding. After feeding, keep Jenny vertical for a few minutes. You seem to be more able than anyone else to calm her.

KATHY: Yes, I think so, too. Rocking her gently in a vertical position has really helped. When she is stiff, the warm bath and gentle massage you suggested have also helped.

DOCTOR: Good, glad to hear that. Just keep alert to her warning signs of overstimulation—yawning, frowns, eye aversion, flailing limbs, whimpering. I know once she starts crying, she is difficult to stop, and prolonged crying may complicate her respiratory problems.

Jenny's movement on Kathy's lap has been gradually increasing during this brief conversation between Kathy and the doctor. She is beginning to stretch her legs forward and her shoulders back. Her restlessness is noted. Kathy shifts her slightly forward in her lap to avoid back arching and potential muscle cramping.

KATHY: I think we are getting ready to leave now. (Both doctor and foster mom pause to observe Jenny.)

DOCTOR: Yes, I'd agree. Jenny is fortunate to be with someone who reads her signals so quickly. I think she is doing well. Kathy, you know that I can't make long-term projections for her, but we will stay in close contact. Play is important for Jenny. Avoid any assistive devices—walkers or jumpers. I'll see you in about ten days; keep up the good work!

KATHY: Thanks! We'll see you then.

Kathy begins to dress Jenny. Jenny's muscle tone has remained relaxed. She makes no attempt, however, to cuddle or hold onto Kathy. And although she is making gurgling sounds, crying does not develop.

It is obvious, even in this brief scene, that with an infant exposed to drug abuse, attachment behaviors are lacking, and handling needs to be slower and more deliberate. Responsiveness and observing infant cues remain *very* important. Few specialists and doctors are willing to make long-term assessments of such babies because each child and situation are unique. The significant point here is that each infant must have the opportunity for attachment to develop. Care that fosters this attachment process needs to be consistent and responsive.

Thought/Activity Questions

1. Imagine a dialogue with a new parent concerning the topic of attachment. What would you like to share about this process? How would your comments change with the parent of a two-year-old?
2. Review table 5.1, Rethinking the Brain, on page 78. Which of the five *new* thinkings do you think is the most important? Why? How might you share this information with a parent?
3. What happens to development if little or no attachment is made? Consider specifically emotional, social, and mental/cognitive growth.
4. Observe in an infant-toddler program when the parent of a toddler is about to leave. What attachment behaviors in the child do you see? How does the parent respond? Consider what changes or additions you might like to see.
5. Describe the kinds of interactions that build attachment.

Notes

1. Rima Shore, *Rethinking the Brain: New Insights into Early Development* (New York: Families and Work Institute, 1997), pp. 16–18.
2. M. Klaus and J. Kennell, *Parent-Infant Bonding* (St. Louis: Mosby, 1982), p. 2.
3. R. Isabella and J. Belsky, "Interactional Synchrony and the Origins of Infant-Mother Attachment," *Child Development* 62, 1991, pp. 373–384.
4. Harry Harlow, "The Nature of Love," *American Psychology* 13, 1958, p. 386.
5. John Bowlby, *Attachment,* vol. 1 of *Attachment and Loss* (London: Hogarth, 1969), p. 386.
6. J. Ronald Lally, "Brain Research, Infant Learning, and Child Care Curriculum," *Child Care Information Exchange* 121, May/June 1998, pp. 46–48.
7. F. A. Goossens and M. H. Ijzendoorn, "Quality of Infants' Attachments to Professional Caregivers," *Child Development* 61, 1990, pp. 832–837.
8. David Kaplan, "Fetal-Infant Crack Addiction," *Foster Parent Training,* conference notes, Daly City, Calif., 1990.

For Further Reading

T. B. Brazelton and B. Cramer, *The Earliest Relationships* (New York: Addison-Wesley, 1990).

Susan Greenberg, "The Loving Ties That Bond," *Your Child From Birth to Three,* (*Newsweek* Special Edition), Spring/Summer 1997, pp. 68–69.

R. Karen, "Becoming Attached," *Atlantic* 265(2), February 1990, pp. 35–70.

J. Ronald Lally, "The Impact of Child Care Policies and Practices on Infant/Toddler Identity Formation," *Young Children* 51(1), November 1995, pp. 58–67.

M. Lamb, *The Father's Role: Cross-Cultural Perspectives* (Hillside, N.J.: Erlbaum, 1987).

H. Raikes, "A Secure Base for Babies: Applying Attachment Concepts to the Infant Care Setting," *Young Children,* July 1996, pp. 59–67.

Joel L. Swerdlow, "Quiet Miracles of the Brain," *National Geographic* 187(6), June 1995, pp. 2–41.

E. Thomas and S. Browder, *Born Dancing: How Intuitive Parents Understand Their Baby's Unspoken Language and Natural Rhythms* (New York: Harper & Row, 1988).

Beginnings Workshop: "Working with Parents of Children with Differing Abilities," *Child Care Information Exchange* 88, November 1992.

CHAPTER 6

The Development of Perception

Infants are immediately involved in the process of gathering information and using it. "Perception" refers to the ability to take in and organize sensory experience. It is an innate tendency to search for order and stability in the world, and it becomes increasingly fine-tuned as we age.[1] Sensory information provides an important link to other areas of development. As infants repeat experiences, they begin to make meaningful connections about objects and people in their world. Neural pathways in the brain are strengthened as they gather, apply, and benefit from their sensory encounters. This chapter reviews these perceptual, or sensory, abilities. It also includes some guides to assist sensory-impaired young children.

The increasing public awareness of early brain development has validated what many parents and caregivers have known for a long time. Learning for infants and toddlers is interrelated; growth in one area influences growth in another. This is certainly clear in the area of perceptual development. As infants become aware of their sensory experiences, they can discriminate between people and make attachments. They also learn to move their bodies in specific ways to accommodate new sensory information. The interrelatedness between motor experience and sensory experience is strong, and it provides the base for cognitive development. Infants need sensory experiences, with opportunities for lots of repetition, if they are to build healthy learning pathways in the brain.

To become more aware of your own perceptions so that you can better understand those of an infant, try the following exercise:

Choose something you like the taste and smell of (a sprig of mint, a piece of apple), and take it to a place where you can be undisturbed.

Block out all your senses except smell and taste. Then pay attention to what you have brought along to smell and taste. Concentrate first on your sense of smell only, then on your sense of taste. When you have fully explored these, put the substance away. Notice how the sensation fades. When the flavor is gone, move on.

Become aware of your body. Sense the places on your body where your clothes touch, where you feel pressure. Pay attention to these sensations. Alter your position, and note the changes you feel.

Be aware of your body in relation to the space it occupies. Feel the space around you. "Sense," without touching, where your body ends and the space begins. Explore the relationship between your body and this space. Try expanding and contracting your body; alter the space it takes up.

Now move your attention from your whole body to your hands. Explore around you with your hands, noticing the textures and forms your fingers encounter. Pay attention only to what your fingertips feel.

Move your focus from your hands to your ears. Pay attention to everything that is coming in through your ears. Now pick out the noise closest to you and listen to it carefully. Next shift your attention to the noise that is farthest from you. Now see if you can concentrate on sounds coming from inside you. Finally, turn on all the noises at once and take them in without sorting them out.

Now move your attention to your eyes. Open your eyes. Look around. Focus on an object near you. See if you can make the object disappear by looking only at the spaces around it and between its parts. Concentrate on these negative spaces for a minute or so. Then take in more objects. Look at them carefully. Then concentrate on the space around and between them. Shift your focus from the space back to the objects and back to the space again. Try concentrating only on background, then on foreground, then on a single object. Let your eyes go out of focus.

Come back to your normal perceptive state.

Now reflect on the order in which you experienced your senses. If you did the exercise the way it was set up, you went from perceiving through very localized physical contact (your taste buds) to generalized physical contact (your skin). Then you went on to perceive with two senses that extend beyond physical contact—hearing and seeing. With these you took in events or objects at a distance.

Infants learn to use their senses in much the same order. They first depend most on perceptions that are direct and physical—especially those that come in through their mouths. An infant's mouth is his or her main learning tool in the first months of life. As infants grow, they learn to "extend" themselves by tuning in to the senses that bring information from a distance.

This ability to tune in to experience and concentrate on certain aspects of it allows an organizational process to develop. This process is neurological—it cannot be seen. But we can see infants adjust to their experiences. Even though all the senses are operating, infants initially do not realize that the information they receive from these senses has continuity. They cannot yet perceive the repetitiveness of events or interpret them. In a short time, however, connections between separate events are clarified. For example, crying infants will calm down as they realize that hearing a particular voice or seeing a particular face means that food or care is about to be given.

This book talks about only five senses, but it is interesting to speculate about possible other senses and whether infants may have many more sensory abilities than we retain as adults. Examine the following passage from *The Metaphoric Mind,* a book that argues that we have not five or six but twenty or more senses.

> Some human beings clearly detect minute changes in gravitational and magnetic fields. Others can detect the energy created by a flow of material in pipes, movement through soil, or electrostatic currents in the air. As adults these people are considered unique, mystical, or deviant in some other way. It may well be that these people have simply retained an awareness of senses they possessed as children.[2]

HEARING

Newborns can hear at birth (and even before). They can sense the direction sound comes from as well as its frequency and duration. Researchers have found that sounds of five to fifteen seconds seem to have the most effect on the infant's level of activity and heart rate (the two measures most frequently used to reflect an infant's awareness of a change in an event). If the sound lasts more than several minutes, the infant becomes less responsive. In other words, an infant is more attentive if you speak and then are quiet than if you make long speeches.[3]

Newborns recognize the sound of their mother's voice. Experiments have shown that infants only twenty weeks old can discriminate between the syllables "baw" and "gah." Listening to people's voices and noting differences seems to be an early skill. Young babies are especially responsive to a high-pitched, expressive voice, using a rising tone at the end of phrases. This describes a speech pattern now referred to as "parentese" (replacement for "baby talk"). Infants' early responsiveness to such sounds and patterns seems to encourage parents and caregivers to talk to them. This interaction strengthens both the emotional tie between them and the infants' readiness for the complex task of language development.[4] The way infants react to sounds or any other sensory stimulation, however, depends a great deal on the situation in which they experience them. A loud or strange noise may be frightening, but the presence of a familiar, comforting caregiver transmits a sense of security and allows the infant to remain calm and open to learning.

Infants need the opportunity to experience a variety of sounds, and they need quiet times in order to appreciate the differences in sounds. If the noise level in the environment is too high, the infant spends a lot of energy tuning out and focusing. The optimum noise level varies with each child. Sensitive caregivers can determine what is more or less right for the individual after they get to know the child. Part of this awareness comes from knowing your own optimum noise level.

Some adults like background music, and others don't. However, a point to consider is this: if you want an infant to focus on a sound, that sound should be isolated and have a beginning and an end. For example, if a music box or record player is constantly playing, the infant eventually stops listening because the sound is no longer interesting. Caregivers should be sure that mechanical toys and other noisemakers do not become substitutes for the human voice. Infants can determine a great deal from the inflection of a person's voice, and attending to the human voice and its inflections is the beginning of language development.

Toddlers have a greater ability to tolerate higher noise levels, so they can be in slightly larger groups than infants. However, toddlers too vary individually, and some children are greatly overstimulated by multiple sounds. These children may be unable to focus when surrounded by noise. One way to help solve this problem is to have quiet spaces where one or two overstimulated children may retreat when they choose to. We've seen pillow-lined closets, tents, and even large wooden boxes available for this purpose.

Toddlers, as well as infants, benefit when the sounds they hear most are live, human voices directed to them personally. Other appropriate sounds in the environment include voices of all sorts (children and adults), music (both live and recorded), and the sounds that naturally go along with free play in a rich environment. Helping children tune in to the sounds of nature, a worthy activity, is often accomplished on short walks, depending, of course, on the environment in which the center or family day-care home is located.

Be aware of talking to one sex more than the other. Boys and girls need equal treatment if they are to grow up feeling like equals.

SMELL AND TASTE

Less is known about smell than about the other senses. Researchers know that it is present at birth. Newborns can distinguish the smell of their own mothers from that of other women who have just given birth, so smell obviously plays a role in attachment. (Mothers also often report that the smells of their babies are pleasing to them.)

Newborns respond to unpleasant strong odors such as ammonia or acetic acid by turning away but seem insensitive to less-interesting odors that are fainter. An increase in breathing rate and activity level can be noted when odors are present in the air, and the greater the saturation of the odors, the greater the heart rate and activity level.

Much animal communication is carried by odors, and it's possible that the infant and toddler smell emotions in others, though that statement is more speculation than fact.

An environment rich in smells adds to a toddler program. They can be part of the daily program, such as food cooking, or they can be introduced by caregivers in such ways as "smell bottles." Be careful of making things that aren't edible smell delicious—such as chocolate shaving cream or peppermint flavoring in play dough—unless the toddlers are well conditioned to the idea that play dough and shaving cream are not for eating.

Taste does not seem to be present at birth, but by two weeks the infant can distinguish between sweet and bitter and prefers sweet. Salt taste is recognized soon after and will be accepted if the infant is hungry. A ten-day-old infant can show surprise if water is substituted for the expected milk, but there seems to be a correlation with whether the baby has been well fed: infants whose diets have been inadequate do not seem to notice taste differences rapidly.

Be careful not to condition infants to the taste of salt and other additives. There is no reason to spice food for the very young—the natural flavors are appreciated and enjoyed if not covered. Most of us have learned that food in its plain state "needs something," and we are suffering for that acquired taste as blood pressures soar and great numbers are on salt-restricted diets.

Tasting can be an important part of the toddlers' day as they are exposed to a variety of foods at meals and snack times. Of course, care should be taken to choose foods that don't present a choking hazard. More about this subject in chapter 12.

TOUCH

Sensitivity to discomfort and pain increases rapidly after birth. Some parts of the body are more sensitive than others. The head, for example, is more sensitive than the arms and legs. Individual babies vary in their sensitivity to touch, and for some touch is unwelcome. Caregivers need to learn ways to handle those "touch-defensive" babies in ways that cause minimal discomfort. One way is to lift such young infants on a pillow instead of picking them up as you would other babies. Some babies and toddlers respond better to strong touch than light touch, which seems to pain them.

Where and how we touch is bound up in culture. It is a good idea to find out what is forbidden or disrespectful in cultures different from your own if they are represented in your program. For example, in some cultures children are never touched on the head, and to do so upsets parents. Consider the message mainstream America gives when one person touches or pats another on the head. How would you feel if your boss patted you on the head? Pats on the head are reserved for the very young or dogs, never for an equal or a superior. Though it seems very natural to most adults, perhaps it would be more respectful to restrain from patting babies and young children on the head.

Be aware if you are differentiating between boys and girls in the way you touch the children in your care. Sometimes people unconsciously touch one sex more than the other. Try to be equal in your treatment of both sexes.

Tactile perception (touch) relates to motor abilities (movement skills). As babies increase in their ability to move around, touch gives them more and more information about the world. And they seek this information almost emphatically. Any environment for infants and toddlers should be all touchable and mouthable (the mouth also gives the very young a good deal of information). And while you are filling the environment with plastic toys (that are both touchable and mouthable), don't forget to provide some natural substances that the children can explore—wood, for example, or wool. (One educational approach, Waldorf Education, believes that young children should experience only objects [toys] made from natural substances because artificial ones—things that look like something else—fool the senses.)

Give toddlers words for what they are feeling—soft, warm, fuzzy, rough, smooth. Be sure they have plenty of soft objects in their environment. Some programs occur in predominantly hard environments because hard surfaces and objects last longer and are more sanitary. Reducing softness is not a way to increase cost-effectiveness because a hard environment changes the whole program. Behavior tends to improve when an environment is softened.

Provide a variety of tactile (touching) experiences for toddlers. Even though they are up and around, they haven't outgrown their need to explore the world with their skin. Here are some ideas for offering toddlers tactile experiences that involve the entire body:

1. A dress-up area filled with silky, slinky, furry, and other textured clothes
2. A sensory tub filled with such things as plastic balls or yarn balls (securely fastened so children don't get tangled in loose ends) to climb into
3. Swimming in plastic pools in the summer
4. Sit-in sandboxes
5. Mud baths (Nothing more is needed than a warm day, a hose, some dirt, and the willingness to clean up afterward. The toddlers themselves know what to do with the mud.)

If you're willing to let children wallow about getting whole body tactile experiences, be careful you don't tread on cultural values. Some cultures have strong prohibitions against children getting dirty or messy.

Other kinds of tactile experiences are designed mainly for the hands (or hands and arms). Some simple, one-step cooking allows children to have a tactile experience. Other possibilities include water play, sand play, play dough, and finger painting (which has several variations, such as shaving cream [not for the youngest toddlers], cornstarch and water, and chocolate pudding [not if food is frowned on as a play medium]). Be sure you emphasize the process and not the product. The point of finger painting is to feel the paint and squish it around, not to make a pretty picture to take home.

Be careful not to exclude girls from these tactile activities because they might get messy. (Some people tolerate messy boys more easily than they do messy girls.) And be aware that some toddlers do not want to get messy. Don't blame parents for this. It may be that the parent has discouraged messiness (for personal or cultural reasons). But sometimes the reluctance comes from the child's personality or stage of development. Many toddlers go through a period of refusing to get their hands messy.

Not all tactile experiences have to be messy. Many excellent programs for toddlers have very limited messy experiences—no one expects you to encourage children to muck around in mud or Jell-O unless you really want to set up that kind of experience. Some simpler but also valuable experiences include a pan of cornmeal with spoons and sifters; a pan of birdseed (just to feel) or birdseed with pitchers, spoons, and cups; and a tray of salt to feel (and perhaps some little cars to run around in it). Just letting children go barefoot provides them with a variety of experiences as they encounter different textures underfoot.

SEEING

We know more about sight than about the other senses, probably because most people depend so heavily on it. Infants can distinguish light and dark at birth. The pupillary reflex (the automatic narrowing of the pupil in bright light and widening in dim light) can be seen at birth, even in premature infants. Within a few hours infants are capable of visual pursuit. Their fixed focus seems to be about eight inches away. In other words, infants are equipped to see the mother's face while breast-feeding.

Within a few weeks, infants can discriminate among colors and prefer warm ones (red, orange, yellow) to cool ones (blue, green). Eye movements are somewhat erratic at first, but they rapidly become more refined. By the end of the second month, infants can focus both eyes to produce a single, though probably blurred, image. By the fourth month, they can focus their eyes and see clearly. Their ability to see is then comparable to that of an adult, though of course they have to learn to perceive and interpret what they are seeing.

Most newborns find all people and objects placed in front of them interesting—though some are more so than others. The human face is the most interesting of all (because newborns' visual abilities are clearly designed to promote attachment).

Infants of all ages need to be able to see interesting things. However, in the first weeks, eating and diaper changing provide sufficient visual input. As infants get older, a variety of visual material becomes more appropriate because it encourages them to move around in their world. Something interesting to see becomes something to reach for and eventually to move toward. Too much visual stimulation, however, can lead to a "circus effect." Infants become entertained observers rather than active participants and grow into passive toddlers who demand entertainment instead of inventing their own. Children used to outside entertainment are drawn toward television—the ultimate entertaining visual experience.

An entertained observer is quite different from a scientific observer. Entertained observers get hooked on a constant flow of novel visual stimulation. They get bored quickly and demand constant visual change. They may become television addicts. Because they experience such a strong assault on one sense (the visual), they ignore the fact that they are not actually involved physically or socially with the world around them. This eventual habit of observation and lack of involvement is detrimental to the development of a wide range of abilities.

Take cues from the infants themselves when setting up an environment that develops visual skills. Otherwise it's hard to know how much sensory input is too much and when interesting new visual experiences will be welcome. If infants cry at certain things, too much may be going on, or they may not yet be ready to leave what they were paying attention to. If they are very quiet, they may be concentrating on something in particular or may be "turned off" by too many events. When infants find their world interesting and are allowed to explore it at their own pace, they learn to entertain themselves in the process of discovery.

Toddlers' visual worlds are larger as they move around more. They also have a better understanding of what they are seeing. To get an idea of what toddlers' visual environments are like, get down at their level and look around. Things look very different down there.

To cut down on visual stimulation for toddlers, put up low barricades to block areas of the room. Adults can see over the barriers in order to supervise, but children experience a visually calming room. (Barriers can also muffle sound to some extent.) Some rooms invite children to really focus on what's available; in others, toddlers get overexcited and have a hard time focusing.

Pictures add visual interest to a toddler's environment (though of course pictures also belong in an infant environment). Hang them low enough for the toddlers to see at their own eye level. Change them periodically, but not constantly, because toddlers appreciate seeing the familiar on a regular basis. Choose pictures that clearly depict familiar objects or other children in action. Be sure to represent different races in your picture display. Also be aware of the sex of the children in the pictures you hang. Don't show pictures that are predominantly little girls looking pretty and doing nothing and little boys involved in engaging activities. We've all been brought up on books that had that particular bias. Let's not pass it on to the children in our care.

One way to hang pictures is with clear contact paper that covers the picture and extends out beyond to stick to the wall. This way the picture is sealed in with no loose corners to pick at and tear and no tacks to swallow.

Aesthetics is a worthy, but often unconsidered, goal when designing a visual environment for infants and toddlers. Children are more likely to grow up with an eye for beauty if the adults around them demonstrate that they value aesthetics.

CHILD WITH SPECIAL NEEDS: SENSORY IMPAIRMENTS

It is clear that infants and toddlers learn a great deal through their senses and that sensory information (perception) provides an important link between all other areas of development. If a young child has a known sensory problem or impairment, there are several helpful things to remember. First, ask about the child's I.F.S.P. (Individual Family Service Plan). A young child who has already seen a doctor or specialist will have this, and it will give you information as to degree of impairment, age of onset, cause, and some curriculum ideas. Always help a child make the most of the abilities he or she already has, and don't focus on the disability. Remember, too, that even if a child has a sensory impairment, there is no doubt still some residual ability in that area. For example, most blind babies see some things, and it is very rare for a deaf infant to hear nothing at all.

Parents can be your most helpful resources. Caregivers and parents working together provide a critical component for the special-needs infant or toddler. You will have valuable information to share with each other. If you suspect that a young child has a sensory impairment, discuss your specific observations with the parent as soon as possible. Early intervention and awareness will be mentioned often in this text. The longer a child experiences deprivation, or the nonrecognition of a disability, the greater the handicap.

Try also to be aware of your own misconceptions and possible myths. A blind baby is not necessarily mentally retarded; a deaf toddler is not necessarily socially withdrawn. Children quickly learn to use compensating skills. But it would be inaccurate to assume that a blind infant has more acute hearing than a sighted child or that a deaf baby will have sharper eyesight than an infant with normal hearing. Sometimes individuals want to "make up for" what they think a child is lacking. Don't feel sorry for children with special needs. Provide a safe environment for them, plan for their specific play needs, and encourage (don't push) their unique strategies or adaptations to help them acquire necessary skills.

The following guides are a little more specific. They focus primarily on young children with either (or both) visual and hearing impairments. This list is not meant to be complete, but it may be helpful to caregivers who have children with special needs in their program.

1. Be aware of signals that may indicate sensory impairments. For example, a deaf infant may be "surprised" by your appearance (did not hear your approach), or he may start babbling (around four months), then stop. A visually impaired infant may not reach for interesting toys (cannot clearly see them), or her creeping may be slow to

develop. Developmental "signals" *depend* on a caregiver's knowledge of the usual sequence of growth.

2. Familiarize yourself with any special devices a young child may be using. Hearing aids do little good if they are inserted incorrectly. Glasses worn at an inappropriate angle may cause additional fatigue for a visually impaired toddler.

3. Be sure when communicating with a child with sensory impairments that you get her attention first. This is appropriate to do with any child, but you may have to be more deliberate with a special-needs child. For example, make sure a deaf child can see you before you begin speaking. It may be helpful for a visually impaired child to hear her name clearly; then pause (allowing the child to orient toward the sound); then continue speaking. These focusing techniques help alert sensory-impaired children to the importance of speech and language as a means of gathering and clarifying information.

4. Guides to foster speech and language for a child with sensory impairments depend on the unique strengths and disabilities of that child. Some guides should be available to you in the child's I.F.S.P. Remember that language development is a complex task (more details on this in chapter 9). When a child's sensory abilities are not intact, that child is at risk for incomplete or delayed concept formation. It is difficult for a visually impaired child to understand fully the "label" of an object he may never have seen. A child with auditory problems may be confused by gestures and facial expressions made in the effort to communicate language he cannot clearly hear. It is important not to overdramatize information you are sharing and to repeat it frequently so the child has time to organize important details in his own way.

5. Young children with sensory impairments may tire more quickly than their peers. Watch for stress signals, and provide for frequent rest periods. A blanket and pillow close by may be all the cues necessary to encourage a busy toddler to pause for a rest. A rested child is readier to pursue and repeat experience from which she will learn.

6. Provide for appropriate play. Support and encourage all areas of sensory learning. Don't limit a child's experience because you think he will not see or hear something. A visually impaired child may be fascinated by the contours of a particular toy he is seeing. A child who is hard of hearing may thoroughly enjoy the song of a music box, no matter how muffled the sound.

Most of the activities presented in this chapter are perfectly appropriate for children with sensory impairments. Consult further with parents and program specialists if you feel an activity needs to be adapted to foster a particular child's abilities.

Caregivers need to be sensitive to each infant's sensory needs and provide for the development of all the senses. The infant's task is to learn to interpret the sensations that come in through the senses. Children don't just take in information; they learn to perceive and organize it. They learn to hear and eventually to listen. They learn to discriminate the feelings on their skin, the various tastes in their mouths, the smells around them, the sights they take in. They learn to "make sense" of sensory information. Responses or reactions to this information from the senses depend on muscles, on motor skills, the topic of chapter 7.

Thought/Activity Questions

1. Look around an infant-toddler environment. List the experiences that you feel foster perceptual development. How can you determine when there is perhaps "too much of a good thing"?
2. Focus on one aspect of perceptual development (one of the senses). Create a "toy" to foster this area of growth. What do you need to consider?
3. Observe a child with a sensory impairment. What adaptations can you see the child making? How is the environment supporting his or her efforts?

Notes

1. J. M. Mandler and L. Douglas, "Concept Formation in Infancy," *Cognitive Development* 8, 1993, pp. 291–318.
2. Robert Samples, *The Metaphoric Mind* (Menlo Park, Calif.: Addison-Wesley, 1976), p. 95.
3. T. G. R. Bower, *Development in Infancy,* 2nd ed. (San Francisco: W. H. Freeman, 1982), pp. 87–99.
4. P. W. Jusczyk and R. N. Aslin, "Infants' Detection of the Sound Patterns of Words in Fluent Speech," *Cognitive Psychology* 29, 1997, pp. 1–23.

For Further Reading

C. F. Abbott and S. Gold, "Conferring with Parents When You're Concerned That Their Child Needs Special Services," *Young Children* 46(4), May 1991, pp. 10–15.
M. Davis, J. Kilgo, and M. Gamel-McCormick, *Young Children with Special Needs: A Developmentally Appropriate Approach* (Boston: Allyn & Bacon, 1998).
Fran Hast and Ann Hollyfield, *Infant and Toddler Experiences* (Beltsville, Md.: Gryphon House, 1998).
Pam Schiller, "Turning Knowledge into Practice," *Child Care Information Exchange* 126, March 1999, pp. 49–52.
T. Sherman, "Categorization of Skills in Infants," *Child Development,* 2nd ed. (New York: American Foundation for the Blind, 1984).
D. Stern, *Diary of a Baby* (New York: Basic Books, 1990).
W. Weiss, J. Salomon, and P. Zelazo, eds., *Newborn Attention: Biological Constraints and the Influence of Experience* (Norwood, N.J.: Ablex, 1991).

CHAPTER 7

The Development of Motor Skills

Movement is the natural, healthy experience of childhood. Most infants and toddlers move a lot! It is through movement, muscular coordination, and the organization of perceptions that young children find out about, and make sense of, their world. Infants' motor skills may seem limited, but sensitive observation reveals competent abilities. Within a year and a half, most infants have learned many of the basic motor skills—arm/hand coordination, walking—that they will need throughout their lifetime. Their sensory experience has given them important feedback. They spend the next years perfecting, expanding, and refining the original postures and movements that they learned early.

This chapter provides an overview of the progression of motor development, including reflexive and voluntary movements and gross and fine motor development. Guides for fostering motor growth are included, as well as some information concerning motor delays in young children.

THE PROGRESSION OF GROSS MOTOR DEVELOPMENT

Reflexive Movements

Newborns can make few voluntary movements beyond the gross random movements of arms and legs. Most of their first movements are reflexive; that is, the muscles react automatically in the presence of different kinds of stimuli. The refined and complex movements that they make are also reflexive in nature.

Reflexes serve several functions. Some, like blinking, swallowing, and clearing the face for breathing, are protective. Others, such as kicking the legs alternately (reciprocal kicking), are precursors of later skills, in this case, walking.

Pediatricians and other infant specialists pay attention to reflexes because they indicate brain growth. As the growth of the brain shifts from the brain stem to the cortex, reflexes change or disappear. Figure 7.1 illustrates some of the reflexes described below.

Reflexes Present at Birth

Normal babies have the same breathing reflex that adults have, as well as a cough and gag reflex that keeps the breathing passage clear. Their eyes blink and squint, and pupils narrow just like adults. They pull away from painful stimuli. They coordinate sucking and swallowing. These are all normal reflexes that are present at birth and remain throughout the person's lifetime.

Other reflexes are specific to newborns and change or disappear as they mature. Some of those are discussed below. The ones outlined here are the most visually obvious and the most often checked when infants are being examined by physicians because they indicate normal development as well as the rate at which the newborn is maturing.

Stepping: If you stand newborns on their feet, they will respond to the pressure by stepping.

Palmar grasp reflex: A newborn's hands curl tightly around any object placed in them.

Babinski reflex: If you stroke the sole of the foot, the toes will fan out, and the big toes will extend.

Moro reflex (also called the startle reflex): If newborns are startled by a sudden change of position or a noise, they fling their arms out with fingers spread wide and then draw their arms (and, to a lesser extent, legs) back toward the body in a clutching motion.

Rooting and sucking: If you touch the cheeks of newborns, they begin to search for a nipple with their mouth. When the mouth is touched, they start to suck.

Hand-to-mouth reflex: If newborns' mouth and palm are touched, they put their hand in their mouth. This is useful for clearing mucus in the early days because when they suck on their fist they can swallow easily.

Righting reflex (also called the china doll reflex): When newborns are held upright, they try to keep their head up and eyes open.

Tonic neck reflex (sometimes called the fencer position): When the newborn's head is turned to one side, the arm on that side extends, and the opposite arm flexes, making the baby look like a fencer. This reflex may eventually help the baby use the sides of the body separately.

Swimming reflex: When newborns are placed in water, they make swimming motions.

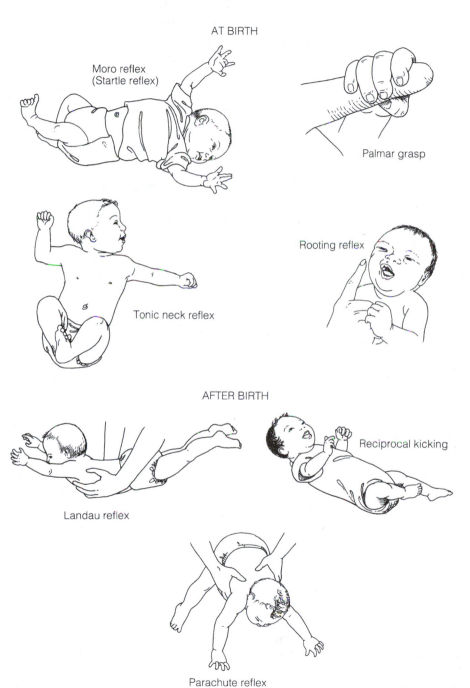

FIGURE 7.1
Reflexes at and after birth

AT BIRTH

Moro reflex
(Startle reflex)

Palmar grasp

Tonic neck reflex

Rooting reflex

AFTER BIRTH

Landau reflex

Reciprocal kicking

Parachute reflex

Reflexes That Appear after Birth

Other reflexes make their appearance during the first few months. As the new reflexes appear, some of the original ones begin to disappear.

> **Reciprocal kicking (bicycling)**: If infants are held out by an adult, they begin kicking their legs alternately. Usually this appears in the first month.

> **Neck righting**: If the infant's head is turned, the body follows. This reflex begins to appear about the time the tonic neck reflex disappears.

> **Parachute reflex**: If infants begin to fall forward from an upright position, they try to catch themselves—arms go forward with hands outstretched. This reflex appears about the time the Moro reflex fades.

> **Landau reflex**: If babies are held under the stomach only, they extend their arms and legs. This extension, which indicates the strength of the back, is a precursor of walking. It is complete at about one year.

Not only is it interesting to see how reflexes serve as the basis for later movement, it is useful for caregivers to know what reflexes indicate about infants' behavior and development. It is sometimes useful to know that babies have not chosen to move in a certain way (for example, rooting before starting to suck), but that they have to do so.

The appearance of certain reflexes, the lingering of reflexes, and the absence of others can indicate differences in development. This aspect of development is complex. When parents or caregivers notice that a baby is showing what seems to be inappropriate reflexive behavior, they may want to discuss what they have noticed with a developmental expert or a doctor.

Voluntary Movements

Eventually, infants make motions that are not automatic but voluntary. These movements are generally divided into two broad types: gross motor, having to do with large muscles and big movements, and fine motor, having to do with small muscles and more delicate movements.

Various large muscles contribute to the infant's ability to move in two directions: up (to an upright position) and around (on a horizontal plane). The two are intertwined because the child needs to get up to move around and needs to move around to get up. Little by little, babies gain control over these muscles. The first muscles to develop are those that control head movements. As babies perfect the skills involved in turning the head from side to side and lifting it up, they strengthen the shoulder muscles. As they begin to move around and squirm, lifting their arms and legs, they develop the trunk muscles. All this preparation is for turning over, just as turning over is preparation for (that is, strengthens the muscles necessary for) sitting up. A child will learn to come to a sitting position without ever having been propped up. The ability to sit comes from developing the muscles prerequisite to the upright position. Infants get ready to sit by learning to move the head and by turning over. The building of the muscle systems is vital; practice at sitting is not.

A general principle involved in motor development is that stability is the means to mobility. Infants cannot move until they gain a good solid base from which to move—whether the movement is vertical, as in sitting and standing, or horizontal, as in crawling and walking. This same principle operates on another level as well. Chapter 5 pointed out that exploration (mobility) is related to psychological stability (trust in attachment).

The plan for developing muscular stability is a part of the infant's makeup—as is the plan for mobility. Nobody has to "teach" either sitting or walking. When normal babies have gone through the necessary muscle development, they will be able to sit and walk without any lessons or practice.

Figure 7.2 shows the major milestones of gross motor development. Use it with caution. Such charts are based on averages, and no individual baby is average. The sequence of motor development is mostly standard, but within it lies a good deal of room for individual variation in timing and style.

BRAIN GROWTH AND MOTOR DEVELOPMENT

Motor development is largely observable; we can see infants refine their physical skills and make more voluntary movements. Now, thanks to neuroscience technology, we can also "see" how the brain changes and grows as young children develop. Everyday behaviors that are observable *do* give us insight into brain growth.

It is important to first acknowledge that the number of neurons (brain cells) a child is born with does not change throughout life. What changes is the number of connections between the brain cells. What also happens is something called "myelinization," a process by which brain fat (myelin) coats and insulates the neural fibers. It accounts for the rapid gain in overall brain size after birth. These neural fibers, or axons, are then better able to transmit electrical impulses (synapses) and make more stable "learning connections."[1] Brain growth in the first year is primarily a process of insulating neural fibers and expanding, or growing, "dendrite trees." As brain growth continues, neural activity increases and moves from the brain stem, in the back of the brain, to the cortex area, in the front of the brain.

This activity can be measured (note: the EEG, or electroencephalogram, detects and measures brain wave activity) and growth in the first year can be seen as surges in brain activity. For example, there is a surge in activity at three to four months, when infants are doing voluntary reaching, at eight months, when they crawl and search for objects, and also at twelve months, when they are walking.[2] Surges are related to the massive production of synaptic connections; the brain is busy making sense of experience. There seems to be clear evidence now that what forms the brain circuitry early in life is *experience*.

FIGURE 7.2
Gross motor development milestones: birth to thirty months

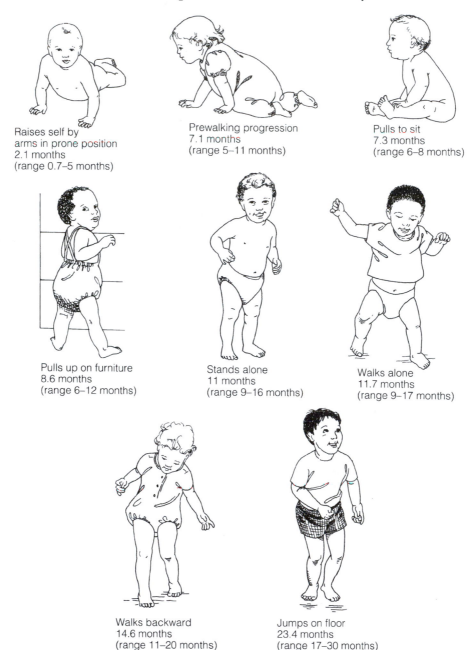

Raises self by
arms in prone position
2.1 months
(range 0.7–5 months)

Prewalking progression
7.1 months
(range 5–11 months)

Pulls to sit
7.3 months
(range 6–8 months)

Pulls up on furniture
8.6 months
(range 6–12 months)

Stands alone
11 months
(range 9–16 months)

Walks alone
11.7 months
(range 9–17 months)

Walks backward
14.6 months
(range 11–20 months)

Jumps on floor
23.4 months
(range 17–30 months)

Some items in this chart were taken from the Bayley Scales of Infant Development.
Copyright © 1969 by The Psychological Corporation, a Harcourt Assessment Company.
Reproduced by permission. All rights reserved.

An additional point should be made. The brain research has clearly indicated that there are *sensitive periods* for development (this will be discussed more in chapter 8, on cognition, and chapter 9, on language). But remember, too, that there is also tremendous *brain plasticity*. The brain is amazingly adaptable. In some cases of early trauma, regions of the brain will take over the function of a damaged area of the brain. While we are still in the process of appreciating more about the vital "windows of opportunity" for learning, don't forget that it is never too late to provide quality experiences for a young child.

FOSTERING MOTOR DEVELOPMENT

Caregivers can do several things to foster motor development in infants, especially gross motor development. Try to keep children in the position in which they are freest and least helpless during their waking hours. Emmi Pikler's research shows that even the youngest babies change position an average of once a minute.[3] So if they are strapped into an infant seat or a swing, they are not able to do what they would do naturally if free. Avoid contraptions that confine infants. (Car seats are, of course, a necessary exception.)

Don't "teach" gross motor skills. Encourage infants to practice what they know how to do. Babies get ready for the next stage by doing thoroughly whatever it is they are doing in the present stage. Trying to teach babies to roll over or walk keeps them from fully exploring and perfecting the skills they already have. They reach each milestone just when they are ready, and their own inner timetable dictates when that will be.

Don't put babies into positions they cannot get into by themselves. The process of *getting into* a position is more important than *being in* the position—the process promotes development. Babies get ready for standing by sitting and crawling, not by being stood up.

Don't shield babies from all physical stress. The body needs a certain amount of stress to grow. Don't *rescue* babies when they get in an uncomfortable position, but wait and see if they can get out of it on their own. Obviously, you don't leave babies in great distress alone and unsupported, but you don't want to always make everything easy for them either. Reasonable—optimum—stress stimulates growth, increases motivation, and strengthens the body as well as the psyche.

Above all, *facilitate* development in the gross motor area—don't *push* it. Because we live in a "hurry-up" culture, some people are most anxious for babies to reach milestones "on time" or even "early." "In time" is a better guide for milestones. Each baby has his or her own timetable. There is no reason to impose someone else's. The question to ask is not "Is this baby progressing rapidly in development?" Note how well babies use the skills they have and if they are progressing in their use of those skills. With these two concepts in mind, you will not have to be so concerned about where they fit on the chart.

Promoting motor development in toddlers follows the same principles as that of infants. Toddlers need freedom to move and experience a variety of ways of using the skills they possess. Large muscle activity cannot be saved for outdoor time but must be both allowed and encouraged inside. A soft environment—pillows, mattresses, foam blocks, and thick rugs (indoors) and grass, sand, pads, and mats (outdoors)—helps toddlers roll, tumble, and bounce around. Various kinds of scaled-down climbing and sliding equipment (both indoors and out) allow the toddler to experience a variety of skills. Wheel toys (these can be saved for outdoors for the older toddler) give a whole different kind of experience as toddlers learn first to walk them and later to pedal them. Large, lightweight blocks encourage building skills as toddlers carry them around, form them into walks, houses, and abstract structures, and then practice gross motor skills on them.

Wandering, carrying, and dumping are gross motor skills that toddlers practice a great deal. Rather than seeing these as negative, caregivers can provide for them in the curriculum. Some programs have things available to dump (and put back). One center even suspends from the ceiling a bucket of objects whose sole purpose is dumping (and refilling). Wandering usually involves picking up objects, carrying them to another location, and putting them down. Sometimes they are actively discarded, and sometimes just dropped—abandoned as if forgotten. The map in figure 7.3 shows the path of a two-year-old over a period of twenty minutes. The black dots represent each time the child picked up or put down an object. Notice the territory he covered and the number of times he picked up and put down objects. This is not unusual two-year-old behavior. Typically, as children get older, they are able to spend more and more time with specific activities. The closer to three years old, the less likely toddlers are to spend good parts of the day moving from one place to another. But early in toddlerhood this constant movement is part of gross motor development, and the environment, both indoors and out, should be set up to accommodate that need.

A word of caution concerning the new brain development information: be alert to any marketing that uses brain research to sell toys and materials. Natural everyday experience—and interactions—are the best way to foster significant neural connections. Interpretation of research must be done with care and sensitivity, and the uniqueness of each child should always be preserved.

Notice whether you are encouraging gross motor movement more in boys than in girls. Girls need strong, skillful bodies as much as boys do. Both sexes in toddlerhood enjoy running-and-chasing "games." The freedom to roll around on the floor, jump onto pillow piles, wrestle, and somersault is just as appropriate for girls as for boys. Music and movement, dance, and circle games encourage all young children to move and have fun. Here is a wonderful place for multicultural ideas, too. Take walks and examine interesting things along the way. Just remember to give children a choice and keep group size small.

FIGURE 7.3
Map tracing the movements of a two-year-old

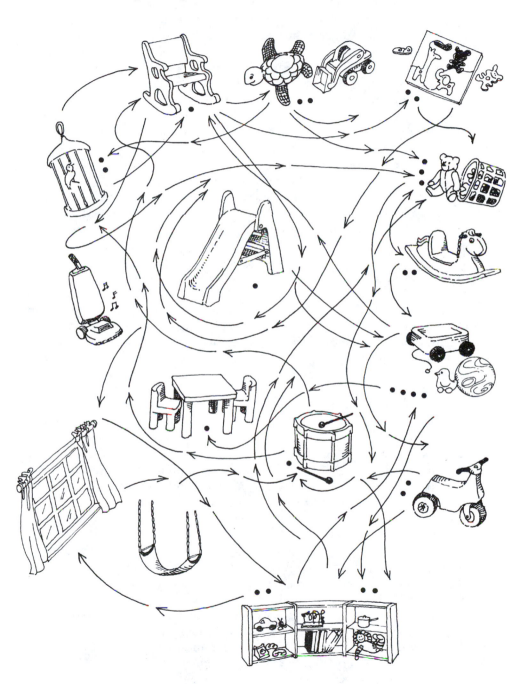

THE PROGRESSION OF FINE MOTOR DEVELOPMENT

The small muscles that a baby gradually gains control of include those of the eyes, mouth, speech organs, bladder, rectum, hands, fingers, feet, and toes. The development of the manipulative skills (hands and fingers) is considered here.

The sequence in which infants learn to manipulate objects shows how complex this ability is. Figure 7.4 illustrates the developmental sequence. At first, newborns generally hold their hands in tight fists (although the clenched fist is more relaxed in those babies who were treated to gentle birth procedures). They hold on to any object put into their hands, gripping so tightly that they can, if held up, support their own weight. But they have no control over their grasp and cannot let go, no matter how much they want to. At some time before six months (usually a little over two and a half months), the tight fists remain relaxed most of the time, and the hands are open.

During the first three months, more of the hand and arm movements become voluntary. Infants begin to reach for objects, first with their eyes, then with open hands. By around three and a half months, they can often close on an object within reach. They may also begin to play with their own hands about this time. The way they grasp at first is distinctive: they use all the fingers together as if they had a mitten on, drawing objects into the palm of the hand. This motion is called the "palmar grasp." Although at this stage the palmar grasp is a voluntary movement, it comes from the earlier palmar grasp reflex present at birth. After learning to pick up objects with one hand, infants soon begin to pass them back and forth between the two hands. By the sixth month, they have begun trying to use thumb and forefinger in what is called a "pincer grasp." They can then manipulate objects with more skill and a variety of motions.

By about the ninth month, infants have perfected the pincer grasp and can pick up small objects with great adeptness. Playing with the hands—picking up and dropping objects for a helpful adult to retrieve and playing pattycake—provides pleasure. The dropping game shows infants' joy in and awareness of now being able to let go. By the ninth month, infants may also be using their forefingers alone—poking, hooking, and probing. Eventually, they can differentiate the use of the hands and can then do two different activities at once (for example, holding something with one hand and maneuvering with the other).

By eleven months, infants can hold crayons and mark on available surfaces, and they can probably get a spoon to their mouths. By a year, the variety of movements has come a long way from the compulsive grasping that was present at birth. Infants can take covers off objects, undress themselves to some degree, take one thing out of another, and take things apart and move them around. They continue to expand their manipulative skills, refining and perfecting their movements. From here on, individuals vary greatly.

Much fine motor development in toddlers comes from encouraging them in self-help tasks. As they get more adept at eating with utensils, pouring

FIGURE 7.4
**Fine motor development: manipulative skills,
birth to twenty-one months**

Grasps and holds ring
.8 months
(range .3–3 months)

Hands predominantly
open and relaxed
2.7 months
(range .7–6 months)

Reaches for dangling ring
3.1 months
(range 1–5 months)

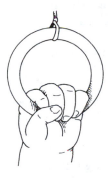

Closes on dangling ring
3.8 months
(range 2–6 months)

Fingers hand in play
3.2 months
(range 1–6 months)

Palmar grasp
3.7 months
(range 2–7 months)

Neat pincer grasp
8.9 months
(range 7–12 months)

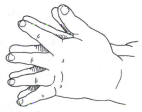

Pattycake (Midline skills
9.7 months
(range 7–15 months)

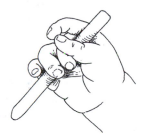

Scribbles spontaneously
14 months
(range 10–21 months)

their own milk, taking off their own shoes, and zipping up their jackets (with a start from an adult), their ability to use their hands and fingers grows.

Toys and materials add to their chances to practice as they play with what you provide them (such as dress-up clothes, dolls and doll clothes, play dough, button and zipper boards, latch boards, stringing beads, nesting toys, simple shape sorters, snap-together blocks, telephones, paint and paintbrushes or water and paintbrushes, crayons, felt pens, scissors, simple paper puzzles, blocks, small figures, cars, and trucks). The tactile experiences mentioned in "Touch" in chapter 6 also promote fine motor development. See appendix B for age-appropriate fine motor toys, materials, and activities. Be sure that you encourage boys and girls to engage equally in fine motor activities. Take a look at Scotty and the number of motor experiences (fine and gross) he is getting in just a few minutes.

> Scotty stands in the sandbox, looking around him. He bends over and picks up a sieve and spoon that are lying at his feet. Then he plops down, legs out straight, and starts spooning sand into the sieve and watching it pour out on his knees. He continues to hold the sieve but drops the spoon as his attention is drawn to a child on a tot bike who has just pulled up to the edge of the sandbox. The child gets off the bike and stands by it, watching something going on beyond the fence. Scotty trips across the sand, sieve still in hand. When he reaches the edge of the sandbox, the sieve drops out of his hand. He seems unaware of that development. He concentrates his effort on getting his feet, first one, then the other, over the board that makes up the edge of the sandbox. He stands by the bike; the child who rode up on it is on the other side of it.
>
> Disregarding the other child, Scotty swings one foot over the bike and straddles it. The other child, who has been watching him, frowns, makes a small noise, and looks around the yard as if to find someone to help him claim the bike. No one responds to his look, so he makes no further protest. Scotty walks the bike away, leaving the child standing there in the same spot.
>
> Scotty alternates between standing and walking the bike and sitting on it and scooting it with his feet. (There are no pedals on the bike.) He keeps on the walk, which is a bumpy asphalt and slightly uphill. He joins a group of two other bikers, and the three move together toward a wide, gentle ramp. They ride up the ramp, stop at the top, and then coast down together. Scotty then leaves the group, walks over to the gate, and stands looking out. He gets off the bike and starts to climb the gate. An adult walks over and gently redirects him to a climbing structure nearby. He starts to climb, but when the adult walks off, he follows her. He stops halfway across the yard when he comes across a group of children washing dolls in dishpans on a low table. He grabs a sponge lying on the table and squeezes it, watching the soapy water drip out. He puts the sponge into the pan, holds it up dripping, and squeezes it again onto

the tabletop. He scrubs the tabletop briefly, then puts the sponge back into the water. He takes a doll out of another tub and puts it on top of the sponge in the tub in front of him. Another child reaches over and takes the doll back, and there is a slight tussle as Scotty tries to keep the doll. He lets go when he hears a call for snack time. He gives the sponge in the tub a pat, which splashes water onto his face. He smiles, pats it again, then races tripping across the yard to the snack table, where he is just in time to pour his own juice from a small, half-filled pitcher.

Scotty encounters many chances to build his skills in walking, running, climbing, and balancing just by being in an environment with equipment and choices. He is also building fine motor skills as he practices grasping, holding, scooping, pouring, and squeezing with the toys and materials available to him. These experiences not only help him develop his perceptual skills but also contribute to cognitive development.

CHILDREN WITH SPECIAL NEEDS: DEVELOPMENTALLY DELAYED

The rate and sequence of motor development for the child with special needs or developmental delays may be slower and more divergent. Reflexes were reviewed in this chapter. They remain an important guide for parents and caregivers because they indicate brain growth and possible brain damage. It is particularly important that their progression be noted carefully during a child's first year.

Motor development may be influenced by a number of handicapping conditions. A blind infant may be slower in his rate of motor growth because limited visual information may reduce his exploration of the world. An infant with cerebral palsy may show poor or limited muscular control because of related brain damage. Infants with motor handicaps or developmental delays show a consistent progression or sequence of motor abilities, but at a much slower rate.

Often it is not totally understood why a child experiences a motor delay. Prenatal care, premature birth, or trauma during or after birth may influence motor development. Early intervention remains the key way to help a special-needs child reach his or her full developmental ability.

Early intervention is based on an understanding of what (developmentally) tends to happen when. An attitude that encourages infants with handicaps to experience and explore the world in a way appropriate for them remains critically important.

Caregivers and parents may find the following helpful:

- Provide for basic play experiences that emphasize use of the senses.
- Provide young children with normally developing role models as playmates.

- Give children some direct instruction or prompting to complete an activity.
- Reduce prompting as the child gains skills through experience.
- Provide nurturance and support for effort.[4]

Consider these guidelines while reading about Peter, a developmentally delayed toddler. He is eighteen months old. He is still crawling and has made no attempt to stand. For unknown reasons, Peter experienced anoxia (reduced oxygen) at birth. Three mornings a week he attends an infant-toddler program for handicapped children.

Peter is sitting on the floor watching two other toddlers and an adult roll a ball to each other. He has been interested in the ball game for several minutes. His eyes carefully follow the ball as it rolls from one person to another, and if the ball leaves the circle, he turns his head to watch one of the toddlers run to retrieve it. He makes no other indication of involvement.

"Peter, would you like to join our ball game?" the caregiver asks. He does not look at her but continues to watch the ball.

"We can move closer to you so that you can play, too." The adult slowly rolls the ball toward Peter. It stops at the edge of his foot. He makes no movement toward the ball but has visually followed it constantly.

"The ball touched you, didn't it, Peter? Would you like to touch it?" the adult says encouragingly. He slowly looks up at her and then to the ball. Peter points at the ball with one finger and "pokes" at it. It moves slightly, and he smiles with pleasure.

Suddenly the toddler sitting next to Peter reaches across his lap and gives the ball a swipe. It rolls back to the adult.

"David must want us to continue our ball game. He has rolled the ball back to me," the teacher comments. "Joan, open your hand a little more this time when the ball comes to you." The teacher demonstrates with her palm up and her fingers curled. "Peter, watch Joan push the ball away." Joan rolls the ball toward Peter. This time it stops near his knee. Peter looks at the ball. This time he does not poke at it but attempts to swing at it with his palm up. Even though his movement is slow and deliberate, he misses hitting the ball.

"Good try, Peter. Do it again," says the caregiver. After two more swings, Peter connects with the ball, and it rolls out of the circle. He follows it with his eyes but makes no attempt to crawl after it.

David jumps up to get the ball. On his way back he notices a bug on the floor nearby and drops the ball. Joan by this time has wandered toward the block area. The adult reaches for the ball. "Peter, would you like me to roll the ball to you?" Peter, who was watching David and the bug, looks back to her and opens and closes and opens his hands.

"You look ready. Here it comes." The ball rolls to Peter. He stops it and holds onto it tightly. He does not lift it or attempt to roll it back to the teacher. Gradually, he moves the ball in a back and forth motion between his hands. After several minutes he lets the ball roll away and turns to watch David, who has joined Joan in the block area. "Would you like to continue playing with David and Joan? You can move into the block area." Peter looks at the teacher. Then he slowly gets into his crawling position and proceeds toward the block section.

Peter will no doubt have plenty of opportunities to play with the ball—and with David and Joan. The adult is providing him encouragement and some demonstration, but she does not push him. Like other children, children with special needs need time and opportunity to practice activities.

It may be helpful at this point to combine some of our information about fine and gross motor coordination with a brief "stage/age" view of physical growth. This is meant to be a supportive guide to all caregivers (whether or not special-needs children are in your program).

Magda Gerber refers to motor skills as an infant's growing "body wisdom." From birth to about eight months, a child has to have basic needs met (food and nurturance) in order to develop in a healthy way. *Trust and security* are growing as a child reaches out to the world. Implications for attachment are clear. Between eight and fourteen months, motor skills have expanded so that *exploration* almost seems to drive the young child. Giving choices, providing safety, and allowing for play are the primary tasks for caregivers and parents at this age. Motor development and problem solving combine for the young explorers, and limit setting and childproofing become issues for the adults. By the time children reach eighteen to thirty months, they may feel they own the world and can do anything. Obviously, their judgment is limited, and parents and caregivers need a lot of energy to keep up with the toddlers! Freedom with guidance is the motto.

This chapter looked at the progression of motor development and provided a brief overview of the milestones of physical growth. Remember that numerous factors may influence the rate of development. Nothing in development happens alone or in isolation. As legs move, sensory perceptions change—a surface touched is hard, cold, soft, or hot. As an adult provides a physical play experience (a rolling ball to chase), a child learns to coordinate hands, feet, and legs to understand and find out about the world. Perceptual and motor skills combine to contribute to cognitive development.

Thought/Activity Questions

1. Review figure 7.2. Suppose the mother of a child in your care found this chart, or one similar to it, in a popular magazine. She wants to discuss its meaning with you. Consider the following and what you would say:

A. Her child is healthy, and motor growth seems very normal. What would you say?

B. You have some concerns about some lags in motor development and have been waiting for such an opportunity. What would you say?

C. The father brings you this chart instead of the mother. What would you say?

2. Invent a toy to foster motor development in infants. Think about and discuss how this toy promotes physical growth.

3. Pretend that you are going to conduct a parent meeting. Outline the details of a discussion regarding how to set up an environment to promote gross motor development. Consider the following:

A. Promoting safety

B. Fostering development, *not* pushing it

C. Teaching parents about developmentally appropriate environments

4. Discuss how you might adapt an infant-toddler environment to meet the needs of a developmentally delayed infant. What would you want to consider?

Notes

1. P. Casaer, "Old and New Facts about Perinatal Brain Development," *Journal of Child Psychology and Psychiatry* 34, 1993, pp. 101–109.

2. M. A. Bell and N. A. Fox, "Brain Development over the First Year of Life," in *Human Behavior and the Development of the Brain,* edited by G. Dawson and K. W. Fischer (New York: Guilford, 1998), pp. 314–345.

3. Emmi Pikler, "Data on Gross Motor Development of the Infant," *Early Child Development and Care* 1, 1972, pp. 297–310.

4. S. Krog, *The Integrated Early Child Curriculum* (New York: McGraw-Hill, 1990), pp. 6–41.

For Further Reading

A. Blenk with D. L. Fine, *Making School Inclusion Work: A Guide to Everyday Practices* (Cambridge, Mass.: Brookline, 1995).

P. A. Chandler, *A Place for Me: Including Children with Special Needs in Early Care and Education Settings* (Washington, D.C.: National Association for the Education of Young Children, 1994).

W. Hayslip and L. Vincent, "Opening Doors to Activities That Include ALL Children," *Child Care Information Exchange* 105, September/October 1995, pp. 43–46.

Mary Benson McMullen, "Achieving Best Practices in Infant and Toddler Care," *Young Children* 54(4), July 1999, pp. 69–76.

Nina Sazer O'Donnell, "Using Early Childhood Brain Development Research," *Child Care Information Exchange* 126, March 1999, pp. 58–62.

Emmi Pikler, "Data on Gross Motor Development," *Early Childhood Development and Care* 1, 1972, pp. 297–310.

Molly Sullivan, *Feeling Strong, Feeling Free: Movement Exploration for Young Children* (Washington, D.C.: National Association for the Education of Young Children, 1982).

Anna Tardos, "The Pikler/Loczy Philosophy," *Educaring* 7(2), Spring 1986, pp. 1–7.

Phyllis S. Weikart, "Facing the Challenge of Motor Development," *Child Care Information Exchange* 121, May 1998, pp. 60–62.

CHAPTER 8

The Development of Cognition

The process of gathering information, organizing it, and finally using it is the essence of the cognitive experience. Knowing and understanding come from active involvement with people and things. Infants and toddlers are naturally active and interactive. They seek experiences that are interesting to them and that eventually lead to problem solving. This chapter focuses on mental, or cognitive, development and how it matures during the first three years. Some of the work of Jean Piaget, the leading Swiss cognitive psychologist, and Lev Vygotsky, the Russian developmental psychologist, will be discussed. Much of the new brain research is confirming how young children learn, and implications of that understanding will be included. The chapter concludes with guidelines for fostering cognitive growth in children, including those with special needs.

Whenever discussing a topic such as mental development and cognitive growth, it is easy also to include such terms as "intellect," "learning," and maybe eventually "academically" related concepts. Most people think of the cognitive process as it relates to IQ score and school-type experiences (including grades!). A quality infant-toddler program will promote cognitive and intellectual growth in young children, but it will not look the same as a traditional classroom setting. Understanding *how* children grow and learn is basic to planning a developmentally appropriate setting that will foster cognitive development.

How do infants develop knowing and understanding? Initially, experience is perceived directly with the senses. For infants to acquire the ability to comprehend this sensory information, they must be able to distinguish between the familiar and the unknown; later they will begin to consider, to formulate, and eventually to form mental images in this process of experiencing and clarifying the environment.

This process is primarily unseen; therefore certain assumptions concerning cognition must be inferred by observing obvious physical movements. Infants begin by exploring the world with their bodies. They internalize what they take in through their senses and display it in their physical movements. Through such simple acts as mouthing, grasping, and reaching, infants gather vital information. You can see infants practicing these acts, repeating them over and over. They rather quickly refine them. For example, when newborns first bring the mouth toward a nipple, the mouth opens wide and ready. With only a few trials, they learn just what size opening the nipple requires and adjust the mouth accordingly in anticipation of what will go into it. They have refined a simple action. Soon they will judge how far to reach and what shape the fingers must take to pick up a cup or a toy. Much later, as adults, they may refine their actions further in order to reach without looking and strike a particular chord on the piano or input data on a computer keyboard. All these muscular refinements had their beginnings in that tiny mouth adjusting itself to the appropriate size for the nipple. In this example, cognition has been tied to fine motor development. You can think of other examples in which cognition is tied to gross motor development, social development, and emotional development. Learning and thinking are behind all areas of development.

The knowing process—cognition—also involves language abilities. As young children use their senses to experience the world, they need labels to categorize and remember these experiences. Once these labels are created, children have increased their ability to communicate and to begin to control their own behavior. These expanded abilities give young children additional opportunities to understand the world.

THE PROGRESSION OF COGNITIVE DEVELOPMENT

The Sensorimotor Experience of Knowing

The theorist who has contributed the most to our understanding of cognitive development in infants and toddlers is Jean Piaget. He was most interested in how children "come to know" about their world. He was not so much interested in how much a child knows (that is, quantity, or IQ), but rather in the quality of a child's understanding and how he can eventually justify or explain it. He named the first stage, birth to two years of age, the sensorimotor stage. This name, which means the coordination of sense perception and muscle movements, is appropriate because that coordination is the beginning of thinking.

These abilities become combined and coordinated—seeing and reaching for the same object, then grasping and sucking the same object. This happens as babies come to recognize cause and effect. These physical movements that lead toward understanding and knowing can be diagrammed as follows:

reflexes → accidental movement → repetition and manipulation → coordination and combination → experimentation and cause and effect → organized, planned thinking behaviors that will be practiced

Gradually, babies come to know that they can control the interaction between themselves and objects. They like this new piece of knowledge, and they keep testing it out. They want to repeat interesting activities. Through this testing, babies come to know that shaking a rattle produces a sound, but shaking a spoon does not. They soon learn, however, that banging a spoon will make a noise, and they like that and keep doing it.

When babies are practicing and combining these first actions, they are in love with their own body—fascinated by what they are feeling and doing. Eventually that fascination moves from their own body to the effects of their actions on the environment. They get interested in what happens when they shove their arm out and hit a toy. A new understanding develops with this shift of focus from self to environment, from action to consequence. Babies begin to realize that they and the objects in the world are separate.

You can see this same progression of development a bit later in toddlers having art experiences. At first, children are most interested in what it feels like when they scribble or scrub with a paintbrush on paper. Later they start looking at the product of their action—the drawing or painting. Some children don't focus on the product until after three years of age.

Knowing they are in a world full of objects and part of it, but not the whole of it, is a great step forward in understanding for infants. Nevertheless, their ideas of objects differ greatly from those of adults. Infants acknowledge the existence only of things they can see, touch, or otherwise know with their senses. When you hide her favorite toy, the infant does not look for it, because she believes it no longer exists. ("Out of sight, out of mind" applies to the thinking of the very young infant.) If you bring the toy out of hiding, it has been re-created for her. This understanding of the world makes a game of peek-a-boo extremely exciting: what power—to create and uncreate a person in an instant. No wonder peek-a-boo has universal fascination. What the young infant lacks is what Piaget called "object permanence." Eventually, infants become aware that objects continue to exist even when they can't see them. But gaining this awareness is a gradual process.

At about one year of age children begin to think in a more sophisticated way and to use tools. Give them a stick and they will use it to gain an out-of-reach toy. Give them a string with something they want at the end and they know just what to do. Novelty becomes an end in itself. Children will deliberately manipulate the environment to find out what happens.

With all this experimenting, children develop some new abilities: the ability to anticipate where an object will be when they drop it, the ability to remember an action after a short interruption, and the ability to predict. Watch an eighteen-month-old child who has had experience with a ball. He may roll the ball off a table and turn his head to the place where it will land.

Or if the ball rolls under a chair, he may look for a way to get it out again. Or if he rolls a ball toward a hole, he will run to the hole to watch the ball drop into it.

The next step in the development of understanding comes when infants can find solutions mentally. After enough experience using their sense perceptions and muscles, they can begin to think of ways of acting and try them out in their head before doing them. They can think of past and future events. You can see they are using mental images and connecting thoughts to experiences and objects that are not present. They can throw an imaginary ball or contemplate the solution to a problem before they begin to tackle it.

The sensorimotor stage can be summarized as follows:

1. Reflexes, simple inborn behaviors (crying, sucking, grasping) (birth to one month)
2. Refines simple behaviors, repeats and combines them (reaching, grasping, sucking on an object) (one to four months)
3. Repeats activity using objects, limited imitation begins (accidentally makes a mobile in crib move, notices it, tries to make it happen again) (four to eight months)
4. Plans (intention) a movement to have something happen (pulls a string to bring a toy closer) (eight to twelve months)
5. Experiments with objects to create new events (a ball rolled from the table will bounce, what will a book do?) (twelve to eighteen months)
6. Imagines events and solves problems, inventions through mental combination, use of words beginning (pretends to throw a ball, calls to caregiver or parent, "here ball") (eighteen to twenty-four months)

Cognition and Language: Sociocultural Influences

The beginning of language and the ability to pretend signal the end of the sensorimotor stage and the beginning of what Piaget calls the preoperational stage. Piaget was not alone in his appreciation of thought and language and their impact on how children come to understand their world. Recently, numerous developmentalists have looked more closely at infant-toddler cognitive growth. The work by Lev Vygotsky gives another perspective on the importance of language (of all people, including children) and how young children acquire problem-solving skills.

The findings by Piaget and Vygotsky suggest that infants and toddlers are competent in problem solving and that their cognitive skills are developing rapidly. A comparison of Piaget and Vygotsky can help caregivers and parents understand cognitive growth and developmentally appropriate practices, especially as to how they pertain to a child's sociocultural world. By highlighting the skills of preoperational children and by reviewing ideas of Piaget and Vygotsky, one can better understand how young children become independent, self-regulating learners.

Preoperational children can use mental images for their thinking processes. Thinking, though still tied to the concrete, is not limited to sense perceptions and body movements. Although toddlers don't practice this very much, they *can* think while standing or even sitting still. (However, they still need to be gathering a great number of concrete experiences *to think about,* so don't let anyone pressure you into sitting toddlers down in order to educate them.)

Because of their increased ability to hold and store mental images, toddlers entering the preoperational stage have increased memory of past events. Although yesterday may not yet be in their vocabulary, they *can* remember yesterday—and the day before.

Their sense of the future also increases as their ability to predict grows with their experience in the world. They continue to use trial and error to gain in this skill, not only in the concrete world ("I wonder what will happen if I pour sand in the sink") but in the social one as well ("I wonder what will happen if I pour sand in Jamie's hair"). Sometimes these experiments are both social and physical and are thought out on the conscious level ("If I pinch the baby, will he cry?"). Sometimes children don't make such clear decisions, but they are still problem solving in a trial and error way ("I wonder if hitting Erin will get an adult over here to pay attention to me" or "If I break enough limits, can I get my caregiver and mother to quit talking to each other so we can go home?"). What appears to be naughty behavior may in reality be this scientific testing.

Step back for a moment (mentally) and review some of Piaget's major points. Piaget believed knowledge is *functional*—it leads to something. The purpose of information (gained from experience) is to help an individual adapt in the world. The most significant knowledge is that which can be used in behavior to accomplish something. (This is particularly important when considering children's *play* experience.) Piaget's view of the young child's cognitive growth contains four major assumptions.

First, interaction with people and the environment is essential. As young children grow and mature, they use experience to "construct" new knowledge. The child's action on objects (sucking, pulling, pushing) is the central force for cognitive development.

Second, Piaget viewed the growth of the young child as gradual and continuous. The concept that objects are permanent grows slowly from the first few days of a child's life. As the "quality" of that concept matures, it provides the memory base, and the language, from which the toddler can create "pretend" play experiences.

Piaget believed that there is a connection between successive periods of development. This third assumption indicates the importance of the *quality* of development in *each* stage of a child's life. A skill or ability later in life depends on the maturing and improving of earlier achievements. In other words, don't push infants and toddlers to be "smarter." The "growth of mental structures," according to Piaget, will foster natural (appropriate) learning.

A fourth basic point Piaget made involves the young child's ability to construct a plan. He believes that this is one of the major competencies to develop during the first two years, and he refers to this as "intentionality." Intentionality gradually emerges as a child selects objects, plays with them, repeats actions on them, and creates a plan. This experience often involves a great deal of absorption; the young child may appear to be "lost in thought."[1]

Take a moment to think about the complexity of creating and using mental images and the ability to construct a plan for thinking. Thinking is not limited to sense perceptions and body movements. It is also a social experience. While infants and toddlers actively explore things in their world, they are often also interacting with other people. Vygotsky believed that cognitive activities have their origins in these social interactions. His work emphasizes the importance of social interaction and adds a significant piece to Piaget's view that mental development occurs only in stages (the child is capable only because biological growth has occurred). By comparing the perspectives of Piaget and Vygotsky, one can better understand how infant-toddler thinking emerges.

Vygotsky, like Piaget, believed that children *construct* their understanding of the world. Infants and toddlers gather and practice important learning constantly. Vygotsky would agree with Piaget that knowledge is functional in that it helps individuals adapt to the world. However, Vygotsky would emphasize that this learning is *co-constructed*. Young children acquire important skills (especially those skills unique to people, such as specific memory and symbolic thought) with the help of another, more experienced learner. This "help" is certainly not always in the form of a lesson. Caregivers who work with infants and toddlers often provide appropriate prompts to help children think about their own experiences. In part 1, particularly in chapters 1 and 4, you read numerous examples of adults supporting children's learning experiences. As mentioned then, timing is crucial. If caregivers step in too early or too late, valuable learning may be lost. Vygotsky's views on "assisted learning," and how learning can lead to development, differ from Piaget's. Vygotsky's focus is that social interaction is a prerequisite for children to develop problem-solving skills and that early language experience is critical to this process. Vygotsky believes that children are constantly learning from others and then they make that learning their own, through play. For Piaget, children *discover* learning through their play experiences, and then take that learning into their social interactions with others. Piaget believed that development precedes learning ("mental structures" mature and foster learning). The "zone of proximal development" is the phrase used by Vygotsky to describe how adults can appropriately assist children's learning. (Like Piaget, Vygotsky used some unique vocabulary!)

Consider an infant who, after crawling under a very low table, tries to sit up. There's no room. He continues to try to lift his head until he realizes that he is stuck. He starts screaming. His caregiver peers under the table, lending her quiet presence. While maneuvering the infant's head, the caregiver talks to him so that he stays low and in a crawling position. She uses verbal and physical cues to guide him out from under the table.

Vygotsky would label the head bumping and squirming the child experienced as the child's "level of independent performance." The way the child got out from under the table was what Vygotsky would call the "level of assisted performance." You might ask yourself, why go to all the trouble? Why not just lift the table off?

According to Vygotsky, if caregivers appropriately assist children in problem solving, children stay with the situation longer and learn more. (Note: The Reggio Emilia schools are proving what Magda Gerber has been saying for years about problem solving. Problem solving and learning work best when in a positive, responsive environment that encourages interactions. The adult, taking cues from the child, assists the child only until he or she can work independently. If the child doesn't need or want help, the adult backs off.)

"Appropriate" is a key word for understanding the concept of helping children. Appropriate help has to do with being respectful and sensitively responsive and always takes into consideration what is best for the child. The approach of this book, which follows Vygotsky's theory, never pushes learning.

A "guided," or socially shared, cognition is at the root of Vygotsky's theory regarding the mental development of children. When caregivers and parents interact with children in collaborative ways, they provide the tools for mental growth that are important to language development. Language, according to Vygotsky, plays a central role in cognition. Language is the first type of communication between infants and adults. Caregiving experiences provide the opportunity for infants and adults to experience these communication opportunities. Gradually, during infancy and toddlerhood, all the gestures, words, and symbols of social interaction that a young child experiences become internalized. It is this eventual communication with self (internalized language) that Vygotsky believed was so important to cognition. Although language development will be discussed more thoroughly in chapter 9, it is important to note here its link to mental growth. Vygotsky's theory acknowledges that cognition and language develop separately, but that they begin to merge within a social communication context. The language of others helps a young child organize her own behavior verbally.[2] How many times have you heard a young child repeat (maybe in abbreviated form) what she has just heard or been told? Vygotsky stressed the importance of this private speech (and, later, make-believe play) to cognition development more than did Piaget.

Today, much thought is being given to the importance of a child's cultural background and how these early social interactions contribute to mental development. In his sociocultural theory, Vygotsky focused on how social interaction helps children acquire the important skills and ways of behaving native to their culture. He believed that the sharing of cultural activities (e.g., cooking) between child and adult contributes significantly to the child's understanding of his or her world. Although some of Vygotsky's ideas may seem obvious to most parents and caregivers, misinterpretations do occur. Some people force children to learn things inappropriate for their age (e.g., math flash cards at three years of age!) and use the work of Vygotsky to justify it. After reviewing some of Vygotsky's concepts, one can't help but appreciate how much he valued the uniqueness of each child and that child's cultural history.

Piaget and Vygotsky have both contributed to our knowledge of the mental growth of young children. Piaget focused on the biological changes that contribute to cognition. Vygotsky stressed how social interaction might transform a child's thinking and problem-solving abilities. Today, neither theory by itself would be enough to completely explain cognitive development. As they grow and mature, children need the support of sensitive adults.

Let's now look at the behavior and play of four children and see how they relate to the biological and social perspectives of Piaget and Vygotsky. Try to determine what might be going on for each child and how the environment might be influencing them. By being able to discuss the ideas of Piaget and Vygotsky, one can resist the pressure to apply inappropriate "school-like" academic experiences to the education of infants and toddlers. Remember, both Piaget and Vygotsky believe that play is extremely important to the child's learning and that pushing a child does not foster real understanding of the world.

The first child is lying on his back on a rug surrounded by a few toys. He turns slightly toward a ball lying near his arm. He stretches, and the movement causes him to accidentally touch the ball. It moves, making a sound. He startles at the sound and looks toward the ball. He lies still again; his gaze wanders. Then he moves his arms again—a big, sweeping gesture—and the ball moves again, making the same jingling sound. He again startles, and a look of surprise comes on his face. You can almost hear his question, "Who did that?" He looks at the ball, looks around, and looks at the ball again. Then he lies still. A few moments later his arms come up and out again, this time tentatively waving. He misses the ball. Nothing happens. He lies still again. He repeats the action—again tentatively. This time his hand passes in front of his eyes, and a spark of interest comes over his face. He looks intently at his hand, and you can almost hear him saying, "What's that thing? Where did it come from?" He moves his fingers, and delight comes into his eyes. "Hey, it works!" he seems to say. His arms continue to wave, taking the fascinating fingers out of his line of vision. He breezes by the ball again, causing it to make just a whisper of sound. His eyes search for the source of the sound.

The second child is sitting on a rug near the first, but they are separated by a low fence. She has a rubber toy in her hand and is banging it up and down on the floor, giggling at the squeaks issuing forth. The toy bounces across the rug as she lets go, and she crawls happily after it. She stops to explore a string with a large bead on the end, but glances to see where the other end is. The string disappears into a pile of toys on the lowest shelf at the edge of the rug. She expectantly pulls the string and laughs delightedly. Then she catches sight of a bright red ball that has rolled out from the pile of toys that fell off the shelf. She crawls over to it and begins to smack it with her hand, making noises while doing so. She seems to expect the ball to move. When it doesn't, she tries again with more force. The ball moves slightly, and she moves after it. She is getting more and more excited, and as she approaches the ball, one hand accidentally swipes it so that it rolls some distance and disappears under a couch in the corner of the room. She watches it roll, starts after it, but stops when it disappears. Looking puzzled, she crawls over to the edge of the couch but does not lift up the ruffle at the bottom to check underneath. She looks a little disappointed, but then she crawls back to the rug and the squeaky rubber toy. As the scene closes, she is once again banging the toy against the floor and laughing at the noise it makes.

The third child stands holding an empty pitcher in his hand. He goes over to a box of toys, reaches into it, and brings out a small plastic bowl, an egg carton, and the lid to a peanut butter jar. He sets these in a row on a low table and pretends to pour something in them from his pitcher. He is careful in his actions and methodically fills each container, including each compartment of the egg carton. Then, seemingly satisfied that the task is done, he tosses the pitcher aside with a joyous shout. He starts across the room in another direction when he notices a plant standing on a table. He immediately runs back to where he left the pitcher and rummages through a pile of dolls and blankets hiding it from his view. He finds it, carries it over to the plant, and carefully pours pretend water into the pot. He abandons the pitcher again and picks up a doll. He scolds the doll, bangs it on the floor several times, then wraps it in a blanket, and lovingly puts it to bed in a box of toys. As he bends over the box, he spies a picture book with fire engines on the cover. He looks at the pictures for a moment, then puts the book on his head and races around the room screaming in what seems to be an imitation of a siren. As he passes by a toy shelf, he sees a wooden fire truck. He pulls it out and proceeds to push it around on the floor. He stops and looks at the holes on the truck where the little firefighters are supposed to sit. No little firefighters are in sight. He pauses for a moment, looks around, then goes to the pitcher once more. The scene ends as he carefully fills each hole in the fire truck with whatever pretend liquid the pitcher contains.

The fourth child is sitting at a table putting puzzle pieces in a three-piece puzzle. When she gets stuck, she looks to a nearby adult, who gives her verbal hints about how to turn the pieces. When she completes the puzzle, she turns it upside down and smiles at the clatter of wooden pieces hitting the tabletop. She works the puzzle again, faster this time, with no help from the adult. When she finishes the puzzle, she puts it back on a low shelf and moves to another table where several other children are poking and squeezing play dough. She asks for a piece, and when none is forthcoming, an adult intervenes, helping each child give her a bit off the hunks they are playing with. She sits contentedly poking and prodding her play dough, periodically conversing with the other children about what she is doing. Her monologue is not in direct response to anything they are saying. There is little interaction at the table, though there is lots of talking. The child we are focusing on rolls her play dough into a ball, then sits looking at it for a minute. Then she begins to pat and shape it, obviously with purpose in her actions. When she has produced a lopsided lump, she sits back, satisfied, and announces to no one in particular that she is finished. She gets up and walks away. As she leaves the table, another child grabs her piece and incorporates it into his own. This act goes unnoticed. The girl, seeing a cart of food being wheeled into the room, runs to the corner to a row of sinks and begins to wash her hands. We leave her thoroughly soaping her hands and arms and obviously enjoying the experience.

It is essential to recognize the importance of play to a young child and how it contributes to his or her cognitive development. When observing children, it is difficult to infer from their physical behaviors and play what they are thinking. By using Piaget's and Vygotsky's ideas of early cognitive development, we can attempt to guess what these children are thinking and how they are being influenced by their environment. We can begin to "see" the transition from unintentional, even accidental, behavior to purposeful behavior that manifests through problem solving, mental images, representational thought, and pretend. We can also see how appropriate adult support can help children learn how to foster cooperation between themselves. Chapter 4 examined the importance of play and provided valuable guides to help plan play sessions. Let's use this cognitive development perspective to reexamine the importance of play.

By the second year, children can think about their world even when they are not directly experiencing it. They also begin to represent things by the use of symbols. Engaging in *pretend play* marks an important step in a child's thinking, and it usually is joined by the beginning of language.

Take the time to observe a two-year-old and a three-year-old involved in pretend play. You may be able to see three different changes or trends that have come about as a result of cognitive growth.

The younger a child is, the more apt he is to be the center of his own pretend play. As he gets older, he gradually acquires the ability to remove himself from center stage. He is then ready to take the role of other imaginary characters. Notice a one-year-old pretending to feed himself. When he gets a little older, he will pretend to feed his doll rather than himself. His doll, however, remains very quiet. By about two years, the child has the ability to make the doll "wake up." Now he can make his doll feed itself. The child can now assume the role of others in his play. He can stand back and consider the other's feeling and one role in relation to another (Is the doll hungry? How much "food" should he supply for his doll?). As he gets older, this becomes more complex and involves other people (for example, several four-year-olds "grocery shopping" in a dramatic play area).

Another change in pretend play can be appreciated when a child begins to substitute one object for another. A very young child needs a real object, or realistic replica, for pretend play. If she is feeding herself, she needs a real cup or real spoon (or plastic replica). As a child gets older (closer to about twenty-two months), she acquires the ability to substitute one object for another. Now perhaps a stick can be used as a spoon, especially when feeding a doll.

At first this substitution is quite limited. Objects need to look like the real thing, and the child may not be able to substitute too many things at one time. Young children need to have available objects to enhance their play. It is important to appreciate that as children get older (closer to four years), it may be difficult for them to substitute a well-known object for something else. A plastic golf club is too much like a real golf club to become a fishing pole. This finding indicates how important it is to have "raw" materials on hand such as tubes, blocks, and an assortment of paper. A paper tube or rolled up newspaper more easily becomes a fishing pole for the young preschooler.[3]

As pretend play continues to develop, a child can invent several actions and combine them. These combinations expand and become more complex as the child gets older. A young child may initially just pretend to feed himself. As he combines actions and integrates them into other experiences, he may eventually pretend to "open a restaurant" and feed several dolls (and no doubt any people who will cooperate).

A toddler's cognitive growth shows, of course, in numerous areas. Pretend play, however, is one of the most dramatic abilities to be observed in a young child. The development of purposeful behavior needs to be planned for and respected by adults.

PROMOTING COGNITIVE DEVELOPMENT IN INFANTS AND TODDLERS

The prerequisite for promoting cognitive development is security and attachment. Through the attachment process, infants develop skills such as differentiation as they distinguish the person(s) they are attached to from others in their world. Attachment also shows intentionality as infants and toddlers use all their behaviors to bring the attached person(s) close and keep them there. Clinging, crying infants or toddlers are exhibiting strong intentionality (a mark of early cognitive behavior) as they try to get the parent to remain. This may be annoying, and it is not usually recognized as cognitive behavior; yet in truth it is very purposeful and intelligent.

Meeting other needs is also part of the prerequisites for promoting cognitive development. Children with unmet needs put their energies into trying to get someone to meet them, which focuses their cognitive development in a narrow way. Children whose needs are met consistently will feel trusting and comfortable. Children who feel comfortable will *explore the environment.* From continual exploration comes cognitive development.

You promote cognitive development by inviting and encouraging exploration in an environment rich in sensory experience. When given the opportunity to play with objects in any way they wish, children encounter problems. As mentioned earlier, problem solving is the basis of infant-toddler education as it is outlined in this book. Allowing infants and toddlers to solve the kinds of problems they run into during the course of a day promotes their cognitive development. Free choice ensures that children find problems that are meaningful to them. Solving someone else's problem is not nearly as interesting to most of us as solving the ones that are related to something that really matters to us.

It helps problem solving if adults do such things as adding words (labeling sensory input—"That rabbit feels soft and warm" or "That was a loud noise" or "That sponge is soaking wet"). In addition, adults can help by asking questions, pointing out relationships, reflecting feelings, and generally supporting the child.

Encourage children to interact with one another during problem solving. The input infants and toddlers get from their peers can both be useful and offer more than one way to a solution. Remember, both Piaget and Vygotsky believe that interaction—with objects and with other people, especially peers—promotes cognitive development.

Include dramatic play props for toddlers. Through pretend, they build the mental images that are so important for the thought process.

Resist pressure to teach or to introduce academic kinds of experiences. Children will learn the names of colors and shapes in the course of normal conversations if you use them naturally ("Please bring me the red pillow" or "Do you want a round cracker or a square one?"). A better use of your time than teaching colors and shapes is to help children learn a variety of approaches to meeting their needs (both physical and social) and making things happen in the world. The concepts will then be imbedded in real life experience and therefore have meaning, rather than ending up as an academic exercise.

Number concepts can also be learned in a natural context. "More" and "less" have real meaning when things are being handed out—such as apple slices. Mathematical concepts come as toddlers play with blocks and sand, compare size and weight of objects, make other comparisons, and figure out relationships.

You will teach reading in your job—but at a toddler level, that is, in a developmentally appropriate way. Your job as a reading teacher of infants and toddlers is not to teach the alphabet but to promote whole language development as well as provide plenty of emergent literacy experiences from which to build concepts so that later, when they see a written word such as "bean," they'll have had many associations with it. It won't be empty of experience and therefore feeling. Children who can recall planting, watering, debugging, picking, snapping, washing, and eating beans really understand what the word means. The word "bean" has meaning as well as rich associations (called connotations). Later, when the children are ready to decode written words, they have real life experience with the words they're reading about.

You can help give children an appreciation of reading and an idea of what it is all about by reading book after book to them. The idea and the joy of reading are important prerequisites to reading itself.

One of the easiest and most effective ways to promote cognitive development is to pay attention to children when they exhibit thinking through problem solving. Of course, many times their choice of solutions gets them in trouble, but even then you can point out that they were problem solving.

Infants and toddlers are naturally creative. If you don't hinder them with too tight limits and an impoverished environment, they will give you lessons in how to use toys and materials in ways you never thought of. Curiosity is part of this push for creativity and needs to be valued and nurtured. Infants and toddlers are newcomers to the world, and they want to know how everything works. They don't want to be told; they want to find out on their own. They are scientists. They don't take anything for granted but rather must prove each hypothesis. Nurture this quality in them!

Infants and toddlers are in the process of creating knowledge (according to Piaget and Vygotsky). They don't just take in information and ideas and manipulate toys and materials. They are not empty vessels to be filled. Instead, they are builders of their own understandings. They use a creative construction process to structure their experiences. And, they need caregivers who understand how to appropriately support and co-construct such experiences.

In this active process of creating knowledge, young children learn to combine known things in their world in new ways. Think about the development of *pretend play*. As a result of exploring and manipulating things, toddlers experiment with new combinations and recombining known "elements" in new ways. This is the essence of "creativity"—the process of combining known things in new ways.

The appreciation of creativity as part of cognitive development emphasizes the importance of planning for it and of not pushing it. When a young child has opportunity to explore and experiment, understanding is fostered. Once children understand how something works (usually as a result of playing with it), they seem naturally to start using it creatively. Exploration is not the same as creativity. Exploration is the beginning point. When promoting cognitive development, try to follow some of the suggestions given in this section. Then step back and watch for the creative, problem-solving process.

BRAIN-BASED LEARNING

The recent brain research that has gotten so much attention nationwide may confirm what many parents and caregivers already know about how young children learn. It may also cause many misinterpretations about development and may fuel marketing strategies for "smart toys" and "super-stimulating" environments. This is an important time to think about young children and to care about how they learn and grow. Consider for a moment your understanding of how young children learn; compare your ideas with Piaget's and Vygotsky's. Pause and review the ten principles of caregiving in chapter 1. Review table 5.1, "Rethinking the Brain," (page 78) in chapter 5. No doubt in the next few years many questions about brain development and learning will be answered. Right now, however, some significant things do seem clear about how the brain learns.

Attachments are primary to development, and learning takes place best in trusting, responsive relationships. The brain functions as an integrated whole; all of the developmental areas are involved. Infants are active learners, and the brain becomes more active when adults respond to infants' cues and signals for attention. Environments are powerful; learning context is as important as learning content. Routines need to be sensitive to relationships (be aware of group size, ratio, and time spent caring for an infant). Meaningfulness of an experience increases the possibility that it will be remembered. Repetition strengthens neural pathways in the brain's circuitry, but don't confuse drill with repetition. Repetition is child-sensitive and comes from the child; drill is adult-directed and adult needs (not the child's) are being addressed.[4]

It is brain density, or neural connections, rather than brain size that contributes most to learning. The brain circuits that have been reinforced and refined translate experience into learning. These branching dendrites in the cortex allow for specific measurement thanks to today's advanced technology. Growth spurts, reflected by increased brain activity, in the first two years actually align themselves with the sensorimotor experiences of Piaget's theory.[5]

More and more we realize that no one theory completely explains how children learn. Piaget's and Vygotsky's theories can be combined to help appreciate cognitive development in the early years. Brain-based learning principles—hands-on, discovery-oriented, collaborative, open-ended experiences—very similar to Piaget's and Vygotsky's ideas, also help us appreciate the essential interconnectedness of young children's learning.

Go back and take another look at the four children playing (pages 128–130). Try to be sensitive to what might be happening in their brains. Can you see neural circuitry being strengthened? Can you see the "magic trees of the mind" (title of Marion Diamond's book on brain growth) growing more dense? Allow yourself to imagine, to wonder. We will certainly be learning more about the brain in the future, but we have much to appreciate today.

CHILDREN WITH SPECIAL NEEDS: RETARDATION

The focus of the chapter has been on how children begin to understand and learn about their world. The most obvious characteristic of "retardation" is a reduced ability to learn. We have already noted that because learning and thinking are internal processes, we must infer what is going on for young children by observing them. The most obvious aspect of development to observe is physical movement. This was discussed to some extent in chapter 7 when we reviewed developmentally delayed children.

Before we go any further, we need to mention "labels." We believe that each child is unique and that labels (per se) tend to categorize and generalize about individuals. In the area of special needs, however, labels can be very important in recognizing children's abilities and limitations. If used appropriately, labels can be guides to caregivers when helping infants and toddlers achieve their greatest potential. Labels, used as identification criteria, also allow programs to seek additional funding resources and community support. We hope labels will always be used in a context that is developmentally appropriate by caregivers who are nurturing and respectful of each child.

"Retardation" and "developmentally delayed" are sometimes used interchangeably. Retardation goes beyond motor assessment and involves more of the cognitive areas of development. For example, specific areas of concern may relate to attention skills, memory, language, and problem-solving abilities. Think about how these four areas link together for a young child. A child who has a limited ability to attend to an experience—become absorbed or deeply involved—may never gather important details to remember. Memory is critical to acquiring labels for these experiences and thus developing language. Language allows for more logical and organized thinking. There is, we might say, a "cognitive" domino effect for the retarded young child.

These abilities, which may be limited, depressed, or nonexistent, also relate to a child's "adaptive" behavior. How well a young child adapts to or copes with the world is, of course, age and situation specific. If an eight-month-old, very recently enrolled in an infant program, cried for the majority of the morning (even though comfort was offered), her behavior could be considered developmentally appropriate. However, if a three-year-old who had been attending a child care program for several months did the same thing and could not be comforted and establish trust, additional questions would need to be asked. "Adaptive" behaviors can be considered "cognitive." They allow a child to predict and therefore generalize trust. These behaviors are significant, and when they are slow to develop, children may experience frustration. Retarded young children tend to have a difficult time adapting to changes. They need more time and the support of a sensitive caregiver.

Trying to assess an infant's or toddler's "intellectual functioning" (IQ score) is very difficult. Few really reliable tests exist. It is generally believed that the younger a child is when tested, the less predictive the results will be. The definition of "retardation" usually involves some degree of assessment in this area. Today, observations and descriptive evaluations are considered the most helpful. It is difficult in the first three years to determine a "mild" cognitive handicap or a concern that may eventually be related to a "learning disability." These milder concerns or processing problems may not be identified until a child reaches school age and is faced with the challenges of reading, writing, and math. More moderate, severe, or multiple concerns will, hopefully, be identified early (before school age), and intervention will be available.

Causes for retardation may be varied or difficult to determine. They may range from genetic (for example, Down's syndrome) to brain damage as a result of infectious diseases (for example, meningitis or rubella). Prenatal environmental hazards such as poisons (for example, cocaine and alcohol used by the pregnant mother) may also result in retardation. The importance of prenatal care cannot be stressed too much.

Promoting the cognitive growth of a retarded young child follows the general guides previously given. You may need to be more deliberate (not exaggerated) with your involvement, and you may need to provide for more "practice" time for the infant or toddler. The infant stimulation programs developed in the late 1960s provided experiences to promote perceptual (motor, language, and social) development. Emphasis was on language and concept formation. Some people became very uncomfortable with such programming because it often involved a great deal of drill. Some felt that things were "done to" infants rather than involving them in appropriate play activities. Our sensitivity has expanded considerably today, and appropriate developmental programming (involving families) is more widespread.

Examine the following guides for preparing environments for and working with retarded young children. Compare them to the ten principles on which this text is based (review chapter 1).

- Provide multisensory experiences.
- Divide learning experiences into small segments or steps.
- Carefully sequence these steps from simple to the most difficult.
- Use concrete examples to teach concepts.
- Provide much practice.
- Give consistent, supportive feedback.[6]

Caregivers of retarded infants and toddlers may need to adapt some aspects of their programs. As with all children, a sensitivity to quality time in which the "whole child's" unique abilities are appreciated is the key. Learning is facilitated when children trust the people around them. Appreciating the quality of his or her accomplishment may be even more significant for a retarded child.

Thought/Activity Questions

1. What behaviors indicate that a child is developing understanding? Describe at least three of them.
2. Discuss Piaget's and Vygotsky's major views about the mental development of children. What guides would you share with parents and caregivers concerning each approach?
3. Design a toy for an infant or toddler that would foster cognitive growth. Include reasons why the toy would be good for this.
4. You are the guest speaker at a parent meeting for an infant-toddler program. The topic is cognitive development. What main points do you want to share?
5. What are possible drawbacks to pushing early learning ("academic"-type activities) for toddlers?

Notes

1. J. H. Flavell, "On Cognitive Development," *Child Development* 53, 1982, pp. 1–10.
2. L. Berk and A. Winsler, *Scaffolding Children's Learning: Vygotsky and Early Childhood Education* (Washington, D.C.: National Association for the Education of Young Children, 1995), p. 22.
3. J. Schickendanz, K. Hansen, and P. Forsyth, *Understanding Children* (Mountain View, Calif.: Mayfield, 1990), p. 196.
4. R. Lalley, "Brain Research, Infant Learning, and Child Care Curriculum," *Child Care Information Exchange* 121, May/June 1998, pp. 46–48.
5. M. Diamond, *Magic Trees of the Mind* (New York: Plume, 1998), pp. 112–120.
6. P. H. Brooks and C. McCauley, "Cognitive Research in Mental Retardation," *American Journal of Mental Deficiency* 88, 1984, pp. 479–486.

For Further Reading

Beginnings Workshop: "Make-Believe Play," *Child Care Information Exchange* 99, September 1994.

L. Berk, "Vygotsky's Theory: The Importance of Make-Believe Play," *Young Children* 50(1), November 1994, pp. 30–39.

J. Gowen, "The Early Development of Symbolic Play," *Young Children* 50(3), March 1995, pp. 75–84.

S. Greenspan, *The Growth of the Mind* (Menlo Park, Calif.: Addison Wesley, 1997).

T. F. Gross, *Cognitive Development* (Monterey, Calif.: Brooks/Cole, 1985).

F. Hughes, J. Elicker, and L. Veen, "A Program of Play for Infants and Caregivers," *Young Children* 50(2), January 1995, pp. 52–58.

E. Jensen, *Brain-Based Learning* (Del Mar, Calif.: Turning Point Publishing, 1996).

R. Kotulak, *Inside the Brain: Revolutionary Discoveries of How the Mind Works* (Kansas City, Mo.: Andrews McMeel, 1997).

J. L. Phillips Jr., *The Origins of Intellect: Piaget's Theory* (San Francisco: W. H. Freeman, 1969).

M. C. Pugmire-Stoy, *Spontaneous Play in Early Childhood* (Albany, N.Y.: Delmar, 1992).

C. T. Tamsey, *Right from Birth: Building Your Child's Foundation for Life* (New York: Goodard Press, 1999).

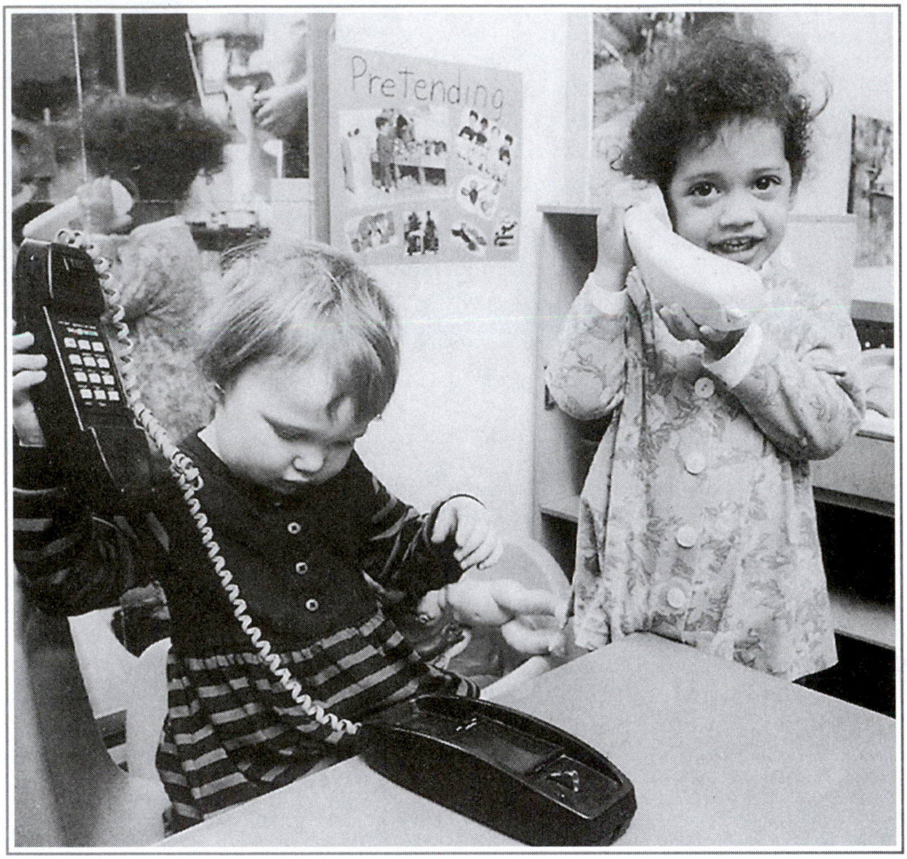
Pretending

CHAPTER 9

The Development of Language

The ability to learn to talk and use language is an amazingly complex process. Very early in life infants begin to coordinate their gestures and make meaningful sounds. They begin to organize their experiences to make themselves understood—to communicate. This ability to develop language involves all the other areas of growth so far discussed in this book (attachment, perception, motor skills, and cognition) and is influenced by emotional and social development (chapters 10 and 11). Through language, children coordinate their experiences and give and receive feedback on these experiences.

This chapter examines the foundations of language growth and what a person needs in order for it to develop. What language allows an individual to do and how the environment may influence language are also reviewed. Brain growth and early language are explored. Guides for fostering language development, bilingualism, and some communication disorders are specific topics within this chapter.

THE PROGRESSION OF LANGUAGE DEVELOPMENT

Infants are born with communication intent; they are not born with language. It is not clearly understood how children acquire the ability to use language. Usually language development is discussed in terms of *what* tends to happen *when* (see table 9.1). No one theory or approach completely explains the development of this ability. It may be more helpful to combine several approaches in an effort to appreciate how language develops. We have already discussed the importance of attachment for infants. Within this responsive

TABLE 9.1
Language Development: What Happens When

Age	Hearing/understanding	Talking
Birth–3 months	• Child will awaken at loud sounds (startle or cry, too). • Child will listen to speech, turn to you when you speak. • Child will smile when spoken to. • Child will recognize your voice and quiet down if crying.	• Child will make pleasure sounds. • Child will repeat same sounds a lot (cooing, gooing). • Child will cry differently for different needs. • Child will smile when he or she sees you.
4–6 months	• Child will respond to tone of voice (loud or soft) • Child will look around for sound (i.e., phone ringing, dog barking). • Child will notice noise/sound from toys.	• Child will make gurgling sounds when alone. • Child will tell you (by sound or gesture) to repeat something. May be a form of play. • Child will use speech or noncrying sounds to get and keep your attention.
7–12 months	• Child enjoys games like peek-a-boo and pat-a-cake. • Child will listen when spoken to. • Child will recognize words for common items like "juice," "cup," "doll."	• Child will use speech or noncrying sounds to get and keep your attention. • Child will imitate different speech sounds. • Child's babbling will have both long and short groups of sounds such as "tata, upup, bibibibi." • Child will have 1 or 2 words (bye-bye, no, dada), although they may not be clear.
12–24 months	• Child will follow simple commands and understand simple questions ("Roll the ball," "Where is the doll?"). • Child will point to a few body parts when asked. • Child will point to pictures in a book when they are named.	• Child can use many different consonant sounds at the beginning of words. • Child can put two words together ("no juice," "more milk"). • Child can use 1–2 word question ("Where kitty?," "go bye-bye?").
24–36 months	• Child can follow two requests ("Get the ball and put it on the table"). • Child will continue to notice sounds (telephone ringing, TV sound, knocking at the door). • Child will understand differences in meaning ("Go–stop"; "in–on"; "big–little"; "up–down").	• Child will ask for or direct your attention to objects by naming them. • Child's speech is understood most of the time. • Child uses 2–3 word "sentences" to talk about and ask for things. • Child has words for almost everything.

Adapted from *How Does Your Child Hear and Talk?*, American Speech-Language-Hearing Association (10801 Rockville Pike, Rockville, MD 20852), 1988. Reprinted with permission.

relationship, infants learn about *social interaction*—a critical component of language growth. When they are cared for and find pleasure in this caring, they *imitate* their caregivers, and their caregivers, in turn, continue to respond to them. This back and forth behavior seems almost to *reinforce* itself.

Infants all over the world begin to develop language in very similar ways. The *ability* to acquire language seems to be inborn, or *innate*. Certain mental and physical skills have to be present for language to progress. As infants grow, *maturation* contributes to the ability to develop words (or labels) and understand symbols. Piaget noted that object permanence sets the stage for language development. Young children have to be able to make sense of, or interpret, their world before using their first words. Vygotsky stressed the sociocultural context of language development. Social interaction helps young children understand the relationship between experiences and appropriate labels for them.[1]

In essence, several important things seem to happen at the same time when children acquire language. Thinking of them as the "three I's" may help. *I*nnate abilities have to be present; a child has to have certain cognitive skills and mental structures to develop language. A child also needs the opportunity to *I*nteract with someone in a responsive way in order to *I*mitate them. This process of imitation, involving interaction, based on innate abilities, should be viewed in a bit more detail. Looking at two developmental levels of language— the receptive (birth to one year) and the expressive (end of first year to beginning first words)—gives more insight into the progression of language.

Receptive Language

Infants share their pleasure in making sounds with their parent or caregiver. They come to associate language with a social occasion. As they coo and babble, they find that they are responded to, which in turn encourages them to respond to and imitate their partner. They become aware of rhythms, pitches, and sounds of words. Language can become a way to excite or to soothe a baby.

Eventually, babies begin to make connections between sounds or sound patterns and events or objects. They notice, for example, that when they are handed a particular object (such as a teddy bear), the same sound pattern occurs time after time. Their storybooks have the same sounds with the same pictures. They notice that whenever their diapers are changed, they hear one of the same sounds and patterns. What the infant takes in and understands is called "receptive language."

From the beginning, of course, infants react to being spoken to, but it is the voice—pitch and tone—rather than the meaning of the words that they respond to. Later, when they begin to respond to the meaning behind the words, this response is true receptive language. Caregivers are sometimes surprised to discover that receptive language is so advanced. When children are spoken to in meaningful ways, they understand what is being said to them much earlier than might be expected.

Expressive Language

As their early cries and vocalizations are responded to, infants learn to refine them, eventually sending more specialized vocal signals. The more they know that their signals or messages are received, the more skilled they become in sending them. From their partnership with a caregiver or two, they learn to convey a variety of feelings—hunger, discomfort, anger, and pleasure. The key to infants' beginning to connect sounds with meaning is the caregiver's responsiveness. If no one responded to their initial cries and vocalizations, infants would have no reason to strive to make signals.

The actual moment a child utters her first word may be quite a surprise to the adult who is present to hear it. One day a little girl may see a banana on a counter and reach for it, saying "nana." She may be surprised by the reaction—such a flutter and flurry of smiles, hugs, and pats, followed by a piece of banana being placed in her hand. She will probably smile back and say her new word two or three more times. Later on she may be asked to repeat her performance as the late shift of caregivers arrives. Perhaps the caregivers, so pleased with this new accomplishment, will report it to the parent. Or maybe they'll keep their pleasure to themselves and decide not to disappoint the parent, who missed the event, by mentioning it, but will let the parent be the one to report the first word when he or she hears it.

Suppose you observed a child who was just beginning to talk, and you wrote down exactly what he or she said. Your notes might look something like this:

> mmmmm mmm (pause) oooo (pause) milk (pause) mimimimimimimi (pause) burrrrr, burrrrrr (pause) ooooooo milk eeeeeee (pause) uhuh (pause) milk!

This may seem meaningless without a context. A description of the whole scene might clarify what the child was communicating.

> A caregiver holds out a cup to a baby seated at a low table. "Do you want a drink of milk?" he asks.
>
> The child answers, "mmmmmmmmm mmm, ooooo, milk!" He reaches for the cup.
>
> The caregiver pours a small amount of milk into the cup. The child lifts it to his lips and takes a sip. Then he says, "mimimimimimimimi, burrrrr, burrrr, burrr" into the cup, delighted in the effect of the movement of his lips on the milk. Milk splashes onto his face. The caregiver reaches for a wet washcloth. The child sets the cup down, and it tips over, making a puddle on the table. "ooooooo milk . . . ," says the child, pointing to the puddle.
>
> The caregiver reaches for a sponge with the other hand and puts it on the puddle while wiping the child's face with the washcloth. "Eeeeeeee." Squeals of protest accompany the face cleaning. When all is in order again, the caregiver reaches for the carton, holds it out, and asks, "Do you want more milk?"

The child answers, "Uhuh, milk!" emphatically, with a vigorous shake of his head while shoving the cup away from him.

This child conveyed a variety of meanings through a few sounds and a single word. In a short time, this same scene might include this verbal sequence:

"Me milk" (meaning "Yes, please, I'd like some milk.")
"Milk spill" (meaning "Hey there, somebody spilled the milk!")
"Me, no" (meaning "No, thank you, I don't want any more milk.")

By the time this child is a toddler, he will be saying the same thing using longer phrases—something like this:

"Give me milk." (perhaps with a "please")
"Oh, oh, Mike, me spill milk."
"Me no want more."

Without ever being "corrected," this child will eventually say:

"I want some milk (please)."
"Oh, oh, Mike. I spilled my milk."
"I don't want anymore (thank you)."

Children refine their language and develop grammatical rules on their own. They don't need corrections or language lessons. They learn by being part of real conversations—ones that move forward. Sometimes conversations just go around in circles when the adult tries to teach by repeating everything the child says in a more correct form. If nothing the adult says adds to the content, these merry-go-round conversations are meaningless. It is more important for adults to realize that as children begin to use longer phrases to communicate, they are also using language as an important tool for thinking.

WHAT LANGUAGE ALLOWS A CHILD TO DO: THE COGNITIVE LINK

The previous scene makes it clear that as a child moves into and through toddlerhood, there is an obvious increase in the ability to communicate. This ability to clarify needs and gather information is expanded as a young child acquires language. In addition to facilitating communication, language has a dramatic impact on thought and cognition.

Infants and toddlers can "think" before they acquire language, but when children really begin to use language, their cognitive abilities take a major step forward. The ability to label experiences, indicating object permanence, allows children to enter into a symbolic realm. Experiences do not have to be "in the moment"; they can be remembered, and a *word* can stand for an object. As children gather labels for experiences, their memories also grow. This memory bank will soon have categories within it. And the categories will eventually allow for a complex classification system. The experience of seeing a cat and learning that label gradually moves into a child's understanding that there are many breeds of cat and that this particular four-legged creature also belongs to a larger category of "animals." Information can be generalized from this understanding, but it all began with the label "cat."

Reasoning and the ability to order experiences are developed as a result of language. Watch (and listen) to a toddler as she plays. You may often overhear her actually telling herself what to do ("Now I'm going to the sandbox. Then I'm going to make a road."). This "verbal instruction" allows a child to plan her own behavior and to move her learning experiences from one situation to another. This ability to organize information eventually allows for abstraction and more formal cognitive thinking. Language increases our adaptation and coping skills. It provides us with the skills to be more clearly understood by others and to understand more concretely events around us. In a world with ever-increasing demands, appreciating how children cope effectively would be a good goal for parents and caregivers.

THE BRAIN AND EARLY LANGUAGE DEVELOPMENT

What is happening in the brain while a young child is trying to acquire language? Some of the new brain research in this area is the most fascinating, and the most specific. Several key findings should be noted. Genes and experiences (nature and nurture) work together for healthy brain growth. As already noted in this chapter, an infant may be physically capable of producing sound, but without nurturing interactions a language delay is likely. These early interactions actually influence the circuitry, or wiring, in the brain. Language development is dependent on the early neural connections (synapses) that are stimulated through responsive interactions with others. And these early experiences seem to be linked to prime times, or optimal periods, for particular aspects of language learning to occur.

During the first few months a child's brain is "neuroplastic," or very flexible and responsive. This is no doubt why young infants initially respond to all the sounds of all languages. But this plasticity lessens with age. Early in brain growth neurons seem to cluster around particular sound patterns called "phonemes" (the smallest units of sound in a language). When these patterns (for example, "pa" or "ma") are repeated, "auditory maps" are formed; neural pathways are reinforced and brain circuitry is made more permanent.[2] This allows an infant to organize patterns of sounds within her native language. By the end of the first year, if certain sound patterns are not heard with regularity, it is very difficult for a child to construct new pathways. (Remember the "pruning process" mentioned in chapter 5.) This is why it is so difficult to learn another language after we get older. Those pathways will never be as easily formed as they are in the first twelve months.

As young children acquire language, their brains become increasingly more specialized for this complex task. Increased electrical activity tends to be concentrated in the left hemisphere of the cortex. Increased brain activity and increased language competency are linked in the second half of the first year. It is at about seven to twelve months that infants join phonemes to syllables and syllables to words.[3] Look back at table 9.1 and the child and caregiver interaction on pages 142–143. Try to imagine brain dendrites, those "magic trees of the mind," expanding rapidly as a young child makes sense of sounds as a result of experience. The first word, usually at the end of the first year, is just the beginning of the language explosion.

Experience also relates to vocabulary. A toddler's vocabulary is strongly correlated to how much interaction she experiences. Infants need to hear words! And these words need to be linked to real events. These are the kinds of experiences that create permanent neural connections. Meaning fosters connecting! Television doesn't do it—TV is just noise to a very young child. The emotional context of language seems to influence neural circuitry, too. Connecting words to pleasant experiences (or negative ones) affects memory. A young child is more apt to remember the label for her special toy or favorite food!

Some debate exists about prime times, or optimal periods, particularly as they relate to language development. Do those "windows of opportunity" slam shut? Probably not. But more is said in the brain research about the specific timing of language than of any other developmental area. Two particular events that are critical to brain development happen in the first two years. The sensorimotor systems are strengthened through myelinization (referred to in chapter 7), and attachment relationships are established. These events dramatically influence brain functioning and growth, and since brain growth is holistic, they must also play a dramatic role in early language acquisition. And these two events may be most significant to our understanding of critical periods of brain growth. Many questions will be answered by researchers in the next few years. In the meantime, appreciating the complexity of language development, and its relationship to what we know about neural circuitry, can help us provide nurturing, appropriate experiences for infants and toddlers.

The following section lists guidelines for fostering language development in young children. As you read it, try to think about what you know about brain growth. How are these guidelines related to what is happening in a child's brain?

FOSTERING LANGUAGE DEVELOPMENT

Caregivers and parents can foster language development in infants by using language with them from the start. *Talk* to them long before they can talk to you. Use real, adult talk. Include them in conversations with other people. Also *play* with them using sounds. Interact with them—create dialogues. Listen to infants, and encourage them to listen, too. Make sure that you have an infant's attention when you are talking together, and be sure to give him or her yours. Even very young infants are very responsive to language. The rhythm of their body movements corresponds with the rhythm of language when engaged in one of these early dialogues. Consider these guidelines for fostering language development in infants and toddlers:

1. Engage in dialogue from day one, during caregiving times and during play time (when appropriate). With younger infants, exchange sounds. This is a natural activity most adults engage in without being told to. They imitate the baby's sounds as well as initiating their own sounds. This kind of dialogue sets the stage for later, when the dialogue on both sides will contain words.

2. Create monologues also. Discuss the present. Describe what is happening as it occurs. Your running commentary will contain the labels children need to learn—labels for people, feelings, actions, objects, and events. When the infant responds, turn the monologue into a dialogue. (It's best always to talk *with* a baby, not *at* him or her.)

3. Discuss the past—remark about what happened just now to infants; with toddlers, you can talk about earlier in the day, yesterday, and last week. The older the child, the farther back you can go.

4. Discuss the future. Knowing what's about to happen helps infants predict events as well as begin to understand labels for things, actions, events, and people. Toddlers can be involved in discussions about the future, including what will happen this afternoon, tomorrow, and next week. The older the child, the farther into the future you can go.

5. Tell stories, sing songs, and recite or create rhymes and poems. Make room in your telling, singing, or reciting for the children's participation or responses. Don't just entertain them; interact with them. They learn language from using it, from being involved, not just from listening.

6. Play games with sounds and words. If you're not good at this yourself, take lessons from the children. Many young children have an outstanding ability to create playfully with sounds and words. This starts early with those first cooings and babblings and continues, if valued and encouraged, until children are creating their own nonsense rhymes and sound games.

7. Be sure older toddlers have plenty of experiences to talk about. The infants will find enough subject matter in the day-to-day play and caregiving routines, but as they grow, their world needs to expand a bit. It's up to you to be sure that expansion occurs. Create "happenings" inside and outside. Bring in visitors. If possible, go on short field trips—a walk around the block can provide conversation material for some time.

8. Read books from infancy on. Read individually or to small groups at any appropriate time when there is an interest. Don't make a daily circle time with required attendance for the whole group. Make it a frequent, short, spontaneous activity accompanied by lots of cuddling and snuggles. Stop when interest wanes, and don't require each child to stay and listen to the whole book. Make this an interactive activity rather than an entertainment. Allow children to "read" to you or to other children. Story or book time for infants and toddlers should resemble what parents do at home more than what preschool teachers do at circle time. The purpose is to familiarize infants and toddlers with books and to create a number of pleasurable associations with books, and eventually with reading. The language goals, though important, are secondary.

9. Bring in pictures, novel objects, and bits of science and nature, and carry on extemporaneous discussions when a child's interest is sparked. Again, these should be dialogues, not lectures.

10. Ask questions—questions requiring a choice. Do you want the square cracker or the round one? Do you want to go for a walk before snack or after snack? Ask questions that have no right answer (called open questions). How does the bunny feel to you? Tell me about Grandma's visit. What did you see on your walk? Closed questions (those with one right answer) are fine, too, as long as the child enjoys them and doesn't feel interrogated. (They are often overused in an attempt to teach language.)

11. Encourage children to ask questions. A favorite game of beginning talkers is "What's that?" They like to ask the question as well as answer it, and in doing so, they practice and collect labels for objects.

12. Encourage children to clarify what they don't understand. Some people try to teach children through questioning them. If pressured for correct answers, children can learn to act as if they understand things they don't. If you encourage an inquiry attitude, they'll ask about words they don't know and then practice them on their own without being taught or pushed.

13. Put language into gross motor activities. Don't regard your language curriculum as something that happens during sedentary times. The way children learn about spatial relations and the prepositions that go with them is through experiencing these concepts with their own bodies. When adults add a label, they help the child classify, store, and remember the concept. "Mario is *under* the box. See him hiding?" "Who's going to sit *beside* you at the table? Oh, Emily's going to." "I see you're *on top* of the steps, Jason. Are you going to stay *up* there, or are you going *down*?"

14. Really listen when toddlers talk to you. Resist the temptation to rush children or interrupt them. Give them time to say what they want to say.

15. Help children listen to each other. Talk for them or interpret when necessary, but keep the focus *off* yourself and *on* the two children who are trying to communicate with each other. "She's trying to tell you she doesn't like you to push her." "Ask her what she wants." "Tell him you want some play dough too."

16. Recognize and respect the parents' ability to understand their own child. Get them to explain or interpret. As you get to know each child's unique method of communicating, you'll no doubt need less interpretation.

CULTURAL DIFFERENCES AND BILINGUALISM

All these guidelines are culturally bound (as is everything else in this book). Some cultures view language practices and the language socialization process differently from the way we have presented it here. They may have different goals for their children regarding language. They may also use different methods from the beginning. You may or may not approve of the cultural approach to language of some of the parents in your program, but you must respect cultural differences and try to understand how values and approaches other than your own may serve the individual in the particular culture.

An example of a cultural difference in language is provided by S. B. Heath, who describes a culture in which babies are made a part of everything that is going on by being held continually but are rarely talked to during the first year. They pick up language by being immersed in it, not by having it directed at them. This shows later in their use of language. They have a holistic view of objects in context. They have difficulty talking about an object out of context, such as sorting out the attributes of that object and comparing them to those of another object out of context. When shown flash card pictures of a red ball and a blue ball and asked, "Is the red ball or the blue ball bigger," children from this culture would have difficulty sorting out the attributes of color and size, though in a real life situation they could determine the larger ball and throw it when asked to do so. Rather than teaching the concepts accepted as important by the mainstream Canadian and U.S. culture (such as color, shape, and size), this culture values the creative use of language, including metaphors. Their children show great skill at creative verbal play and use of imagery.[4]

Children in child care are influenced by the caregiver's culture. Children who grow up in two cultures and incorporate both are said to be bicultural. Whether or not those two cultures conflict and cause the child to feel torn between them depends on the child, the parents, the caregiver, and the cultures themselves. Sometimes children seem to get caught *between* two cultures and experience a lot of pain in their upbringing.

A child can be bicultural and still be English speaking, as are many children in this country and other parts of the world. Many bicultural people, however, speak more than one language.

Infants can learn two languages from day one, and by the time they are toddlers, they can be very skilled at switching back and forth between them to different people and in different contexts. Bilingualism is a skill to be valued and nurtured. Day care can provide excellent opportunities for this skill to develop as children of one language background come into contact with caregivers of another. Take advantage of any chance you have to help children become bilingual (with the parents' permission, of course). You can do this by talking to them in your own language (if their family speaks a different one) or another language (if you are bilingual yourself).

Keep in mind the "language relationship." The language relationship is established without fanfare when two people meet for the first time. For two monolingual English-speaking people, there is no option; the language of their relationship is English, and they never even think about it. But when two bilingual persons meet, the situation is different. There is a choice, and once the choice is made, the two feel most comfortable when they speak the language of their relationship to each other, though both may be fully capable of speaking the second language.

When a bilingual caregiver meets a young infant, the choice of language is present to some extent because the baby is not yet a full-fledged member of a language community. If bilingualism is a goal, establishing a relationship in the target language from the beginning is quite simple.

Establishing this relationship is a little more difficult with a child who is already partway along in his or her language development because of the difficulty in communicating until the child learns the second language. The strength of the bilingual goal and the extent to which children feel secure and are able to get their needs met should determine whether to establish a language relationship in a language other than the child's own with the primary caregiver. When both caregiver and child are skilled at nonverbal communication, the choice isn't so difficult. Once the language relationship is established, there is a motivation to learn the second language, and it isn't long before verbal communication is established. It is important, however, to remember that, although some children seem to "pick up" language fast, language acquisition doesn't happen overnight. Communication is necessarily weak at the beginning and often for a long time afterward. It's very hard on some older babies and toddlers to be put into situations where they can't understand what is said to them. Just imagine how you would feel being totally dependent on someone who didn't speak your language.

When bilingualism is a strong goal and the child is liable to suffer from the initial lack of communication, it is best to have two caregivers to relate to the child. One can then establish a relationship in the second language while another is present to establish a language relationship in the child's own language. Thus the child can become bilingual in a secure situation. This way of ensuring bilingualism is common practice in many families in different parts of the world.

Be careful that you don't ask bilingual or limited English-speaking parents to speak English to their children when their inclination is otherwise. If you do, you are disregarding the language relationship. And you may be impairing the communication between parent and child. Magda Gerber, a bilingual person herself, says that it is natural for parents to speak to their children in the language they themselves were spoken to in infancy and toddlerhood. Even parents who have become proficient in English may find that the words of caring come more easily in the language of their own beginnings. Be careful not to hinder parents' ability to communicate caring and tenderness to their children.

Be concerned about the quality of verbal communication in your environment or program if bilingualism is a goal. Unless you are proficient in the language you are using to communicate with the child, the goal of bilingualism may get in the way of communication. If your ability to express yourself in the target language is limited, you should weigh communication and the child's language development against the goal of bilingualism.

As already mentioned, a solution to this problem, if there is more than one adult and bilingualism is a goal, is for one to establish relationships in one language and the other to establish them in the second language. In this way, children establish a relationship with someone who is proficient in one language and are assured of good communication while they progress in a second language. Without someone to communicate with who is proficient, the child misses out. With one proficient speaker and one less than proficient one, the child can gain some added benefits without losing out on first language development. This scene shows how bilingualism can work in a family day-care home.

> It's late in the afternoon, and a woman is heating tortillas on the stove. A three-year-old watches her from the kitchen table. He tells her that he is hungry—in Spanish. She smiles and answers him in Spanish, at the same time handing him a warm, soft, rolled-up tortilla. Another three-year-old appears at the doorway, requesting a tortilla in English. She obliges with a second tortilla and again answers in Spanish. Both children stand by the table chewing their tortillas, obviously relishing the flavor.
>
> A man enters the kitchen. "Ummm, something smells good," he comments.
>
> "Yes," replies the woman. "Guess what?"
>
> "Tortilla. It's yummy," says the first child, holding his out to show the man.
>
> "Want a bite?" asks the second child.
>
> "Here's one for you," says the woman, handing the man his own fresh, hot tortilla.
>
> All three chew contentedly. Then the man says, "How about Grandma? Go ask her if she wants a tortilla."
>
> The first child runs from the room, calling, "Abuelita, Abuelita, quieres tortilla?"

This child, only three years old, is managing to learn two languages and, further, is learning when to use each one. The other child is getting exposure to a second language and developing his receptive language skills. Depending on the circumstances, he may begin to use it himself one day. In the meantime, he's in a situation where he can use and be understood in his own language while learning another one.

The skill of using language appropriate to the situation is not limited to children using two languages. All speakers learn early to distinguish between language styles. Listen carefully to the difference between the way two three-year-olds talk to each other and the way they talk to adults. Listen, for example, to the way children "play house." The one playing the mother talks the way she perceives adults talk; the one playing the baby speaks in a different way altogether. Clearly, they have learned that there is one style for talking to peers and another for talking to adults. Children also distinguish among the adults they speak to. The way they talk to mother may be different from the way they talk to father, caregiver, or a stranger on the streets.

Language is culturally bound and influences our lives immeasurably. Infants and toddlers learn to use language in natural settings when they are spoken to, responded to, and listened to. Language influences how they perceive the world, organize their experience, and communicate with others.

CHILDREN WITH SPECIAL NEEDS: COMMUNICATION DISORDERS

The process of acquiring language is clearly complex. Numerous factors affect its development. Communication disorders, therefore, are particularly complex. Many aspects of a child's environment may contribute to a communication problem. It is important that parents and caregivers have an overview of healthy language development (as in table 9.1). If they suspect a problem, they should quickly consult a speech-language therapist. Early intervention is vital if a young child experiences communication difficulties.

Communication disorders tend to occur in two major areas: language production and speech patterns. Language is a code, or symbol system, that we learn in order to share ideas. It allows us to send and receive information. Speaking and gesturing (and eventually reading and writing) are forms of language. Speech is the spoken aspect of language. It is the forming and sequencing of sound. Language disorders are generally more serious for a child. For example, a young child may have no problem producing speech—his voice is appropriate and the muscles around his mouth and lips are coordinated. But this same child may not be able to make sense when talking or not understand the meaning of what he hears. A delay in language or speech generally means that words or sounds are not understood or made correctly at the expected age. Each child is unique in learning language, but all children should follow

---

BOX 9.1
Milestones and Warning Signs

Young Infants (Birth to Eight Months):   Young infants communicate initially to get their needs met and then expand their communication to include playful exchanges, learning the rhythms of interacting with their caregivers. Warning signs for the young infant include the following:

- A general lack of interest in social contact (infant avoids eye contact, holds body rigidly)
- Lack of response to the human voice or other sounds

Mobile Infants (Six to Eighteen Months):   Mobile infants playfully experiment with language and communicate with purpose. At this stage, one often hears first words. Mobile infants will practice newly acquired words over and over and try to use them whenever they can. Warning signs for the mobile infant include the following:

- At eight to nine months, the child stops babbling (infants who are deaf babble at first and then stop).
- The child does not show interest in interacting with objects and caregivers in familiar environments.
- At nine to ten months, the child does not follow direction of point.
- At eleven to twelve months, the child does not give, show, or point at objects.

From "Early Messages," Child Care Video Magazine. Reprinted by permission of J. Ronald Lally, Far West Laboratory for Educational Research and Development and California Department of Education.

(within several months) developmental guides for language growth. Delays may happen for a variety of reasons. A child may have a physical impairment. The lack of muscle coordination (especially the small muscles in the face, mouth, and throat) will cause a delay in speech production. Brain damage or mental retardation will impair cognitive abilities, which will in turn affect language. Hearing loss (a sensory problem) will result in some language concerns. Emotional and social deprivation can also cause a communication disorder. All areas of growth support children in their efforts to acquire language, and a problem or concern in any one of these areas may result in a language delay.

A parent or caregiver may wonder at what point to be concerned about a child's language development. Some of the following guides may help. Use

- At eleven to twelve months, the child does not play games such as pat-a-cake or peek-a-boo.

Older Infants (Sixteen to Thirty-six Months):   There is typically a language explosion at the beginning of the older infant stage. The number of words that toddlers know increases rapidly, and they start to use simple grammar. Warning signs for the older infant include the following:

By 24 months, the child

- Uses 25 or fewer words

By 36 months, the child

- Has a limited vocabulary
- Uses only short, simple sentences
- Makes many more grammatical errors than other children at the same age
- Has difficulty talking about the future
- Misunderstands questions most of the time
- Is often misunderstood by others
- Displays fewer forms of social play than other children at the same age
- Has difficulty carrying on a conversation

caution when applying any measure of development to a child. Individual differences or special circumstances need to be accounted for.

Normal speech in a young child that has some "interruption" in speech flow is often referred to as "stuttering." Be careful about calling normal disfluency—repeating or stumbling on words—stuttering. It is not unusual for young children (under four years) to pause frequently when trying to think of how to say something. Labeling this behavior incorrectly may cause unnecessary frustration to the child. And it may result in inappropriate behavior from the adult. Only about 1 percent of children and adults are considered stutterers.[5]

The treatment of a communication disorder obviously depends on the child. If there is a structural problem (a cleft lip or cleft palate), it needs to be corrected. Ear infections need to be treated promptly. Early intervention programs (especially for children under three years old) usually involve helping parents and caregivers create responsive play experiences with appropriate verbalizations. It means talking to a child about objects and experiences in the way most mothers talk to their babies. In general, the more severely disabled the young child, the more responsive and repetitive the practices of the caregiver must become.

Communication is intertwined with all areas of a child's development. Intervention plans or treatment strategies must be made a part of a child's everyday world. The guides for fostering language development mentioned in this chapter certainly are relevant for most children with a communication disorder. Interactions that are part of a child's daily routines, and appreciative of individual effort, seem to be the most effective.

Thought/Activity Questions

1. Review table 9.1. A parent asks you about her eight-month-old child's language growth. How might this chart's information help you? How might it be used inappropriately?
2. Visit the library in your area and review the children's section. Select at least five books that you think are appropriate for toddlers. Justify your choices.
3. Observe a child under three years of age. What language behaviors do you see? How does this child get his or her needs met? What does language allow him or her to do?
4. Imagine that you have a child with some communication disorder in your program. What would you need to consider? List several appropriate language activities.

Notes

1. L. Vygotsky, "Play and Its Role in the Mental Development of the Child," in *Play: Its Role in Development and Evolution,* edited by J. Bruner, A. Jolly, and K. Sylvia (New York: Basic Books, 1976).
2. S. Begley, "How to Build a Baby's Brain," *Newsweek,* Spring/Summer 1997, 28–32.
3. D. L. Mills, S. A. Coffey-Cornia, and H. J. Neville, "Variability in Cerebral Organization during Primary Language Acquisition," in *Human Behavior and the Developing Brain,* edited by G. Davidson and K. W. Fischer (New York: Guilford, 1994), pp. 427–455.
4. S. B. Heath, *Ways with Words: Language, Life, and Work in Communities and Classrooms* (Cambridge: Cambridge University Press, 1983).
5. G. Stiames and H. Rubin, eds., *Stuttering: Then and Now* (Columbus, Ohio: Merrill, 1986).

For Further Reading

K. Barclay, C. Benelli, and A. Curtis, "Literacy Begins at Birth: What Caregivers Can Learn from Parents of Children Who Read Early," *Young Children* 50(4), May 1995, pp. 24–28.

Magda Gerber, "Babies Understanding Words," *Educaring* 3(4), Fall 1982, pp. 5–6.

B. Gleason, ed., *The Development of Language,* 3rd ed. (New York: Macmillan, 1993).

K. Hakuta, *Mirror of Language, the Debate on Bilingualism* (New York: Basic Books, 1986).

D. Hallahan and J. Kauffman, "Communication Disorders," in *Exceptional Children: Introduction to Special Education,* 5th ed. (Englewood Cliffs, N.J.: Prentice-Hall, 1991).

B. Hearne, *Choosing Books for Children* (New York: Bantam Doubleday Dell, 1990).

A. Honig, "Singing with Infants and Toddlers," *Young Children* 50(5), July 1995, pp. 72–78.

J. Ronald Lally, Peter L. Mangione, and Carol Lou Young-Holt, eds., *Infant/Toddler Caregiving: A Guide to Language Development and Communication* (Sacramento, Calif.: Far West Laboratory for Educational Development and California Department of Education, 1992).

M. Nash, "Fertile Minds," *Time Special Report: How a Child's Brain Develops,* February 3, 1997, pp. 48–63.

R. Richman Jr. and C. Patterson, "Cultural and Educational Variations in Maternal Responsiveness," *Developmental Psychology* 28, 1992, pp. 614–621.

L. Vygotsky, *Tools of the Mind* (Englewood Cliffs, N.J.: Prentice-Hall, 1996).

C. Willis, *Your Child's Brain: Food for Thought* (Little Rock, Ark.: Southern Early Childhood Association, 1997).

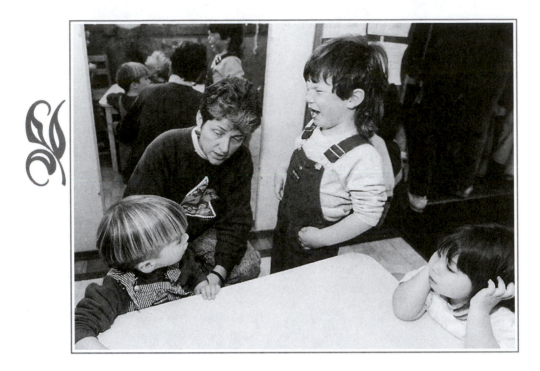

CHAPTER 10

The Development of Emotions

Emotions and feelings are linked early in a child's development. What they are and where they come from can be of special interest to caregivers and parents. The word "emotion" comes from a Latin word meaning to move away and to disturb or excite. Emotions come from within an individual, though they may be triggered by an external event. A "feeling" refers to a physical sense of, or an awareness of, an emotional state. It also involves the capacity to respond to that emotional state.

The point is that emotions and feelings are real. They may be triggered from the outside (for example, by someone else), but the feelings themselves belong to the person experiencing them. One should never discount another's feelings. A young child may be in distress over something you consider very minor. But his or her feeling is real and should be acknowledged and accepted. From this acceptance base, young children can learn to value their own emotions and feelings, to calm themselves, and to act in ways that are considered socially acceptable. When caregivers and parents help infants and toddlers recognize their own feelings and cope with them, they are contributing to children's inner sense of self-direction and competence.

This chapter focuses on emotional development and how feelings in the very young grow and change over time. We will review factors that influence this development, as well as how emotions affect brain development. Specific attention is given to helping infants and toddlers cope with the feelings of fear and anger. Caregiving guides for special-needs children with temperament difficulties and emotional concerns are also included.

THE PROGRESSION OF THE DEVELOPMENT
OF EMOTIONS AND FEELINGS

Feelings and emotions develop. Newborns' emotions are related to immediate experiences and sensations. Newborns' emotional responses are not very defined but are rather a general stirred up or calmed down response. Refined responses depend on development that occurs after birth. Memory and the ability to understand and anticipate are examples of how emotional expression evolves through the cognitive development that occurs gradually during the first two years.

That newborn infants do have emotions from the first moments of life is a concern of the gentle birth advocates, such as Frederick Leboyer, the French obstetrician. Until Leboyer advertised his gentle birth techniques, it was widely believed that babies do not feel much at birth. If they have sensations, the possibility that they have emotional responses was discounted. We know now that infants do have the use of their senses at birth. Consequently, researchers and caregivers are not questioning the emotional aspects of what infants feel. Although infants cannot talk about what they experience emotionally at birth, we can see physical reactions. Evidence exists that they react to harsh stimulation with tenseness. We once thought that the panicky birth cry and the tightly clenched fists were normal and even necessary. Now that Leboyer and others have demonstrated what happens when you reduce such harsh stimuli as bright lights, loud noises, and abrupt changes in temperature, we know that a newborn can be relaxed and peaceful. Some babies born under Leboyer's method even smile right after birth.[1]

In the first weeks of life, infants' emotional responses are not very refined. Either very young infants are in a stirred up state or they are not. They may cry with great intensity, but it is hard to put any labels on what they are feeling. As they mature, however, the stirred up states begin to differentiate into familiar adultlike emotions—pleasure, fear, and anger. By the second year, you can see most of the finer variations of these basic emotions. Toddlers express pride, embarrassment, shame, and empathy.

Sometimes people want to divide feelings into two categories: good and bad. However, all feelings are good; they carry energy, have purpose, and provide us with messages that are important to our sense of self-direction. A better way to divide them is into "yes!" feelings and "no!" feelings.

Some examples of "yes!" feelings are joy, pleasure, delight, contentment, satisfaction, and power. Infants and toddlers should experience plenty of these kinds of feelings. Power is a feeling you might not expect to find in a list of "yes!" feelings in infants and toddlers; yet it is vital to very young children. Power comes as they discover they can make things happen in their world— they can influence the objects and, most especially, the people around them. Attachment is one means of ensuring a sense of power in infants. Child care programs should be very aware of whether each child is feeling powerful and take steps to remedy the situation if some are not.

The "no!" feelings, especially fear and anger, are the ones that command the most attention, and we discuss them here at length.

HELPING INFANTS AND TODDLERS COPE WITH FEARS

The scene that follows shows a child who is afraid.

> A baby is sitting on the floor playing with a soft rubber ball. She stops playing for a moment and looks around the room, searching. She finds her mother close by, a look of relief passes over her face, she gives a big smile, and she continues to play. She hears a door open and sounds coming from the other room. Two people enter. The baby freezes. One of the people approaches her enthusiastically—holding out her arms, talking warmly and excitedly. The baby stiffens. As the person moves nearer, the baby's whole body attitude is one of moving back, away. She remains in suspended animation until the moment the person's face arrives close to hers. She then lets out an enormous howl. She continues to scream and stiffen even though the person talks soothingly and moves away slightly. She stops only when the caregiver moves away and her mother comes in close to soothe and comfort her. She clings to her mother, swallowing her last sobs while keeping a suspicious eye on the stranger.
>
> "I'm sorry I scared you," says the caregiver, gently keeping her distance. "I see that you are really afraid of me." She continues to talk in a quiet, calm, reassuring voice.

This child is obviously attached and experiencing strong feelings of fear that result from her cognitive ability to distinguish her mother from strangers. Stranger anxiety is a common and perfectly normal fear. The caregiver in this scene found it effective to back off from the infant. Next time she will probably approach more cautiously and slowly, allowing the child time to "warm up to her." She will discover what it takes for this particular child to accept her. Some children will allow a direct approach; others do better when the stranger ignores them but remains near enough so that the child can decide to approach, when he or she is ready to do so.

The causes of fear change as infants grow into toddlers. After the first year or two, the fears of noise, strange objects, unfamiliar people, pain, falling, and sudden movements decrease; but new sources of fear take their place (for instance, imaginary creatures, the dark, animals, and the threat of physical harm). Notice that the movement is from immediate events and sensations to more internal events, imagined, remembered, or predicted. This change is related to the child's growing ability to think and consequently to understand potential dangers. Consider the caregiver's response in this scene.

> The toddler room is full of activity. A jack-o-lantern on the shelf gives a clue to the time of year. Three children are on a low loft in a dramatic

play area putting on hats and shawls and other dress-up clothes. A child enters the room, holding onto his father's hand. He is wearing a mask. He sees the three children in the loft and immediately comes up to join them. Two children go about their business, but the third one takes one look at the mask and begins to cry quietly. He backs off and tries to hide behind the box of dress-up clothes. He keeps his eyes on the masked face. A caregiver, seeing his distress, approaches quickly.

She speaks matter-of-factly to the masked child. "Kevin, Josh doesn't like your mask. He needs to see your face." She takes the mask off Kevin and holds it out toward Josh. "See, Josh, it's Kevin. He had a mask on. That's what scared you." Josh still looks nervous as he glances from the mask in the caregiver's hand to Kevin's face and back to the mask. "Here, do you want to see it?" She offers to hand it to him. Kevin protests, grabs the mask, and puts it back on. Josh looks terrified again. The teacher firmly removes the mask. "I won't let you wear that, Kevin, because Josh is scared." She hands the mask to another caregiver and asks him to put it away. Kevin protests mildly and then gets occupied trying on a furry hat and admiring himself in the mirror. Josh then crawls out from behind the box, watches the mask disappear across the room, and looks at Kevin's face. Then he picks a hard hat out of the box, puts it on, and goes to stand by Kevin to look in the mirror. The caregiver, seeing the situation is over, leaves to mop up a spill at the drinking fountain.

This caregiver, like the first one, understood and accepted the child's fear. Acceptance is vital if children are to come eventually to recognize, identify, and accept their own feelings.

Compare the following two responses to a crying, fearful infant:

"I know you're afraid right now. I will be here if you need me to help you."

"Oh, poor baby . . . don't be afraid . . . I'll make everything all right. . . ."

By saying "Don't be afraid," the caregiver in the second example is telling the baby that his feelings are not all right or appropriate. Instead of offering security and helping the infant find his own ways of coping, the caregiver in the second quote is "saving" the baby, teaching him that he cannot manage on his own. Comforting should be done in a way that leads children to learn to comfort themselves and to know when to ask for help.

Sometimes it helps if an infant can "relearn" a situation that was once frightening. (This relearning is called "conditioning.") For example, a particular object or activity that provokes fear can be proved harmless if it is presented along with something that is pleasant or if a loved person is present to explain the situation. It may take several introductions. Stop if the child seems highly anxious, and try again in a few months.

Here is a summary of guides on how to help infants and toddlers cope with their fears:

1. Accept all fears as real and valid. Do not minimize the child's feeling, even though the incident that provoked it may seem insignificant to you. Acknowledge the fear.
2. Give the child support, and show confidence that he or she can find ways to cope.
3. Use foresight to prevent fearful situations when possible. The caregiver in the first scene could have approached more carefully. The caregiver in the last scene could have met Kevin at the door and taken the mask. (In a toddler program, there is sure to be at least one child who is afraid of masks.)
4. Prepare toddlers for potentially frightening situations. Tell them what to expect.
5. Break frightening situations into manageable parts.
6. Couple the unfamiliar with the familiar. A comforting person or object can help a child cope with a new, potentially frightening situation.
7. Give young children time to adjust to something new.

Think about how you deal with your own fears. Do you use withdrawal and avoidance techniques as well as seeking comfort and security? Do you find that expressing your fears helps you cope with them? Perhaps you can discover something about your own coping devices that will help you respond to a fearful child.

Consider the following situations. Would knowledge of your own coping techniques help you respond to these children?

A nine-month-old child has just been left in the center by his mother, who is late to work. Although she did stay with her son a few minutes before handing him over to the caregiver, who happens to be a substitute and new, he started screaming when she hastily said good-bye to him and hurried out the door. He is now sitting on the floor, terrified, alternately screaming and sobbing. What is the probable meaning of this child's behavior? How would you respond if you were the substitute?

A two-year-old is looking through a stack of books lying near at hand. She is on a soft cushion looking very relaxed. Next to her is a caregiver, who is holding another child who is also holding a book, looking at the pictures. The child on the cushion picks a book and flips through it. She comes to a picture of a clown, slams the book shut, and sits looking terrified. How would you interpret this child's behavior? How would you respond if you were the caregiver?

A two-and-a-half-year-old is making an enclosure out of large plastic blocks. She stands inside looking very proud of herself, saying, "Look at my house, teacher." A siren screams outside in the street. She freezes.

Then she races to the stack of cots and crawls under the bottom one, squeezing her body almost out of sight. What do you make of this behavior? How would you respond if you were the caregiver?

In your responses, did you acknowledge the children's feelings? Did you have the urge to rescue them, or could you find ways to give them some help in discovering their own methods for relieving their feelings? Can you see what purpose the fear might serve in each of these situations?

In general, fear protects the individual from danger. In infants, it is fairly easy to see how fear functions, because infants react to falling, to harsh assaults on their senses, and to separation from the person primarily responsible for their well-being. Fear can protect them from danger. Toddlers have more complex fears because their cognitive development allows more to go on inside. When they are frightened, both infants and toddlers often protect themselves by withdrawing, as contrasted to angry infants and toddlers, who more often lash out.

HELPING INFANTS AND TODDLERS COPE WITH ANGER

Anger, like fear, may make life hard for caregivers. Look at the following example:

> The scene is a family child care home. A two-year-old is taking the toys off a low shelf and putting them in a cardboard box. She wanders off from this activity and stops briefly to look out the window—touching her tongue to the cold glass. Then she meanders over to a three-month-old who is lying on a blanket beside a caregiver. Dropping down heavily, she reaches for the baby's head. The caregiver reaches out and touches the toddler's head softly, saying, "Gently, gently. You may touch, but you have to be gentle." Her abrupt motion turns into a light touch, and she strokes the infant for a minute the way she has just been stroked. But then she gets more energetic, and her stroking becomes a heavy pat. Her hand is held back by the caregiver, who once more says, "Gently, gently," as she strokes her head again and holds her hand. But this time the child's response is different, and she lifts her free hand to hit the infant, an expression of determination crossing her face. She is prevented by the firm grasp of the adult. Thwarted in her desires, she turns on the adult, eyes flashing, and begins to struggle. At the same time, she starts to make protesting noises. The scene ends with a very angry little girl being removed from the vicinity of the helpless infant. The last thing you hear is the caregiver's calm voice saying, "I know you're angry, but I can't let you hurt little Trung."

Notice that the adult dealt respectfully with both children. She protected the infant, but in doing so made the other child angry. Nevertheless, she treated her anger with respect by accepting the fact that she was angry and by acknowledging the fact to her. She did not allow her to act on her anger by hurting Trung.

Although the cause of this toddler's anger seemed to be being thwarted, causes are sometimes not related to the immediate situation and come from some deeper place. It is harder to accept an infant's or toddler's feelings as real and valid when *you* do not see any good reason for them. When the cause for anger is not as obvious, or considered by adults as not valid, they tend to make remarks like, "Oh, that's nothing to get mad about" or "Oh, come on now, you're not really mad." But feelings are real even when the cause isn't obvious or doesn't seem valid. Respectful caregivers treat them as such. They do not contradict the feelings an infant or toddler expresses, even if their own experience is otherwise. They pay attention and try to reflect what they perceive coming from the child. They neither tease nor distract the child by changing the subject. This approach says to the child, "What you feel is important." Nothing is done to discount or minimize the importance of recognizing and accepting feelings. One should not have to justify feelings—that they are there is enough.

To accept and reflect feelings, caregivers must manage somehow to be serene, tolerant, and self-controlled. They must be able to be empathetic. But, at the same time, they must not deny their own feelings. Just as was stated in the sixth principle in chapter 1, caregivers should be honest about how they feel and be able to decide when it is appropriate to express their feelings. Good caregivers also learn how to set aside their own feelings when appropriate in order to understand what a child is feeling. This is the empathetic relationship. It is important in helping children recognize, accept, and then cope with their own feelings.

In addition to responding by accepting a child's feelings and expressing their own when appropriate (which teaches by modeling), caregivers can deal with infants' and toddlers' anger in several other ways. Prevention is sometimes possible. Be sure that infants and toddlers do not confront too many frustrating problems during their day. For example, toys should be age appropriate. They should also be in good repair. Toys that don't work or have missing parts can be frustrating. Don't remove all sources of frustration, of course, because that eliminates problem solving.

Provide for infants' and toddlers' physical needs. A tired or hungry child is more easily angered than one who is rested and full. Short tempers hinder problem solving because the child gives up in unproductive anger.

Think about how you deal with your own anger. You might even list the ways you express and cope with it. Are you satisfied with how you cope? Can you teach infants and toddlers to cope with their anger in some of the same ways? Do you find that you often express anger in different ways? Do you find that you often do not express anger when you feel it—especially when you cannot act upon it? A difficulty arises when the built-in responses for emotions are inappropriate and one cannot use the energy that rises with the anger. Then the feelings, and the energy, are blocked. That energy is released through action or expression. Some adult ways of directly expressing anger are through words and actions. Some indirect ways are physical activity, such as jogging or chopping wood, or some artistic pursuit, such as painting, music, or writing poetry.

Young infants have limited resources for expression. Crying may be all they are capable of. However, crying is a good release valve for infants because it involves both sound and physical activity. The early crying can later become refined physical activity and words as infants grow in their ability to use their body and language. Caregivers who allow infants to cry in anger are also able to direct angry toddlers' energy to pounding clay, throwing beanbags, and telling people how they feel. This way neither infants nor toddlers learn to deny or cover up their anger in an unhealthy way.

Look at the following situations and think about how the caregiver might respond. Here's a situation with an angry two-year-old:

> The boy is playing with a plastic rake next to a low fence in the yard of an infant-toddler center. He sticks the rake through the fence and twists it. When he tries to pull it out again, he finds it stuck. He pulls and twists, but the rake doesn't come loose. He shows frustration on his face. His little knuckles are white from holding onto the rake handle. His face is getting red with anger. He kicks the fence, then sits down and cries.

Here is another two-year-old—angry for a different reason:

> The girl is dragged into the center, screaming and kicking. Her exasperated mother gives the unwilling little hand to a caregiver, tells her daughter good-bye, and walks briskly out the door. The child runs after her mother, begging her not to go. As the door shuts, she grabs the handle and tries to open it. When she finds she cannot, she lies on the floor right in front of it, screaming and kicking.

Sometimes anger mobilizes extra energy for problem solving or gives motivation to keep on trying. Not all problems have satisfactory solutions, of course, and in such a case the anger can be used only as an expression of the frustration felt. This expression can be seen as an aspect of asserting independence.

A caution: some cultures have different ideas about expressing anger and do not see independence as a goal. It is important to consider what each parent wants for his or her child.

Self-Calming Techniques

Most infants discover ways to calm themselves and use these devices into toddlerhood and beyond. It is important that children not rely solely on others to settle their emotional upsets. Most infants are born with varying degrees of abilities to do this. These abilities are called self-calming devices. At first the techniques are quite simple, just as the infants' emotions are also simple (though intense). The most commonly seen self-calming device is thumb sucking, which may start at birth (or even before). As infants' emotions become more complicated, so do their abilities to deal with them. The variety of self-calming behaviors seen in an infant-toddler child care setting will give you an idea of how these behaviors work.

Twelve children are engaged in various activities. Two infants are asleep in their cribs in a blocked-off corner of the room. One six-month-old is on the lap of a caregiver, taking her bottle. Two three-month-olds are lying on their backs in a fenced-off corner of the room watching two toddlers who are poking toys through the slats of the fence. These children are being watched by one adult, who also has her eye on a toddler who is headed for the door, apparently intent on some outdoor activity. In another corner of the room, four toddlers are eating a snack, seated at a table with another adult. Suddenly, a loud bang from the next room interrupts all activity.

One infant wakes up, starts to cry, then finds her thumb, turns her head down into the blanket, and goes back to sleep. The other sleeping infant startles without waking up, twists around slightly, and goes back to sleep.

The six-month-old taking her bottle stops, looks intensely at the caregiver, gropes with her free hand for something to hang onto, and hangs on tight.

The two infants on their backs start to cry. One struggles to change his position, gets involved in his effort, and stops crying. The other continues to cry.

The two toddlers who have been watching them stop their activity. One sits down and starts twisting her hair. The other heads for his cubby, where he knows he will find his special blanket. The child who was headed to the door runs to the caregiver, picking up a doll on the way. He stands by the caregiver, stroking the smooth satin dress of the doll.

Of the children who were having a snack, one cries and cannot comfort himself until the caregiver's voice soothes him saying, "Yes, that was a loud noise, and it scared you." One cries for more food, one cries for mommy, and one climbs under the table, whimpering.

Some self-calming behaviors are learned; others, like thumb sucking, appear to be innate. A newborn who is tired or frustrated will suck even when no nipple is present. When children are a bit older, thumb or finger sucking still serves in times of stress. Knowing that someone they trust is nearby and checking in with them by glancing toward them or calling to them helps children calm themselves.

This growth of self-calming behaviors, from one as simple as sucking to one as complex as sharing important feelings, is a process influenced and supported by social relationships.

What do you do to settle yourself down when you are upset? Are you aware of your own self-calming devices? How are your self-calming behaviors similar to or different from those of the infants and toddlers in the previous scene?

DEVELOPING SELF-DIRECTION

Emotions, and the resultant attempts at self-calming, are related to a sense of self-direction. Each of us has within us a force that provides the natural thrust toward maturity, guides growth, and gives direction to our life (both in the long term and from day to day). This force guides growth toward health and wholeness, the integration of all aspects of development.

C. G. Jung described this force as "an inner guiding factor that is different from the conscious personality. . . . It is a regulating center that brings about a constant extension and maturing of the personality."[2]

Abraham Maslow also recognized this self-directing force. He saw it as a process and called it "self-actualization." He argued that healthy people are always in the process of self-actualizing. That means they are aware of their potential and, at least at times, make choices that move them toward it instead of away from it. Maslow says self-actualizing people perceive reality clearly, are open to experience, tend to be spontaneous and expressive, have a sense of aliveness, function well, are able to be objective and detached, tend to be creative, have the ability to love, and, above all, have a firm identity, autonomy, uniqueness—a strong sense of self.[3] (Chapter 13 contains more about helping children develop a sense of self and self-concept.)

Maslow makes it very clear that people come to have these characteristics only when their physical, emotional, and intellectual needs are met. He sets out five levels of needs (see figure 10.1). Only when the needs on one level are satisfied can a person move on to deal with those on the next level.

What are the implications for caregivers of Maslow's levels of needs? Levels 1 and 2 are of primary concern in an infant-toddler child care program. The needs of those levels are usually regulated by licensing requirements (in states that have licensing requirements). Levels 3, 4, and 5 are more often left up to the staff of the center or the caregiver(s) in a family day-care home. This book has taken as its primary focus the top three levels. A look at the principles in chapter 1 shows little focus on the physical needs of infants, but rather assumes that caregivers will provide for these needs first. They are, after all, the obvious needs. The aim here has been to bring out the needs that must be met after the basic ones have been satisfied. The aim in chapter 2 was to show how to serve physical needs in ways that respond to higher needs at the same time.

Although Maslow stresses the importance of meeting needs, he also points out that overindulgence is not good. That means if most of the time children's needs are met promptly, sometimes they can wait a bit. He says,

FIGURE 10.1
Maslow's hierarchy of physical, emotional, and intellectual needs

LEVEL 5

Self-Actualization

(needs that relate to
achievement and self-expression,
to realize one's potential)

LEVEL 4

Esteem   **Self-Esteem**

(needs that relate to maintaining satisfying
relationships with others—to be valued,
accepted, and appreciated, and to have status)

LEVEL 3

Love   **Closeness**

(needs that relate to love, affection, care,
attention, and emotional support by another)

LEVEL 2

Safety   **Security**   **Protection**

(needs that relate to physical safety to avoid external
dangers or anything that might harm the individual)

LEVEL 1

Sex   **Activity**   **Exploration**   **Manipulation**   **Novelty**
Food   **Air**   **Water**   **Temperature**   **Elimination**   **Rest**

(needs that are essential body needs—to have access to food
water, air, sexual gratification, warmth, etc.)

Source: Abraham H. Maslow, *Motivation and Personality* (New York: Harper & Row, 1970), p. 72.

"The young child needs not only gratification; he needs also to learn the limitations that the physical world puts upon his gratifications. . . . This means control, delay, limits, renunciation, frustration-tolerance, and discipline."[4]

All creatures have a need for stress, for problems. A lack of problems creates deficiencies. *Optimum* (not maximum or minimum) stress gives children an opportunity to try out their own powers, to develop their strength and will by pushing against something. Problems, obstacles, even pain and grief can be looked upon as beneficial for development of a sense of self-direction. What else can caregivers do to help a child develop a sense of self-direction? Here are some suggestions. First, help children pay attention to what their perceptions, feelings, and bodies tell them. As stated earlier, don't contradict their perceptions with statements like, "That soup is not hot!" or "That didn't hurt, now did it?"

Second, don't interrupt when children are obviously deeply involved in something. When you break in, you are asking them to pay attention to *you*. Children have the ability to get the most out of whatever it is they experience, so let them fully experience it. And be sure to allow periods without stimulation. Let children have peace and quiet so they can hear their inner music, feel their inner urges, and see their inner images.

Third, don't push development. Provide a prepared environment and good relationships, and then trust that children's sense of self-direction will ensure that they will do what they need to do when it comes to conquering developmental tasks like crawling, walking, or talking. When they have very thoroughly done what they need to do at one stage, they will become bored and will move on. When pushed, children lose touch with their own inner sense of direction.

Fourth, give choices. Maslow says, "In the normal development of the healthy child, it is now believed that, much of the time, if he is given a really free choice, he will choose what is good for his growth. This he does because it tastes good, feels good, gives pleasure or *delight*. This implies that he 'knows' better than anyone else what is good for him."[5]

Fifth, encourage children to develop independence and become self-sufficient. Growing means letting go. One learns to walk only when one is willing to let go, to take risks. Caregivers can help children let go by allowing them to take reasonable risks and by providing warmth, confidence, reasonable safety, and a home base. The choice of when to let go is up to the child.

You may notice that these suggestions are related to and in some cases restatements of the principles of caregiving listed in chapter 1. All of them involve respecting the child, which is what the principles are based on. The child's sense of self-direction is nourished by the respectful child-adult relationship that these principles promote.

THE EMOTIONAL BRAIN

Many of the current findings related to brain development clearly validate the caregiving principles that are the philosophical base of this book. Understanding what is happening to the brain from an early developmental perspective can sharpen our awareness of just how important sensitive, responsive care is to a young child's healthy growth. We know that the brain is impressionable; it has plasticity and clearly responds to a variety of experiences. The brain is resilient; it can compensate for some negative experiences if they are not unduly prolonged. And the brain is *emotional*! It reacts to, and processes, emotions.

Before language develops, early emotional exchanges between babies and their parents or caregivers serve as the basis for communication. These early emotional exchanges actually foster brain growth. When a responsive relationship has been established, an infant experiences delight in seeing that person. Visual emotional information is processed through the neurons in the right hemisphere of the cortex and brain activity increases. This arousal in the brain usually causes an increase in the infant's physical activity. And if the cues that result from this behavior are responded to correctly by the parent or caregiver, brain growth is encouraged. A sensitive adult influences not only an infant's expression of emotion but also the neurochemistry of that young brain.[6]

It was noted earlier in this chapter that "optimum" stress can provide growth opportunities for young children. Stress may be necessary for development, but how much is too much? What happens to the brain when a very young child experiences too much stress for too long?

Frequent and intense early stress experiences (poverty, abuse, neglect, or sensory deprivation) actually cause an infant's brain to reorganize itself. The infant's "stress regulation mechanism" is set to a higher level to help him or her cope more effectively (related to the "fight or flight" experience often referred to in psychology), and certain chemicals are released in the brain. One of the best understood neurochemicals is the steroid hormone called cortisol. It can be measured in saliva. During times of stress, cortisol is released in the brain. It alters brain functioning by reducing the number of synapses in certain parts of the brain. If these neural connections continue to be destroyed by cortisol, developmental delays in cognitive, motor, and social behavior result. The good news is that very young children who have warm, nurturing care in the first year of life are less likely to produce high levels of cortisol in times of stress.[7] The attachment experience acts as a protective buffer to stress.

So much of the current information about the brain emphasizes the importance of attachment and nurturing, responsive care for healthy neural development. We've acknowledged what can happen if a child receives too much stimulation, or too much stress. But what happens when a baby is with a depressed parent, and the infant's cues for emotional interactions are ignored? Over time the baby also develops depressive behavior and is less active and more withdrawn. The young child may also begin to turn inward for self-stimulation and self-soothing. When tested, these babies had elevated heart rates, elevated cortisol levels, and reduced brain activity. Infants whose parent(s) are depressed are at greatest risk for long-term developmental delays from the age of six to eighteen months. This is also the prime time for emotional attachments. An important note to add is that when the parent was treated and went into remission, the baby's brain activity returned to normal.[8] This is clearly an example of how important family support is when considering the overall healthy development of young children.

For all of us, and especially for young infants, emotions amplify experience. Strong troublesome emotions need a supportive context if an infant is to learn to tolerate and adapt to such feelings. Don't forget that joy and delight are also strong emotions and can create an attitude that the world is full of wonderful things to discover. Respectful relationships are prerequisites for healthy emotional growth.

CHILDREN WITH SPECIAL NEEDS: EMOTIONAL DISORDERS

Sometimes, however, no matter how respectful a caregiver is, a child may not seem to be developing a sense of self-direction. Or his or her ability to self-calm seems almost lacking, the child remaining upset for long periods in spite of the comfort he or she is given. It is important to recognize that some infants and toddlers may have particular emotional difficulties. These may be organic, inborn, or environmental. The caregiving principles within this text certainly still relate to most of these children, but their special needs require some additional comment.

Whenever discussing special needs, it is important to try to clarify (describe) the abilities and limitations a child may have as quickly as possible. If this has not already been done for a child in your program (for example, the I.F.S.P., Individualized Family Service Plan), you need to work in partnership with the parents. A "label" should be applied carefully, but we discussed the significance of doing this in previous chapters. Trying to determine if a child may have an emotional disorder is particularly difficult for several reasons.

First, there is no clear definition of "normal" emotional health. The earlier you look at behavior (in this text, under three years), the more you look at a *wide range* of behaviors. Each infant and toddler is unique, and his behavior may be perfectly appropriate for where he is at that moment. You have to get to know a baby (at least for a short time) to determine emotional health.

It is also difficult to determine the cause of an emotional disorder, especially in a very young child. It may be genetic or environmental. What we say is a "disorder" might be the child's unique way of coping with stress. She may have to learn very early how to adjust to an unhealthy parent or to an unsupportive environment. If a child has another disabling condition (for example, deafness or retardation), the definition of an emotional concern for that child is further confused. Which disability is the "primary" one?

Current efforts to define "emotional disorder" focus on behavior that has several common features (and for our purposes can be applied to young children):

- Behavior goes to an extreme (not just a little different from the usual).
- The problem is long lasting or chronic.
- The behavior is unacceptable (for social or cultural reasons).
- The child's inability to learn cannot be explained by intellectual, sensory, or health factors.
- The child cannot build or maintain a satisfactory relationship.
- The child's mood is generally unhappy or depressed.[9]

The specific behaviors most frequently referred to include distractibility, short (or no) attention span, hypersensitivity, anxiousness, repetitive speech or behavior, and extreme restlessness.

A caregiver or parent will no doubt immediately realize that any one of these behaviors could be perfectly appropriate at a particular time. If a child is upset or has a mild illness, any of these behaviors could be seen. It is when these behaviors (usually two or three together) go on and on that a parent or caregiver should seek the assistance of a specialist.

Temperament (inborn characteristics that incline us toward specific emotional responses) can help us understand why there are differences in infants' crying, activity, cuddliness, and so on. The best-known work in this area was done by Thomas, Chess, and Birch in the early 1970s. They described three basic temperaments that can be observed early in life. The *easy* baby is adaptable, approachable, and positive in mood. The *slow-to-warm-up* baby is at first negative in new situations but, with time and patience, eventually adapts. Such children may seem withdrawn, but with time, they adjust just fine. The *difficult* child (approximately 10 percent of babies) often is in a negative mood, is unpredictable (especially regarding eating and sleeping habits), and has intense and irritable reactions to new settings and people.[10]

Infant temperament does incline babies to express themselves in particular ways. We now know, however, that temperament characteristics at birth often don't last. Such characteristics don't necessarily predict later behavior. But the temperament research has shown us (again) the importance of attachment. Personality is shaped by the constant interaction of temperament and environment. A difficult baby requires a lot of extra effort and patience. Parents and caregivers may be at risk for "care burnout" with such babies, especially if they do not understand their developmental needs or are threatened by them. Any baby with a possibly difficult temperament may be at risk for developing attachment problems. Attachment problems often lead to emotional disorders.[11]

Think for a moment about an infant or toddler in your care who was difficult. Describe the child's behavior. What were your reactions? What would you try to do now?

The issue here is prevention. If parents and caregivers know that a baby may be difficult, but otherwise healthy, they should be more sensitive and responsive to that baby's demands. Caregivers and parents, working together and being supportive of each other, can help a difficult baby develop self-calming skills. Sensitivity to attachment needs and early intervention are the important concepts to be appreciated.

Review some of the points about attachment made earlier in this text. Attachment provides the base for trust, security, and emotional health. Infants and toddlers with special needs often have additional attachment issues and concerns. If they are slow in their responses, caregivers may assume that they are unresponsive and may not interact as much with them. If they cannot hear or see adult signals, they may miss vital cues for interaction. In all cases, their emotional needs may remain unmet.

Some very young children today have special attachment needs. A chronically ill child or any child forced to remain in the hospital for long periods runs a risk of emotional deprivation. Helping such children experience as full a life as possible is a current concern. *Morning Glory Babies: Children with AIDS* by T. McCarroll is a particularly sensitive account of caregiving. The issue of caring for AIDS babies remains controversial, but this gentle story demonstrates how wisdom, strength of spirit, and unconditional love can be part of any child's life.

The following general guides may help caregivers work with children who have emotional concerns. Be sure you are aware of additional community resources and specialists in your area who may assist you.

- Be sensitive to the child's environment. Limit the noise level and visual stimuli when necessary.
- Become a good observer. Watch for behavior that may indicate a child's growing irritability.
- Provide free play times for impulsive children. Choices for these children may need to be limited.
- Maintain physical closeness or a gentle touch to help children maintain control.
- Do not permit aggressive behavior. Firm consistency helps children develop trust (in you and in themselves).

Help all children feel good about themselves. Even when children have emotional concerns (and behavioral problems), they need opportunities to develop self-direction. Sensitive caregivers reassure children that they are worthy human beings. They give all children the opportunity to express their feelings appropriately and socialize with others.

Thought/Activity Questions

1. Review your definition of attachment. What role does it play in emotional development?
2. How would you help calm a fearful eight-month-old infant? How would your behavior change if a two-year-old was fearful?
3. How would you help a toddler cope with anger? Describe a recent experience with an angry toddler and what you did in response.
4. How does your mood affect the way you interact with others? Why is this of special concern when dealing with infants and toddlers?
5. How can you respond to infants and toddlers in ways that promote individuality? Consider special-needs children, too.

Notes

1. Frederick Leboyer, *Birth without Violence* (New York: Random House, 1978).
2. M. L. von Franz, "The Process of Individuation," in C. G. Jung et al., *Man and His Symbols* (New York: Doubleday, 1964), p. 162.

3. Abraham H. Maslow, *Toward a Psychology of Being*, 2nd ed. (New York: Van Nostrand, 1968), p. 157.
4. Ibid., pp. 163–164.
5. Ibid., p. 198.
6. L. Gilkerson, "Brain Care: Supporting Healthy Emotional Development," *Child Care Information Exchange* 121, May 1998, pp. 66–68.
7. R. Shore, *Rethinking the Brain* (New York: Families and Work Institute, 1997), pp. 28–30.
8. Ibid., pp. 41–43.
9. D. Hallahan and J. Kauffman, *Exceptional Children, Introduction to Special Education*, 5th ed. (Englewood Cliffs, N.J.: Prentice Hall, 1991), pp. 176–178.
10. A. Thomas, S. Chess, and H. Birch, "The Origin of Personality," *Scientific American* 223, 1970, pp. 102–109.
11. B. Egeland and E. A. Farber, "Infant-Mother Attachment: Factors Related to Its Development and Changes over Time," *Child Development* 55, 1984, pp. 753–771.

For Further Reading

C. F. Abbott and S. Gold, "Conferring with Parents . . . Special Needs Services," *Young Children* 46(4), May 1991, pp. 10–15.

J. Belsky and D. Eggebeen, "Early and Extensive Maternal Employment and Young Children's Socioemotional Development," *Journal of Marriage and the Family* 53, 1991, pp. 1083–1110.

Madga Gerber, "Helping Baby Feel Secure, Self-Confident and Relaxed," *Educaring* 1(4), Fall 1980, p. 4.

D. Goleman, *Emotional Intelligence* (New York: Bantam Books, 1995).

S. Greenspan and S. Weider, *The Child with Special Needs: Encouraging Intellectual and Emotional Growth* (Reading, Mass.: Addison-Wesley, 1998).

J. Kagan, *Galen's Prophecy: Temperament in Human Nature* (New York: HarperCollins, 1994).

J. Kuebli, "Young Children's Understanding of Everyday Emotions," *Young Children* 49(3), March 1994, pp. 36–47.

A. Leiberman, *The Emotional Life of the Toddler* (New York: Free Press, 1993).

T. McCarroll, *Morning Glory Babies: Children with AIDS and the Celebration of Life* (New York: St. Martin's Press, 1988).

A. Saplosky, *Why Zebras Don't Get Ulcers: A Guide to Stress, Stress-Related Diseases, and Coping* (New York: W. H. Freeman, 1994).

M. E. Schreiber, "Time-Outs for Toddlers: Is Our Goal Punishment or Education?" *Young Children* 54(4), July 1999, pp. 22–26.

A. Thomas and S. Chess, *Temperament and Development* (New York: Brunner/Mazel, 1977).

CHAPTER 11

The Development of Social Skills

Socialization connects us to other people. It is the learning process by which we become acceptable members of our society. Social skills foster cooperation and interdependent relationships. Human beings have to learn social skills; they aren't born with them, and they don't just unfold as do gross motor and language skills. Social skills are special to the culture from which they come, and they are learned only from other people.

The development of social skills in infants and toddlers is dependent on other areas of development. A secure attachment base allows a child to trust and therefore separate from parents with some degree of ease. Muscle and motor development provide for social skills that range from toilet training to self-feeding. Cognitive and language skills combine to help young children solve problems and make their needs clearly known to others. A sense of self and a growing ability to manage feelings provide the base for the development of empathy. And it is through empathy, this feeling with another, that we become a connected and caring society.

We need to provide experiences for young children that will foster the social skills we value as a culture. Children learn these skills from responsible adults who care about them and consistently show them respect.

This chapter looks at the progression of social development from infancy through toddlerhood. Special emphasis is given to Erik Erikson's stages of trust, autonomy, and initiative. Practical applications of his theory are discussed as they relate to discipline and prosocial behavior. Practical applications are also included for healthy brain growth. The special needs of all children are reviewed in a summary set of guides for caregivers and parents.

At no time in history has the development of social skills been so important. We can't afford to raise a generation to believe that might is right. We need to teach young children how to resolve conflicts without resorting to force. This teaching starts with infants.

EARLY SOCIAL BEHAVIORS

Infants come equipped with a set of social behaviors that start to work right from the beginning to involve the people around them in the socialization process. In fact, just hours after birth, you can see babies interact with synchrony by moving their bodies to the rhythm and body movements of anyone who talks to them. The dancelike movements are minute, but they are present, in spite of the fact that the speaker is usually unaware of them. They occur only in response to language (any language, not necessarily that of the baby's family) but do not show up in response to other kinds of rhythms.[1]

Another early social behavior is imitation. Babies' inclination to imitate serves the socialization process well as they copy or imitate adult social behavior (which means, of course, the adult must be aware of modeling prosocial behaviors). This imitating behavior starts very early. In the first weeks, babies will imitate such behavior as opening their eyes wide or sticking out their tongue.

Another evidence of early social behavior that seems by nature designed to involve the adult in the socialization process from the beginning is smiling. Whether the first smiles are "real" smiles—social smiles—is still debated. Whether truly social or not, smiles almost always elicit a social response from the adult smiled at.

By the time they are a few months old, most babies are effective at nonverbal communication with the people to whom they are attached. As they get better and better at communication with particular people, they develop fear when around people who don't know their unique communication systems. This fear, called "stranger anxiety," often appears around the sixth month. It seems to be strongest in babies who have excellent communication with their partner(s). The fear is intensified when the stranger tries to communicate with the babies. Often the fear is lessened when the stranger remains silent and noncommunicative. If you think of how you would feel when confronted with someone speaking a foreign language who seems most anxious to tell you something, you may understand the infant's upset when faced with a communicative stranger.

By the second year of life, babies are already making communicative social gestures that predict to some extent which of them will be well-liked preschoolers and which will have difficulty with peer relationships. The infants who will probably become well-liked preschoolers already have a number of *friendly* gestures that they exhibit regularly, such as offering toys, clapping hands, and smiling. Infants who regularly use threatening or aggressive gestures or a mixture of friendly and unfriendly gestures to their peers are more likely to grow into less-liked preschoolers.[2]

Attachment is the prime factor in the development of social skills. From a primary relationship come the skills for developing other relationships.

STAGES OF PSYCHOSOCIAL DEVELOPMENT

The theorist who has the most to say about social development is Erik Erikson. In *Childhood and Society,* he describes three stages of what he calls psychosocial development that apply to children under three.

Trust

The first stage of psychosocial development is trust. Sometime during the first year of life, if infants find that their needs are met consistently and gently, they decide that the world is a good place to be. They develop what Erikson calls a "sense of basic trust." If infants' needs are not met consistently, or are met in a harsh manner, they may decide that the world is unfriendly and develop mistrust instead of trust. Such infants can carry this outlook into adulthood if nothing happens to change their view of life.

If infants are in day care, the adults in the program have some responsibility for ensuring that the children in their care come to gain a sense of basic trust. That means that their *needs* must be a primary concern of everyone from the director down. There is no way to run an infant program that emphasizes anything but individual needs—infants are not like older children, who can put group needs before their own and wait for lunch or snack or wait an hour to go to the bathroom. Infants cannot be treated as a member of a group but must be responded to as individuals.

The importance of developing a sense of basic trust also means that infants in day care need small groups with consistent caregivers. Stability in programs contributes to the infants' well-being and building sense of trust.

Part of developing trust means coping with separation. As attachment strengthens, so does the pain of being away from the person(s) to whom the child is attached. Day-care workers spend a lot of time and energy helping children manage the feelings separation brings forth. Here is an example of a child experiencing some of those feelings.

A mother enters the room carrying a child who has a tense look on her face. She has both arms around her mother's neck and is hanging on tight. Her mother puts her diaper bag into a cubby by the entrance, then speaks briefly to the caregiver. She bends to remove her shoes, then walks into the play area, stopping on a rug. The mother bends over to put her daughter down, saying, "I have to go pretty soon, Rebecca. You're going to stay here with Maria. She'll take care of you while I'm gone." Maria has come close to the pair and kneels down, waiting.

The child clings tighter. The mother sits down on the floor, Rebecca still in her arms. They both sit there for several minutes. The child begins to relax a bit. She reaches for the handle of a push toy, which her mother hands her. She runs it back and forth across the rug while still in her mother's arms. Finally, she gets down, and, sitting right next to her mother, Rebecca begins to bang a plastic hammer on a pounding bench. She gets absorbed in her activity and moves slightly away from her mother. With that her mother gets up, looking over to Maria, who is across the room by now. She then leans down, kisses her daughter, and says, "It's time for me to go now. Good-bye." She walks over, slips her shoes on, then moves quickly to the door. Her daughter follows her with a distressed look on her face. At the door her mother turns once briefly, throws her a kiss, turns back, opens the door, and is gone. At the sound of the door closing, Rebecca lets out a wail, then collapses in a heap, sobbing.

She looks up as a hand touches her shoulder. She sees, kneeling beside her, Maria, the caregiver. She moves away from the touch. Maria continues to stay close by her. "I see you're upset that your mom left." Rebecca begins to scream again.

Maria remains close, but silent. Rebecca's screams subside, and she goes back to quiet sobbing. She continues to sob for a while; then she spots her diaper bag where her mother left it in her cubby. She reaches for it; her tear-stained face has a look of expectancy on it. Maria gets it out for her. Rebecca clings to it. Maria reaches inside and pulls out a stuffed bear wrapped in a scarf. Rebecca grabs the bear, hugging it fiercely. She strokes the scarf, holding it to her nose periodically and smelling it. Her face gets more and more relaxed.

Maria moves away from her. Rebecca doesn't seem to notice. Maria comes back with a box of dolls and blankets, which she arranges on the floor near Rebecca. Rebecca crawls over immediately, tips the box over, and crawls inside. The scene closes as Rebecca is wrapping a doll in a blanket and putting it to bed in the box next to her bear, which is covered with the scarf.

Notice how Maria helped Rebecca cope with separation. She stated the situation and the feelings. She was available but not pushy. She was sensitive to Rebecca's responses to her touch and to her words. She encouraged Rebecca to find solace from familiar belongings. She set up the environment to entice Rebecca from her feelings.

Helping Children through Separation   Here are some more ideas about how to help children through the process of temporary separation as they say good-bye to parents.

1. Be honest. State the facts, including the emotional facts. Say something like Maria did or something like this: "Your mom had to go to work, and you're unhappy about being left." If the feeling you perceive is anger, you can state that.

2. Handle the situation with the appropriate degree of seriousness. If the suffering is minor, don't make it more serious than it is. But don't make light of it either. Don't underplay the importance of the relationship of child to parent and the degree of suffering the child may be experiencing. You may think to yourself, "This is nothing—you'll be taken care of—there's nothing to be afraid of here." But the child doesn't know that and in spite of your reassurance may not believe it. It will take time for the child to discover that is the situation—there really is nothing to be afraid of. In the meantime, if the child is terrified, accept that fact.

3. Provide a balance of kindly concern and matter-of-fact confidence. Somehow convey the attitude that it hurts now, but you'll survive it—and grow from it. Be careful about being overreassuring. If you make promises, the child may begin to wonder if you're really positive that his or her parent will return.

4. Offer support and help with coping. Physical closeness may help. Some infants and toddlers do better with an adult close by; others move from parent to a toy or interesting material put out to be enticing. Sometimes children will play out their feelings with a toy.

5. Welcome things from home. Some children find comfort in a link to home provided by a familiar object. This may be some special attachment object such as a blanket or stuffed animal, or it may be something that has no emotional significance other than the fact that it came from home. One toddler felt great comfort in the fact that his mother left her purse (an empty purse) by his diaper bag. It seemed that he wasn't sure she would come back for him, but he *knew* that she would come back for her purse!

6. Allow children individual ways of feeling comforted. Some children refuse to remove a sweater, a hat, or other piece of clothing. Something about wearing it seems to make them feel more secure when away from home. Or maybe it has to do with feeling the stay is only temporary as long as they don't take off the piece of clothing—something like the message adults give when they enter a room and keep their car keys in their hands the whole time they are there.

It's hard to be attached and dependent and be away from home. Can you remember feeling small, helpless, and separated from the person you were attached to? Think about what it was, in your experience, that helped you cope with being apart from the people you were attached to. Has another person been helpful to you during a difficult separation? If so, can you remember what it was that person said or did? Use your own experience to help you promote coping skills in infants and toddlers.

It is important to deal with separation even with a child who is not terribly upset. Coping with loss and separation is a lifetime task, not something we get over when we are babies after the first separation from parent(s). All our lives we lose those we are close to as friends and family grow away from us (or we from them), move to another city, or die. The coping skills we develop in our first years serve us for the rest of our lives. When children learn to cope with fears of loss and separation, they get feelings of mastery. When they don't learn to cope, they feel failure and mistrust.

Adult Issues with Separation   Sometimes it is difficult for adults to deal with infants' and toddlers' feelings about separation because of their own experiences. They may have old issues around separation—unfinished business, so to speak, that they aren't ready to deal with. So they may prefer not to reopen old wounds. In that case, they may feel uncomfortable around children who are suffering a sense of loss. Instead of trying to understand the feelings and help the children cope, they wish the feelings would just go away. They may distract children from their feelings, hoping they will forget the pain. But the pain doesn't just "go away." Children need to learn to cope with the feelings. Separation skills are a competency infants and toddlers build; they don't usually arrive in a program already competent. So when separation is an issue, separation is the curriculum, and that's where the adult focus should be.

Recognizing the range of feelings that comes with separation can be helpful for caregivers. The feelings of loss may range from mild discomfort and anxiety to sadness, even grief. Fear and anger are other reactions common to a separation situation. A feeling of loneliness is another reaction. A child may be feeling all of these at once or may feel just one. All of these feeling words have been used by adults to describe their reaction to a loss that came from being apart, temporarily or permanently, from someone they were attached to. Though infants and toddlers aren't necessarily competent at describing feelings, it is easy to detect that they feel the same range as adults feel.

An additional issue that caregivers often have to face is that of parental behaviors around separation. It is common to hear caregivers complain that parents magnify separation problems and even create additional ones. This happens when parents have as much (or more) pain at leaving their children as their children have at leaving them. Because of these feelings, parents may act in ways you don't approve of. Some prefer to sneak away because they can't stand saying good-bye. Others prolong the good-byes until everyone is in pain, though the child has already shown he or she is better off with a quick, uncomplicated departure. Some parents suffer because the child cries when they leave; others suffer because he or she *doesn't*. Be sensitive to parent feelings, and realize that separation is hard on them too. The parents' difficulties may be compounded by a sense of guilt at leaving their children. Give them all the support and help you can. (There's more on this subject in chapter 14.)

An additional factor when looking at separation in infant-toddler day care is that of attachment to caregivers. As shifts change, personnel changes, and adults come and go, infants and toddlers may have to deal with separation from a beloved caregiver before they say hello once again to a beloved parent.

In fact, a day in a day-care center may be full of hellos and good-byes because of breaks, lunches, and assorted responsibilities that may call a particular caregiver out of the room. These comings and goings are usually less of a problem for infants and toddlers in a family day-care home.

Autonomy

Erikson's second stage of psychosocial development, autonomy, occurs as the growing infant reaches the second year and begins to move around in the environment. When infants become toddlers, they begin to perceive themselves as separate individuals—not just a part of the person(s) they are attached to. They discover the power they possess, and they push toward independence. At the same time, their developing capabilities allow them to do more for themselves. They learn self-help skills.

Readiness for toilet learning, discussed in chapter 3, is an example of the coming together of increased capabilities and the push for independence. The necessary capabilities lie in three separate domains—the physical (control), the cognitive (understanding), and the emotional (willingness). The goal is to get the movement toward independence working for you and not against you. If you get too demanding or pushy, you may find yourself in a power struggle over toilet learning, and then the child, in the name of independence, feels the need to oppose you. Independence becomes linked in the child's mind with diapers or "accidents." Far better if the child sees you as a support and an aid rather than an obstacle to his or her own developing capabilities and independence.

Language provides clues about another area of autonomy. The "NO!" for which toddlers are so famous is a further clue to the push for separateness and independence. They differentiate themselves from others by what seems to be contrariness. If you want them to go in, they want to stay out. If you want them to stop, they want to start. If you're serving milk, they want juice.

Granted, caregivers don't usually see as much of this kind of behavior as parents do. The tie between parent and child is a much stronger, more passionate one. Many children feel more secure and therefore free to express themselves in words and actions at home than they do in day care. It is important not to make parents feel they are doing something wrong because more defiant and rebellious behavior comes out when they are present. Rejecting behaviors are normal—even good—for toddlers to exhibit. They show that the child's growing sense of autonomy and separateness is strong.

Demanding only "good" behavior in toddlers may cause a great deal of frustration for children. If a toddler program does not allow children to feel normal rejecting behaviors, what do they do with those feelings? Are they getting their needs met in day care? What might it do to their relationship with their parents if they have to concentrate all their rejecting behaviors into the few hours they spend with them?

Language provides further clues about other areas of autonomy that are part of the toddler period. "Me do it!" shows that drive for independence. By capitalizing on this drive, you can promote the development of self-help skills. When children want to "do it," set up the situation so they *can*.

Because we want children to grow up being cooperative and sharing individuals, we sometimes push them to share before they are ready. Children who have no sense of possession can't understand the concept of sharing. Children who have some sense of possession still may not be ready to share. Some take a long time to develop a feeling that something *belongs to them*. If they spend most of their waking hours in an environment where everything belongs to everybody or to the program, it may take a good deal longer.

Sometimes, in the name of fairness, children are constantly asked to give up a turn or a toy before they are finished with it. When this occurs in an environment where there are no private possessions, rather than learning to be a sharing person, some learn just not to care. It doesn't matter to them whether they play with this toy or that or for how long. They learn to stay uninvolved rather than face the pain of being constantly interrupted and sidetracked. Think what it would be like to be a child who never gets a chance to play out a fantasy or an interest or reach a point of satisfaction by being allowed to have a toy or material in your possession until you are really through with it. How would this situation affect attention span? Do some children learn to have short attention spans because some caregivers overstress sharing?

Initiative

Erikson's term for the stage of older toddlers as they approach preschool age is *initiative*. The focus on autonomy eventually passes. The energy that has previously gone into separating and striving for independence, and which often results in defiance and rebellion, is now available for new themes. This energy pushes children to create, invent, and explore as they seek out new activities. At this new stage, toddlers become the initiators of what happens in their lives and gain enthusiasm from their newfound power.

The caregiver should respond to this need to initiate by providing information, resources, freedom, and encouragement. Although older toddlers still very much need limits, the caregiver can set and keep the limits in such a way that toddlers don't feel guilty about this powerful push they feel to take initiative. People with initiative make valuable citizens. They gain this quality early in life when the people around them encourage them to be *explorers*, *thinkers*, and *doers*.

GUIDANCE AND DISCIPLINE

The socialization process in infants comes about as adults meet their needs. Infants require no guidance or discipline. Limits come naturally from their own limitations. Control may be a minor issue at times. Usually, meeting a specific need will take care of their lack of control, or they may need to be held close and tight. An example of providing control when an infant needs it is when newborns cry in distress that is not hunger. Sometimes they quiet down when wrapped tightly in a blanket. The blanket seems to provide the control that they do not have as their legs and arms hang free under loose covers.

This same theme, tightness providing control the infant lacks, looks different in the toddler stage. Toddlers may also appreciate a "feeling of tightness" when control comes from the outside, in situations when their own underdeveloped ability to control themselves gives way. Holding out-of-control toddlers tightly usually enables them to regain inner control.

Limits for Toddlers

Toddlers need to feel that there are limits even when they do not need the tightness of outside control. Think of limits—rules of behavior—as invisible fences or boundaries. Because they can't see these boundaries, children need to test in order to discover them. And they have little faith in words alone. Just as most of us are compelled to touch the surface behind the "wet paint" sign, so are toddlers compelled to bump up against a limit to see if it is really there and to make sure it will hold. Some children will do more testing than others, but all children need to know that there are limits. The limits provide a sense of security, just as the tight blanket does for the newborn.

To illustrate the security that limits provide, think of yourself driving across a high bridge. You probably have done that more than once in your life. The limits on the bridge are the rails on the sides. Can you imagine yourself driving across that bridge if the rails were removed? You don't physically need those rails, you know. After all, how often have you actually bumped the rails while driving across a bridge? Yet the thought of the bridge without the rails is terrifying. The rails provide a sense of security, just as the limits set for toddlers provide security in their lives.

Any discussion of limits, guidance, and discipline in toddlers quickly brings forth a discussion of what to do about such behaviors as biting, hitting, throwing things, and negativism. No single answer covers all behaviors in all situations with all children. The only single answer that applies is "It depends. . . ."

Biting   Let's look at biting. Start by asking, "Why is this child biting? What is behind the behavior?" If children are very young, they may be biting out of love. Sometimes when adults model playful nibbling, chewing, or "eating up" as a way of demonstrating affection, infants imitate their actions by biting those they love. This is not hard to understand if you relate to feelings implied in the expression "to sink your teeth into something." Mouths are expressive organs, and when a child is too small to convey the intensity of a feeling with words, biting may do it.

Of course, not all biting is done for love; some is done for power. When a child is small, physical power is minimal. But the jaws have powerful muscles, and little teeth are sharp. Even a very young child can do real damage with a bite. Some children learn this as a means of getting their own way with children who are bigger than they are.

Some biting may be done out of curiosity. Just as infants mouth and bite objects, so may they mouth and bite people. They do this with no malice intended—they are merely exploring.

Some biting is done as an expression of anger. Adults clench their jaws and grind their teeth; infants and toddlers sink their teeth into any available arm.

Some biting may be a means of gaining attention. Imagine yourself a toddler in a program where adults are available but are spread thin, and you get focused attention from one of them rarely and then only briefly. Or imagine that you do get focused attention, but the adult tends to be cold and rather vacant. There's more of a shell than a real person. No matter what you do, you can't seem to tap the real person inside the shell. Then one day you discover that by merely putting your teeth into a child's leg, you can get an adult to come over and touch you—even pick you up, hold you tight, look you right in the eye, and talk at length to you. This adult, who was all fluff before, becomes hard and real as the exchange provides passion and intensity. The message is that you finally did something that *mattered*!

Some young children need this kind of strong interaction. It tells them that you care what they do, that their behavior matters to you. If they can't provoke an intense interaction any other way, they may continue to bite, just to get it.

The way to stop biting is to prevent it, not try to deal with it after it happens. Biting is too powerful a behavior to allow to continue. It's too painful for the person bitten, and it's too frightening for the biter to have that much power to do harm. When biters can't control their own behavior, it's up to you to control it. A useful technique after waylaying the biting is to redirect the urge. Give these children something to bite on that is made for biting— teething rings, cloth, or rubber or plastic objects. Offer these as choices, saying something like, "I can't let you bite Craig, but you can bite the plastic ring or this wet washcloth." Don't do this in a punitive way.

What else you do besides control the behavior and offer biting alternatives depends on the origins of the biting. If it is being modeled, try to cut off the modeling. If it is an expression of a feeling (love, frustration, or anger), teach alternative means for expression. Help children redirect their energy into positive ways of expressing the feelings. Redirecting the biting to objects is a start, but go beyond that. If a power issue is involved, teach children other techniques for getting what they need and want. If it is an attention issue, find ways to give children the attention—the intense interactions they need—without biting being the trigger. None of these is an easy solution, and it may take a good deal of brainstorming, discussion, cooperation, and teamwork even to identify the origins of the behavior and the appropriate approach.

Biting is an example of an aggressive (intent to harm) behavior. Other aggressive behaviors that cause toddler caregivers problems are hitting, kicking, shoving, hair pulling, throwing objects, and destroying toys and materials. To figure out what to do about these behaviors, you must go through a problem-solving process, looking at the particular child, the possible origins of the behavior, the message behind the behavior, the way the environment may contribute to the behavior, the way adult behavior may trigger the aggression, and the resources the child has for expressing feelings. Beware of advice that advocates any one simple solution. Behavior is complex, as are children. No one approach is right for everyone all the time.

Negativism Another category of difficult behaviors caregivers of toddlers deal with is negativism. A frequent complaint from caregivers is, "They won't do what I say." Part of the problem may be that toddlers can't always translate word messages into physical control, even when they understand what you want. Another part of the problem is that when toddlers are faced with demands or commands they often do the opposite.

The secret to dealing with negativism is to stop issuing challenges. Stay out of power struggles. Try not to be boldly confronting. If you approach a toddler who is outside a limit, say a girl climbing on a table, start by being calm and matter-of-fact rather than confrontive. Don't issue a challenge (such as "Get off the table"). State the limit in positive terms, such as "The ramp is for climbing" or "Feet belong on the floor." One particularly talented teacher simply says, "You can put your feet right here," patting the appropriate place. Nine times out of ten the feet go directly to where they belong! Something about the way she says it conveys such a confident and positive attitude that there is no challenge issued.[3]

TEACHING PROSOCIAL BEHAVIOR

There is another half to discipline and guidance besides setting limits—that is, developing prosocial behavior. Prosocial behavior doesn't just automatically occur by putting infants and toddlers in groups and setting limits. You have to plan for it to happen. You have to *make* it happen.

Some children have natural inclinations toward kindness and compassion from the early years, but most have to be taught. We used to think that the egocentricity of preschool age children kept them from seeing another person's perspective. We know now this is not true. Even infants cry in empathy for other infants, and many toddlers will offer a toy or a pat to a child in pain, obviously trying to comfort or help. Here are some ideas about how to promote and teach prosocial skills.

1. Whenever you set a limit, explain *why*. Let children know the effects of their behavior on others—that hitting hurts, that grabbing toys causes unhappiness.
2. Notice children who show they care about other children. Mention the behaviors. Call attention to the behaviors you wish to occur more often. Use such simple statements as "I see how you are being very careful with the doll," "I liked the way you gave Chelsea her blanket when she was crying," "I noticed you tried to help Joanie solve that problem," or "I bet you feel good about giving that toy to Sammy when he asked you for it." Remark about specific behaviors rather than making global judgments (such as "good girl!").
3. Model prosocial behaviors yourself. Say thank-you when someone shares something with you. Be kind and considerate not only to the children you work with but to other adults they see you with.
4. Take a problem-solving view rather than a power stance when there is a conflict. You will want not only to model conflict resolution with other adults but to help the children in their dealings with one another. Encourage them to talk to one another rather than to you. Give them the words to use if they need them: "Tell Jesse you don't like it when he takes the toy away from you." Then turn and see what Jesse says in response. Help him make himself understood if he needs help. Help the children see one another's points of view and come to some kind of conclusion. Don't solve their conflicts for them; teach them to solve conflicts themselves.
5. Encourage cooperation. Have cooperative activities where children do things together rather than separately. Instead of individual art projects, try taping butcher paper to a table, making felt pens or crayons available, and letting children create a group picture.
6. Pay special attention to children who are constantly picked on or rejected by their peers. They need extra help with social skills. Both aggressor and victim need your extra attention (but not when they are aggressing or being victimized). Teach aggressors other ways of getting what they need or want, and teach victims how to stand up for themselves.
7. Avoid punishment. Punishment may work to curb antisocial behaviors, but it works against teaching prosocial ones. And it is never appropriate to inflict pain on a child.

Promoting social development and teaching social skills are not easy. Often you end up undoing what you've been trying to do. Some undesirable behaviors are impossible to ignore, but by paying attention to them, you ensure that they will continue. You're also bound to model behavior you don't want the child to pick up. The message is far stronger if you model the behavior you are after. As human beings, we can't be perfect, which in itself is an important message to infants and toddlers. As you forgive your own less-than-perfect social skills, so, perhaps, can you forgive theirs.

PROMOTING HEALTHY BRAIN GROWTH

Planning for healthy brain development may be the best way to establish the neurological base for prosocial behavior and to avoid the possible misinterpretations of the new brain research. The importance of early social contact has been emphasized a great deal by the current information on the brain. Social development discussed in this chapter has its beginnings in the early attachment experiences, and these cause an amazing sequence of activity related to brain function. The early circular interactive patterns in the brain indicate that babies develop their first sense of self through contact with others. How we use the new research to encourage appropriate contact between caregivers and infants is the challenge.

Ron Lally, a pioneer in planning environments for infants and toddlers, has been a leader in interpreting brain research as it relates to quality care for very young children. He has identified seven "gifts" that are vital for healthy social growth. The following guides are practical behaviors that encourage caregivers to appreciate the importance of child care as the foundation for social, and brain, development. As you review these seven guides, reflect on the seven points on teaching prosocial behavior on page 186. What similarities do you see?

1. *Nurturance* is caring and giving. Because each infant is unique, nurturance means responding to every baby individually. When a baby feels a caregiver's responsive nurturance, comfort and security are established. It is the comfort of this connection that is vital for attachment.
2. *Support* is the context of care that a child receives. To support a young child means that the caregiver must respect a child's various feelings. Caregivers offer support by acknowledging a child's frustrations, by encouraging curiosity, and by enforcing rules that promote social interactions with others.
3. *Security* is related to both nurturance and support, and it is what makes a child feel safe. Caregivers provide security when they provide reliable, responsive care and when they enforce safety rules consistently.
4. *Predictability* is the "gift" that is vital for a child's sense of security and mental growth. Predictability is both social and environmental. A child needs to be able to rely on people and to be able to find things and places. Predictability avoids both confusion and rigidity. It allows a child to feel secure and to seek challenges.
5. *Focus* supports very young children's attention in their environment. An infant or toddler's attention span will increase if there are not too many toys, too many interruptions, or too many other people. Their opportunity to focus on meaningful experiences needs to be respected.
6. *Encouragement* from a knowledgeable caregiver tells a young child, "I appreciate your efforts; you are becoming a competent person." A child's own learning is reinforced through encouragement. It is a

response that understands the importance of child's imitation, experimentation, and discovery as critical links to learning.

7. *Expansion* of a child's experience involves "bathing (not drowning)
the child in language." Watch for the young child's cues and build on
his or her unique experiences. Involvement in fantasy play, talking
along with a child, and responding to activities are all ways to demonstrate to young children the value of learning.[4]

The child care setting that offers these seven gifts provides a base for the
practical application of brain research and for the secure social development
of a child. The current research has emphasized just how early neural circuitry
is formed and how critical social development is to that formation. The
healthy brain is a social brain!

THE SPECIAL NEED OF ALL CHILDREN: SELF-ESTEEM

Considerations involving special-needs children have been included at the end
of the chapters in part 2, "Focus on the Child." Special-needs children do have
a variety of conditions that influence their interactions with people and things.
Their specific challenges may place extra demands on parents and caregivers
who are trying to promote healthy interaction and social skills. The unresponsive child, or the one with a sensory impairment or with retarded, inconsistent
communication, needs a caregiver who understands the vital significance of
interpersonal relationships.

Although the study of special-needs children seems to be a study of "differences," it is also a study of "similarities." Special-needs children are more
similar to other children than they are different. The most important characteristics of special-needs children are their *abilities*. And a very important
need for all children is that they *feel good* about their abilities. This sense of
inner positiveness is a prerequisite for mental health and competent social
interaction.

Social skills and the socialization process have been the focus of this
chapter. As noted numerous times in this text, the foundation for interacting
with others is attachment. From a nurturing attachment experience, children
learn to value themselves and others. This valuing of self is called "self-
esteem." Self-esteem is vital for *all* children. And it is important for caregivers
creating quality experiences for children to appreciate it.

The definition of self-esteem is complex. As we grow and develop, it is
being constantly reshaped while we interact and experience our world. It is a
personal assessment of positive worth. But it is not the "me, my, mine" sense of
worth. An individual with self-esteem is confident, optimistic, and sensitive to
the feelings and needs of others. The roots of this lifelong process are clearly
taking hold in infancy and toddlerhood.

Two types of experiences are most significant to the development of self-esteem. As an infant experiences attachment that is secure and nurturing, his self-concept begins to develop. Self-concept is formed by the infant's feelings about himself as they are reflected in his interactions with others. When a baby is responded to and is part of a loving relationship, his self-concept is positive and trusting.

The second important experience that contributes to self-esteem is the successful accomplishment of tasks. As a toddler explores and interacts with her world, her self-image is growing. Self-image is a more personal assessment of one's experience. If a toddler lives in a world with lots of "No's" and has little opportunity to test her skills, her image of herself may be low. Her inexperience limits her view of her own competence.

Very young children need secure relationships (with others) and opportunities to actively explore the world (on their own). When the self-concept is positive and trusting and the self-image is vital and active, children experience life as accepting and meaningful. This is the beginning of self-esteem. Children's ability to feel themselves as loving and competent allows them eventually to see others in a similar way.

Pause for a moment and think about how the work of Erikson and Piaget relate to children's positive feelings about themselves. Erikson emphasized the establishment of trust (through relationships with others) and autonomy (through experiences with everyday events) as vital to healthy development. Piaget viewed children as active participants in their own world. And this physical activity leads to cognitive activity, eventually resulting in coping skills. Individuals with self-esteem tend to have very good coping skills.

As young children experience the challenges and limits of life, they need the stability of a personal base within themselves. This is important for all children; it may be even more important for special-needs children. We all need a place to "come home to," a place that is accepting and renewing. The ability to create such a place is the essence of self-esteem.

How can adults help children develop self-esteem? The importance of a secure attachment has already been mentioned. Adults who feel good about themselves tend to pass that feeling on to their children. It is important that caregivers and parents see self-esteem as a lifelong process and that they are contributing to their own needs for nurturance and challenge.

Certainly the ten principles on which this book is based promote self-esteem. The principles support independence while providing a loving base. They respect individual needs and stress appreciation of problem-solving efforts.

Adult feedback to children should be real, or authentic. Persistently positive information, like persistently negative, does not prepare children for the *real* world. They will not be ready for the challenges of peers and school if caregivers and parents have not given them honest information. Remember to trust their competence and encourage their resiliency.

No doubt every adult has had the experience of not feeling respected by others. Your self-respect and self-esteem are as valuable as your attitude toward children. Cultivating your own self-worth and getting to know yourself better are worthy goals (for children and for all of us). The following poem by Kahlil Gibran, with its appreciation of uniqueness and individual growth, provides a summary for this chapter and for the developmental section of this book.

Your hearts know in silence the secrets of the
days and the nights.
But your ears thirst for the sound of your
heart's knowledge.
You would know in words that which you have
always known in thought,
You would touch with your fingers the naked
body of your dreams.
And it is well you should.
The hidden well-spring of your soul must
needs rise and run murmuring to the sea;
And the treasure of your infinite depths
would be revealed to your eyes.
But let there be no scales to weigh your
unknown treasure;
And seek not the depths of your knowledge
with staff or sounding line.
For self is a sea boundless and
measureless.
Say not, "I have found the truth," but
rather, "I have found a truth."
Say not, "I have found the path of the
soul," say rather, "I have met the soul walking upon my path."
For the soul walks upon all paths.
The soul walks not upon a line, neither
does it grow like a reed.
The soul unfolds itself, like a lotus of
countless petals.[5]

Thought/Activity Questions

1. What do you think are the most important social skills in our society? How would you begin to teach them to infants and toddlers?
2. How can caregivers respond to infants and toddlers in ways that promote individuality?
3. You are writing a brochure for your new infant-toddler day-care program. In it you want to include a statement about your philosophy on "discipline." What do you want to share with parents on this topic? Try writing several statements.
4. List behaviors that you think indicate positive social development. How can caregivers and parents encourage these behaviors in the first three years?
5. Review the ten principles in chapter 1. Clarify how each one promotes self-esteem.

Notes

1. T. G. R. Bower, *Development in Infancy*, 2nd ed. (San Francisco: W. H. Freeman, 1982), p. 256.
2. Jaipaul L. Roopnarine and Alice S. Honig, "The Unpopular Child," *Young Children*, September 1985, p. 61.
3. Doyleen McMurtry, early childhood instructor, Solano College, Suisun, California.
4. R. Lally, "The Art and Science of Child Care," *Program for Infant/Toddler Caregivers*, WestEd, 180 Harbor Drive, Suite 112, Sausalito, Calif.
5. Kahlil Gibran, *The Prophet* (New York: Alfred A. Knopf, 1923).

For Further Reading

B. Caldwell, "Early Experiences Shape Social Development," *Child Care Information Exchange* 121, May 1998, pp. 53–59.

M. Carter, "Building Self-Esteem: Training Teachers of Infants and Toddlers," *Child Care Information Exchange* 92, July/August 1993, pp. 59–61.

S. Crockenberg, "How Children Learn to Resolve Conflicts in Families," *Zero to Three*, April 1992.

N. Curry and C. N. Johnson, *Beyond Self Esteem: Developing a Genuine Sense of Human Values* (Washington, D.C.: National Association for the Education of Young Children, 1990).

Erik Erikson, *Childhood and Society*, 2nd ed. (New York: Norton, 1963).

K. Freiberg, ed., *Educating Exceptional Children*, 7th ed. (Guilford, Conn.: Dushkin Publishing Group, 1994).

A. Gordon and K. Browne, *Guiding Young Children in a Diverse Society* (Boston: Allyn and Bacon, 1996).

P. Greenberg, *Character Development: Encouraging Self Esteem and Self Discipline in Infants, Toddlers, and Two Year Olds* (Washington, D.C.: National Association for the Education of Young Children, 1990).

R. Lally, "The Impact of Child Care Policies and Practices on Infant/Toddler Identity Formation," *Young Children* 51(1), January 1995, pp. 58–68.

M. Meyerhoff, "Of Baseball and Babies: Are You Unconsciously Discouraging Father Involvement in Infant Care?" *Young Children* 49(4), May 1994, pp. 17–19.

M. Pratt, "The Importance of Infant/Toddler Interactions," *Young Children* (54)4, July 1999, pp. 26–29.

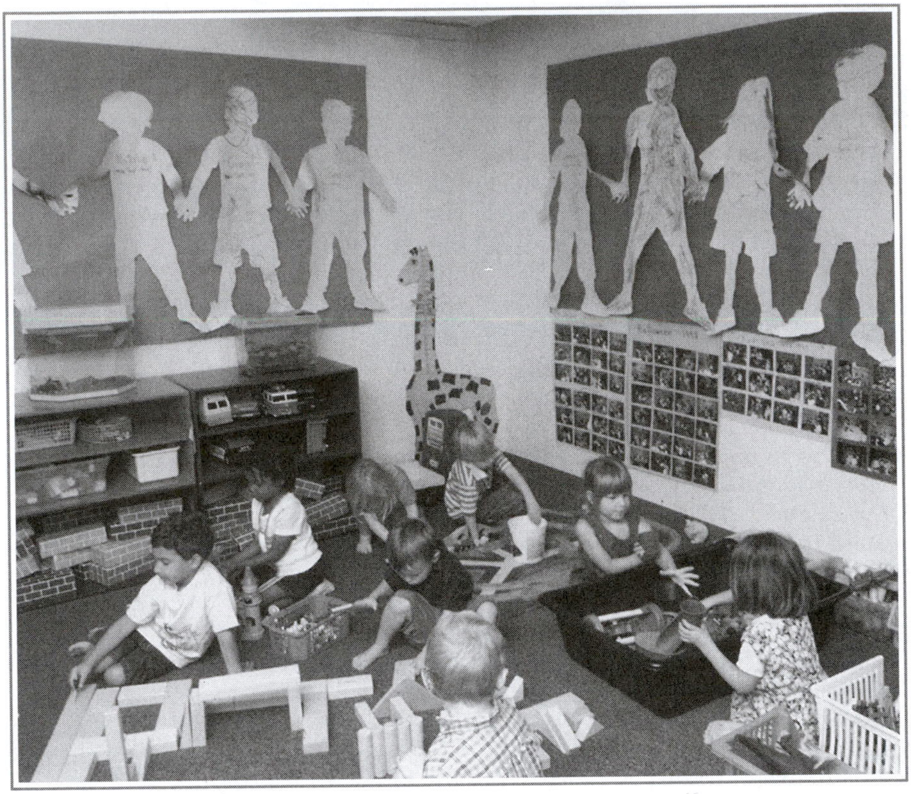

CHAPTER 12

Physical Environment

The environment as it relates to play was discussed briefly in chapter 4. This chapter covers the total environment: health and safety considerations and setting up for caregiving activities. We also include an expanded look at setting up for free play for infants and toddlers, plus a look at responding to the needs of chronically ill or disabled children. Much of what is discussed applies to family day-care settings as well as centers.

The child development associate assessment process defines quality settings for infant and toddler care as those that are safe environments that promote health and learning. Each of those components is examined in turn, and the chapter ends with a set of dimensions for a general assessment of the environment for infants and toddlers in programs or in family day care.

A SAFE ENVIRONMENT

Safety is a first consideration in planning for infants and toddlers. Group size and adult-child ratio are important factors in creating a safe environment. The Far West Laboratory for Educational Research and Development, in conjunction with the California Department of Education, has created the guidelines shown in table 12.1.[1]

Creating a Safe Physical Environment: A Checklist

- Cover all electrical outlets.
- Cover all heaters so children are kept well away from them.
- Protect children from all windows and mirrors that aren't shatterproof.

TABLE 12.1
Guidelines for Group Size and Adult-Child Ratios

Group Size Guidelines (Same-Age Groups)			
AGE	RATIO	TOTAL SIZE	MINIMUM NUMBER OF SQUARE FEET PER GROUP*
0–8 months	1:3	6	350
8–18 months	1:3	9	500
18–36 months	1:4	12	600

Mixed-Age Guidelines (Family Child Care)			
AGE	RATIO	GROUP SIZE	MINIMUM NUMBER OF SQUARE FEET PER GROUP*
0–36+ months	1:4**	8	600

*The space guidelines represent minimum standards of adequate square footage per group; the amounts shown do not include space used for entrance areas, hallways, diapering areas, or napping areas.

**Of the four infants assigned to a caregiver, only two should be under twenty-four months of age.

Developed by Far West Laboratory for Educational Research and Development and the California Department of Education. Reprinted by permission of J. Ronald Lally, Far West Laboratory.

- Remove or tie up all drapery cords. (Long strings, cords, and ties of any kind should be eliminated to prevent strangling.)
- Get rid of all slippery throw rugs.
- Get some instructions from your local fire department on how to put together a plan in case of fire. Consider the number and location of fire extinguishers, easy exit, and methods for carrying children who can't walk. Then schedule periodic fire drills.
- Make sure there are no poisonous plants in the environment. (Many common house and garden plants are deadly poison. If you don't know which ones are, find out!)
- Make sure all furniture is stable and in good repair.
- Remove lids from toy storage boxes to prevent accidents.
- Make sure all cribs and other baby furniture meet consumer protection safety standards (that is, slats are close together so babies can't get their heads stuck. Crib mattresses must fit tight so babies can't get wedged between mattress and side and smother).
- Keep all medicines and cleaning materials well out of reach of children at all times.

- Beware of toys with small parts that can come loose and go into mouths (such as button eyes on stuffed animals).
- Remove all broken, damaged toys and materials.
- Be sure no toys or materials are painted with or contain toxic substances.
- Know first aid and CPR.
- Keep a first aid kit at hand.
- Keep emergency numbers handy by the phone along with parent emergency information. Update parent emergency numbers frequently.
- Make sure the equipment you have is appropriate for the age group served. For example, climbing structures should be scaled down for toddlers.
- Supervise children well and allow them to take only minor risks but not risks with grave consequences. (Don't differentiate between boys and girls in the degree of risk you allow.)

If you have special-needs children in your program, you have to do a safety check that includes their special circumstances or disabilities. Are there ramps of an appropriate degree of slant for wheelchairs? Is some equipment safely adaptable for their special needs?

HEALTHFUL ENVIRONMENT

A healthful environment is as important as a safe one. Good light, comfortable air temperature, and ventilation contribute to the health and well-being of the infants and toddlers in the environment.

Creating a Healthful and Sanitary Environment: A Checklist

- Wash hands often. Hand washing is the best way to keep infections from spreading. Wash after coughing, sneezing, wiping noses, and changing diapers and before preparing food. Use dispenser soap instead of bar, paper towels instead of cloth. Avoid touching faucets and waste receptacles after washing. (Foot-controlled faucets and trash cans with a foot-control lid opener eliminate the probability of recontaminating clean hands.)
- Wash children's hands regularly also—especially before eating and after diapering or using the bathroom.
- Do not allow children to share washcloths or any other personal item.
- Clean toys and play equipment daily for any group of children who are young enough to mouth objects.
- Wear socks or slippers rather than street shoes in areas where infants lie on the floor.

- Vacuum rugs and mop floors regularly.
- Be sure each child has his or her own bed, cot, or pad, and change sheets regularly.
- Take routine precautions in changing diapers to prevent the spread of illness. Provide a clean surface for each changing by washing down the waterproof diaper changing area with disinfectant solution, and/ or provide fresh paper each time. Wash hands carefully after each changing.
- Take routine precautions in food preparation, serving, and cleaning up. Wash hands before handling food. Store food and bottles in refrigerator until right before using them. To wash dishes and bottles, use extra hot water. (Dishwashers with the hot water heater turned to high help eliminate germs.) Use a weak bleach solution if you don't have a dishwasher. Date all stored food. Clean out the refrigerator regularly, and throw away old food.
- Be sure all children in your care are up to date on their immunizations.
- Learn to recognize the signs of common illnesses.
- Make clear policies about which symptoms indicate when a child is too sick to be in your program. Parents' and caregivers' ideas and needs often differ when it comes to this subject.
- Require permission slips before you administer any medicine, and then be sure to give prescriptions only to the child with his or her name on the bottle.

Although you do not want to compromise health practices, be aware that cultural differences may arise concerning health matters. Try to be sensitive to parents who have ideas different from accepted practice about the paths to good health.

Also be sensitive to the special needs of chronically ill children, who sometimes have immunity problems. They may need extra protection from the spread of virus and bacteria that other children in your program carry. Examine your health and sanitary practices carefully to be sure you give these children the protection they need. Resist criticism from those who accuse you of being overprotective.

Offer good individualized infant nutrition, or ask the parents to provide nutritious food and bottles. Some guidelines agreed upon by most pediatricians are to wait on solids for three to six months, then introduce them slowly, one at a time, working up from a spoonful to a reasonably sized infant helping. Most pediatricians have a favorite order in which they advise introducing solids, starting with cereal. Most advise waiting to introduce those solids that may trigger allergies, such as egg white and orange juice. Stay away from mixtures (like casseroles) that contain several foods, in case one causes an allergic reaction (you won't know which one). Stay away from all additives—salt, sugar, and artificial colors and flavors. Infants need pure, natural, unseasoned food. Don't serve infants under a year old honey or corn syrup, because it may contain a certain kind of spore that causes a food poisoning only infants are susceptible to. Avoid foods that infants can choke on, such as raw carrots and popcorn.

Nutrition for toddlers follows many of the same guidelines. Choose food that is pure and natural—not processed with additives. Toddlers (and infants too) enjoy finger food. They need a break from purees and cereals. Give fruit or vegetable snacks rather than cookies or highly salted crackers. Give apple slices and carrot sticks (and then be cautious of apple peels) only when children have enough teeth and the ability to chew them. Avoid such foods as popcorn, nuts, peanut butter, hot dog rounds, grapes, and other foods on which toddlers might choke. Cut hot dogs lengthwise and then in small pieces. Avoid rounds! Cut grapes at least in half, and cut big ones in fourths. This particular caution goes double for those special-needs children whose reflexes may not be totally developed and who may be more prone to choking or breathing difficulties.

LEARNING ENVIRONMENT

Much of the structure of an infant-toddler program comes from a well-planned environment. According to Louis Torelli, "A well-designed environment . . . supports infants' and toddlers' emotional well-being, stimulates their senses and challenges their motor skills. A well-designed group care environment promotes children's individual and social development. It is comfortable and aesthetically attractive to both children and their caregivers."[2]

Research shows that behavior is influenced by environment.[3] A structured environment gives us clues about how to behave in it. You know that yourself. Just compare the library with the workout room in the gym. Or think of how the grocery store communicates what's expected, with carts at the door and open shelves and checkout stands, compared to a jewelry store, where you sit at a glass counter and someone offers you things from behind lock and key.

Infants and toddlers also get messages from the environment if it is well planned and consistent. In fact, learning to receive those messages is an important part of their socialization process as they learn about expectations for various behavior settings.[4]

Children with physical limitations will get specific messages if the learning environment isn't adapted to their special needs. For example, if a child in a wheelchair isn't able to go outside or across a thick carpet, his experiences in the program will be limited. If toys or equipment aren't at his level, he gets the message that they're not for him to play with. Make accommodations in the environment for *all* the children in the program, including those with special needs.

Although much learning goes on in the play area of the infant-toddler environment, it is not confined to that space. The whole environment, including caregiving areas, is the learning environment in an infant-toddler program. See the sample classrooms in figures 12.1, 12.2, and 12.3.

FIGURE 12.1
Infant classroom

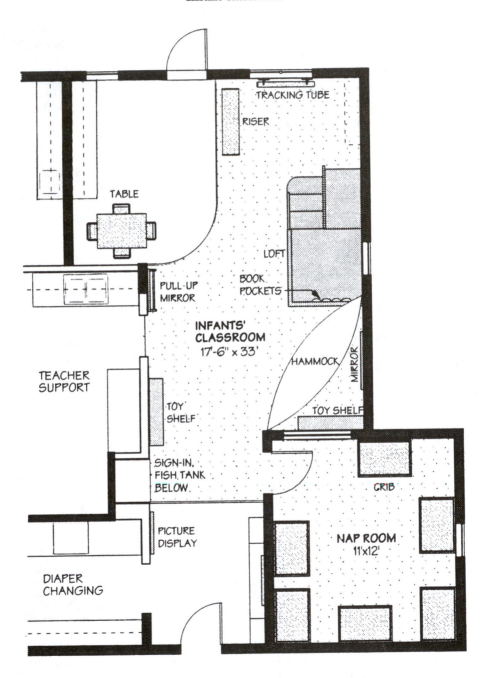

TRACKING TUBE

RISER

TABLE

LOFT

PULL-UP
MIRROR

BOOK
POCKETS

INFANTS'
CLASSROOM
17'-6" x 33'

HAMMOCK

MIRROR

TEACHER
SUPPORT

TOY
SHELF

TOY SHELF

SIGN-IN,
FISH TANK
BELOW.

CRIB

PICTURE
DISPLAY

NAP ROOM
11'x12'

DIAPER
CHANGING

FIGURE 12.2
Toddler classroom

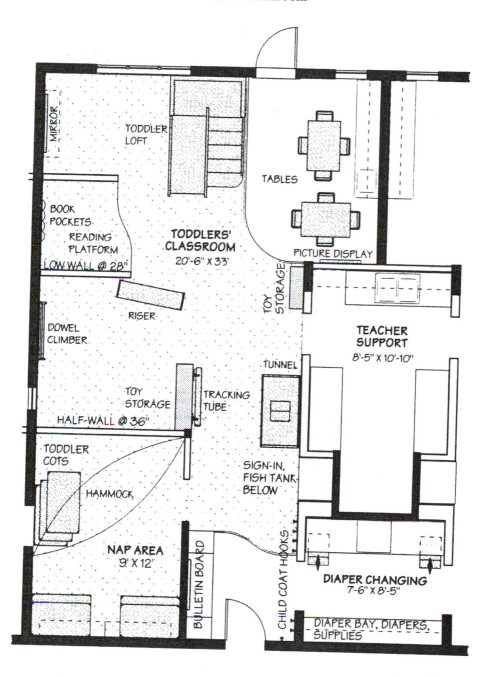

MIRROR

TODDLER LOFT

TABLES

BOOK POCKETS

READING PLATFORM

LOW WALL @ 28"

TODDLERS' CLASSROOM
20'-6" X 33'

PICTURE DISPLAY

TOY STORAGE

RISER

DOWEL CLIMBER

TEACHER SUPPORT
8'-5" X 10'-10"

TUNNEL

TOY STORAGE

TRACKING TUBE

HALF-WALL @ 36"

TODDLER COTS

HAMMOCK

SIGN-IN, FISH TANK BELOW

NAP AREA
9' X 12'

BULLETIN BOARD

CHILD COAT HOOKS

DIAPER CHANGING
7'-6" X 8'-5"

DIAPER BAY, DIAPERS, SUPPLIES

FIGURE 12.3
Combined infant/toddler classroom

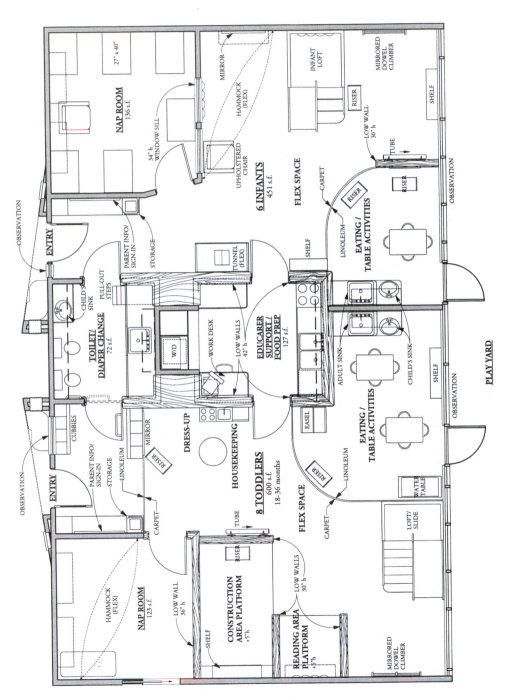

LAYOUT

There are some general rules for setting up an environment for infant-toddler care, whether in a center or family day-care home. You should have a designated place for arrivals and departures. Near this area should be storage for children's belongings. The sleeping area should be apart from the play area and should be subdued in atmosphere—restful colors, quiet, nonstimulating. The eating area also should be somewhat separate from the play area, though the two may overlap at times because you use eating tables for various other kinds of activities. The eating area should, of course, be close to a kitchen or other warming or cooking facility. The diaper area should be away from the eating area and close to a bathroom, or at least a sink. The indoor play area should be cheerful and well lighted and should invite exploration. There should be an outdoor play area as well that is equally inviting to explore. (It's appealing to some to have eating and sleeping areas outdoors also.) Storage and office space (at least a desk and phone) are also usually a part of the environment. Infants and toddlers come to learn what is expected in each space if the spaces are distinct from one another.

The furniture, equipment, and materials for caregiving activities vary somewhat with the philosophy and goals of the program. The following corresponds to the philosophy of this book.

Eating

Refrigerator and provision for warming food either in the room or very nearby are essential. Sink and counter also are essential. A dishwasher is handy. Tools and utensils for food preparation are needed as well as unbreakable dishes, cups, and spoons, in addition to bottles and nipples (which the parents may send with the children). The eating and food preparation area needs storage for food, dishes, and utensils. Small, low tables and chairs that children can get in and out of themselves add to feelings of independence. (Some children eat better in smaller groups because small groups are less stimulating, which is something to consider when choosing tables.) Some programs feel high chairs are a necessity, but others find they can get along without them. It takes some training on the part of the caregivers to get the children to eat at the table if children have a choice to leave. If provision is made for adults to eat in comfort—whether in the room or somewhere else—it makes them feel more at home than if they always have to stand at a counter or squat in tiny chairs.

Sleeping

The sleeping furniture depends on the age of the child. The youngest infants are more secure in bassinets or cradles; the older infants need cribs. Toddlers can sleep on cots or pads on the floor. Children should not share cribs, cots, or bedding, but each should have his or her own.

Although sleeping separately is standard practice in infant-toddler care, for cultural reasons and for health considerations, it is important to recognize that some cultures do not consider separate sleeping arrangements for infants or toddlers either normal or healthy.

Diapering

The diapering area needs counters or tables to change diapers, with storage of all equipment right at hand. Equipment includes diapers, cleaning supplies for disinfecting the changing surface after each diapering, and sanitary storage or disposal for soiled diapers.

Toileting

Toddlers appreciate child-size toilets, and they need access to sinks with soap and paper towels (or a sanitary way to use cloth towels). This area should be convenient to play space, both indoors and outdoors.

AGE APPROPRIATENESS

The most important factor in a learning environment is that it be developmentally appropriate for the age group. Infants are not served in an environment planned only for toddlers, just as toddlers do not behave the same in an environment designed solely for infants or for preschoolers. Developmental appropriateness is vital.

Often you have to be extremely flexible when you have infants and toddlers in the same room. The environment not only has to respond to the needs of the particular age constellation but also must respond to changes as the children grow and develop over time.

Jim Greenman illustrates this notion of flexibility in an interview in *Child Care Information Exchange*:

> Flexibility comes from rethinking the usual, like a couch. For infants, a couch provides a perfect space for two caregivers to sit and hold babies. As children learn to crawl, the couch can be moved out from the wall to create an interesting path. When children want to practice walking, the same couch provides a soft walking rail. Once toddlers become fascinated by more complex kinds of spatial games like hide-and-seek, the couch can become the base for a slide or for tunnels made from blankets. This process of designing and redesigning an environment creates a caring and a working space which keeps pace with changes in the children.[5]

Another example of flexibility is what one caregiver did with a set of shelves that holds toys. She found the children constantly dumping the toys on the floor and trying to climb up the empty shelves, so she laid the unit down on its back, and it became a piece of gross motor equipment as children crawled in and out, curled up between the shelves, and "drove" in it like a truck. This supine bookcase provided wonderful opportunities for the young imaginations in this program.

Appropriate Environments for Infants

How is the environment different for the infant and for the toddler? Partly it is size. The younger the child, the smaller the group and the space around should be. For the newborn, space can be frightening, and very confined space is appropriate—like a bassinet. The older immobile babies need expanded space, but not enormous space. They need to be on the floor, but protected from walking feet that appear as if they might step on or trip over the helpless infants. This is the age for which playpens are most appropriate. As babies begin to move around, either by rolling or crawling, they need even more space. The playpen is too small. When they first get upright, they need support for cruising—rails or furniture to hang on. In a home environment, coffee tables, end tables, chairs, and couches provide this support. In an infant center, other provisions must be made. (The *outside* of the playpen will work for this purpose.)

A word about cribs: cribs are not good learning environments—they are good sleeping environments. When the message is consistent about what cribs are for, some babies learn early to associate them with sleeping and have less difficulty going to sleep when put down. But if the crib is lined with toys and hung with mobiles, music boxes, and bags of goldfish, a mixed message is given. The environment is stimulating, not conducive to sleep. Better to give the message that playing happens outside the crib. Cribs are too small for all but the youngest babies to play in anyway. Better to use them only to confine tired children, not alert, awake ones. Awake ones need a different environment.

Appropriate Environments for Toddlers

Toddlers, of course, need even more space and gross motor challenges appropriate to their age level. They also need an environment that encourages independence—steps up to the sink so they can wash their hands, swings they can get in and out of themselves, pitchers to pour their own milk and juice, cloths so they can wipe up their own spills, a dishpan at hand so they can bus their own dishes. Toddlers also need an environment that invites them to explore using gross and fine motor skills and all their senses.

The play space should contain a variety of age-appropriate toys and equipment that encourage active, creative, whole-body play as well as manipulative skills. It should suit the mood of all children at any given time on any given day—those who feel energetic, those who feel mellow, those who want to be alone, and those who feel sociable.

Family Child Care and Mixed Age Groups

Setting up a child care environment for children of varying ages in a home is different from center-based program environments where children are grouped by age. Family child care homes have some distinct advantages that centers find hard to come by. There is less likely to be an "institutional feel" to them. The small scale of a home environment can be a great comfort to children who are easily overstimulated. There is a richness in a home that results from the greater variety found in an environment set up for mixed age groups as well as used by adult family members. A home naturally provides a variety of textures, sounds, and activities as life in the home continues in the presence of the children. Some of the advantages of being in a home are also some of the challenges that providers face as they try to make their homes safe, comfortable learning and care environments for children. Seeing how family members use their time may be a wonderful experience for children as they watch the teenage family member fix her car, or grandma sort her stamp collection. But the activities that the family members engage in may not necessarily be good for children. For example, if the same teenager comes in and plops down in front of the television, that may be a problem the provider will have to deal with.

Unlike the carefully designed center layouts shown in figures 12.1, 12.2, and 12.3, family child care depends on a preexisting floor plan that is for family living rather than specifically for child care. Providers make choices about which rooms to use for children's activities. Some choices are obvious, like bathrooms for washing and toileting, kitchens for cooking and perhaps eating. In the other chosen rooms, rearrangement of furniture may be necessary to make space for play. Some providers create play spaces in the living room, family room, dining room, a spare room, a basement, a converted garage, or a combination of rooms. Furniture may be moved back to make room for children to move around, or it may be rearranged as dividers to create sections for storing and use of specific children's toys and materials. Area rugs can also be used to define play spaces. Good use can be made of loft beds as spaces where older children can go to be away from younger ones. On the other hand, cutting off the legs of a loft bed to a safe height makes a low climbing space for younger children as well as perhaps a small area to crawl under. Low shelves make toys accessible to everybody, so in mixed age groups, care must be taken to put only appropriate and safe toys and materials on them that are suitable for even the very youngest child. Mixed age groups present a special set of challenges. The provider must be diligent about providing a safe environment that allows play and exploration for all ages. That means putting things at different levels for different age groups. Infants and toddlers who still explore by mouthing must be protected from small parts and fragile toys. Activities not suitable for the youngest children can be done at the kitchen table or counter to keep them out of reach of little hands. The materials must be stored up high. Nobody wants a toddler pulling out the hundred-piece puzzle and chewing on the cardboard pieces. Storage for toys is important so everything isn't out every day. Rotating ensures that the novelty of stored toys brought out for use creates new interest in old things. Some toys should be rotated and others left out all the time to give children a sense of consistency.

What Should Be in the Play Environment

As to what should be in the play environment (toys, equipment, and materials), age appropriateness is again the key (see appendix B). Newborns and very young infants need little in their play environment. A few things to look at are enough. The most interesting object in their environment is the live human face. Recognize that fact, and don't try to replace it with toys, pictures, or even television. They need responsive people more than they need any animate or inanimate object. (They also need lots of peace and quiet and minimal stimulation.)

As infants get older, they need a limited variety of soft, washable, brightly colored toys to be looked at or sucked on. Bright scarves and soft beach balls are easy to grip and wave around. Rattles, squeeze toys, plastic keys, and large plastic beads are interesting to babies who are learning reaching and grabbing skills. Toys that are responsive and make noise encourage babies to try different kinds of manipulations.

By nine months of age, infants enjoy a wide variety of objects, including cloth or cardboard books, a variety of hats and other head gear, dolls, plastic or wooden cars and trucks, play or real telephones, and nesting toys. They also like objects from the adult world—wooden spoons, pots and pans, and real telephones. Crawlers are very interested in exploring, manipulating, and testing the world of objects.

Beginning walkers enjoy push-and-pull toys in addition to all the things already mentioned. They spend more time walking around carrying and dropping toys than manipulating them at this stage, when they are practicing their walking skills. Large, very lightweight blocks are a hit. Children enjoy hauling them around, stacking them, and building enclosures.

By eighteen months, toddlers are still enjoying all of the above in addition to playing with more dress-up clothes (besides hats), as well as using available objects for dramatic play. By making available such things as housekeeping tools and equipment, toy stoves, brooms, plastic dishes, dolls, and steering wheels, you encourage their dramatic play.

Two-year-olds are even more sophisticated in dramatic play and need a larger variety of objects to encourage it. They also enjoy small figures, doll houses, snapping blocks, and beads to string. Two-year-olds also enjoy books and can use real ones as well as babyproof ones. Simple puzzles, lock-and-latch boxes, button and zipper boards, and other manipulative devices appeal to them. The closer to three the child is, the more the environment can resemble a typical preschool environment.

Toys and Materials for Inside

The list of appropriate toys and materials in the inside environment can be almost endless. Practically anything you can think of that is safe and interesting can become a learning tool for infants and toddlers. Here is a general list of things for the inside environment you might not have thought of:

- Beanbags. They can be hauled around, put in things, dumped and thrown. They don't fall off when stacked. (They do sprout when sucked on, though.)
- Plastic margarine tubs with damp sponges cut in different shapes.
- Blocks of all sizes—especially large, lightweight, plastic-covered foam ones that allow even the youngest toddlers to build, stack, and produce structures and enclosures with them.
- Shoe boxes with lids. Children love to take lids off and put them on again. You can put a surprise inside—bubble packing or a piece of white tissue paper.
- Scarves, scarves, scarves. Fun for all ages—even the very youngest.
- Books, books, books. Babyproof ones are needed for the youngest children; regular ones are fine for older toddlers.
- Muffin pans with a ball in each cup (a beginner's "puzzle" that even the very youngest can be successful with).
- Water. The possibilities are endless: scooping, pouring, straining, floating objects (soap, sponges), and dolls to wash are a few ways to use water as a learning medium.
- Flannel boards with felt pieces. Make them available to toddlers, and watch them explore, experiment, and talk as they move the pieces around.
- Paper to tear. Toddlers have very long attention spans when paper tearing is an activity.[6]

Toys and Materials for Outside

The outside environment should give infants a feeling of being safe and should give toddlers plenty to do. Younger infants need a shaded, grassy, protected place to lie on a blanket. Crawlers need safe spaces to crawl and explore, with textures to feel that don't hurt their knees. A hint for protecting knees comes from a reviewer of this text. Take adult-size tube socks and cut off the toes. Double and pull up over crawler's knees to create instant, cheap, knee pads! Crawlers need safe objects to manipulate and mouth. Beginning walkers need smooth surfaces that aren't too challenging as well as push-and-pull toys. Wheel toys are good for this age group, too.

Here are some ideas of what to have in the outside environment for toddlers:

- Truck inner tubes. These are usually free. Don't inflate fully. They make great bouncers.

- Knotted ropes to swing on.
- Trapezes made of a dowel suspended from ropes. Wrap the ends of the dowel with duct tape.
- Sling swings hung very low for the child to swing on belly down.
- Milk crates, big wooden boxes, thick planks, sawhorses, and ladders to make whatever climbing structure strikes your fancy.
- Wheel toys, including riding toys, push toys, and wheelbarrows and wagons to haul things around.
- Small slides they can go down head first.
- Various elevations—especially a hill. The hill is always fairly dry, even after a rain, and it's a challenge to walk up and down it. If you can get grass to grow on the hill, it makes a good place to roll.
- Rocking toys that children can get off and on by themselves.
- A sandbox with all sorts of containers and shovels and funnels, big and small.
- Water in all sorts of containers—little plastic swimming pools, big saucers, cement-mixing pans, baby bathtubs. Make available containers, funnels, hoses, sponges, cloths, and paintbrushes. Painting with water is always a favorite.
- Straw provides additional softness for outside. Children can jump into it and haul it around.[7]

ASSESSING THE QUALITY OF AN INFANT-TODDLER ENVIRONMENT

Besides looking at age appropriateness, there are other ways of assessing the quality of a learning environment.

In their book *Dimensions of Teaching-Learning Environments, II, Focus on Day Care,* Elizabeth Jones and Elizabeth Prescott defined five dimensions of a learning environment: soft-hard, intrusion-seclusion, high mobility–low mobility, open-closed, simple-complex.[8]

The soft-hard dimension is fairly self-explanatory. Assess this dimension of an infant-toddler environment by asking the question, Is the learning environment full of softness? In their indoor environment, infants and toddlers need thick rugs, soft blankets, stuffed animals, cozy furniture, mattresses, pads, cushions, and laps. In the outside environment, they need grass, sand, water, soft balls, pads, and laps. A soft environment is *responsive*. Many centers tend to have less softness than infants and toddlers need—partly because it is harder to clean soft materials and surfaces and partly because they tend to wear out. Day-care homes usually do better than centers on the softness side of the dimension because a home usually has the stuffed furniture and curtains that centers lack.

Is there also some hardness, or is every inch of floor carpeted, every inch of the yard in lawn? Hard floors and smooth cement present a different feel to the crawler, are easier to walk on for the beginning walker, and make nice noises for the older toddler. Some hard surfaces and hard toys and materials belong in infant-toddler care, but the emphasis should be on softness.

The environment should provide for both optimum intrusion and seclusion. Desirable intrusion comes as the outdoor environment comes inside, providing interest and novelty. Low windows allow children to see what is happening outside, in back or on the street, but protect them from the dangers and noise. Desirable intrusion also occurs as outsiders come into the infants' and toddlers' environment—the telephone repair person, parents picking up children, visitors. Caregivers should maintain an optimum level of intrusion.

Seclusion should be provided so children who need to be alone or with one other child can find spaces to do that. Of course, supervision must always be a concern, but there are ways to make private spaces that adults can still see into. One simple way is to move a couch out from the wall. One center has a series of topless wooden boxes against one wall, with holes to crawl into. The sides screen the crawlers and toddlers from the rest of the room, but adults can see into them.

Louis Torelli talks about the importance of being able to break away from the larger group:

> A multi-level design, for example, varies the floor height with appropriately scaled platforms, lofts, "nests" and canopies. These mini learning environments set up a landscape for safe exploration in which infants can handle a toy, look at a book, stack blocks, crawl up steps, or simply watch the adults and other children from a cozy, semi-enclosed "private space."[9]

For some children with special needs, a place to escape what may be for them too much stimulation is imperative. Be aware of these children's needs for seclusion and minimal stimulation and provide for those needs.

High mobility and low mobility should both be encouraged in an environment for infants and toddlers. Children who are old enough should be able to move around freely. Children should not have to wait for outdoor time to engage in vigorous movement. That means, of course, that group size must be on the small side. Eight is big enough for an infant-toddler group. Two- to three-year-olds can manage in a slightly larger group—twelve—if the environment is well planned. Children with special needs may benefit from being in even smaller groups than other children.

The open-closed dimension has to do with choices. An example of openness in the environment is low open shelves that display toys to choose from. Closed storage is also appropriate to regulate or reduce choices and to get rid of a cluttered atmosphere.

Openness also has to do with the arrangement of furniture and dividers. A good arrangement is to have openness from your waist up so you can supervise, but some feeling of closed space below so infants and toddlers aren't overwhelmed by large expanses.

The open-closed dimension also has to do with whether a toy or material has one right way to do it (like a puzzle, form board, or graduated stacking rings) or whether it encourages all kinds of exploration. A stuffed animal and play dough are both open, as is water play. Children under three need many more open materials and toys than closed ones. Older toddlers may enjoy some closed materials and tasks, but younger ones and infants disregard their intended use and make everything open. They find ways to use all toys and materials (closed ones as well as open ones) that adults never dreamed of. For an infant, the concept of the wrong way to use a toy doesn't exist.

The simple-complex dimension is more of a concern for caregivers with older toddlers. The more complex a material or toy (or combination of materials and toys), the more things toddlers can think of to do with them. Sand, water, and utensils combined present lots more possibilities for action than any one of the three by itself. Caregivers who explore this dimension find attention span increased when complexity is introduced into the environment.

In "Designing Infant/Toddler Environments," Jim Greenman mentions some additional dimensions to consider when planning learning environments for infants and toddlers.[10]

Scale

Greenman points out that just as adults feel small in environments designed to promote that feeling (such as courtrooms or cathedrals), so infants and toddlers feel small in any environment designed for other age groups. Even a preschool environment will add to the infant's and toddler's feeling of smallness. When they sit in chairs that leave feet dangling, swing in swings they can't get into or out of, or play at chest-high tables, they feel smaller than they need to feel. Infants and toddlers need rooms, ceilings, furniture, and spaces scaled down for them. You want them to feel big and capable, not small and inadequate. The physical environment can make a difference in their self-concept.

Aesthetics

Infants and toddlers should spend their time in a place that is visually appealing. Lighting is an important factor in visual appeal. If possible, avoid the over-lit and even effect of fluorescent lighting. Natural and incandescent lighting give variety and add warmth. Color and its different emotional qualities should be considered, as should visual noise. In most infant-toddler environments, there is so much going on—so much to see—that the background should be calm, warm, and neutral. Greenman suggests avoiding the usual riots of color and design when planning walls, surfaces, curtains, and other fabrics. With a neutral backdrop, the people, toys, and materials stand out better, allowing children to find them and focus on them. The children are less distracted.

Acoustics

Noise can be a real problem where infants and toddlers are together in a group. Every effort should be made to lower the noise level and protect the children who need quiet from those who are shouting, crying, or engaging in noisy activities. Group size has a lot to do with noise level, which is an important reason to keep groups small. Dividing the space helps, too, as does providing plenty of softness to absorb sound (carpets, stuffed furniture, pads and cushions, curtains, and acoustical ceilings). Be aware of background noises and their effect on the children and adults as a group and individually. Some lights emit a high-pitched sound that irritates sensitive ears. Noise from fans or other machinery can be soothing or irritating, depending on the sound and the room.

Order

Relating to both aesthetics and acoustics is a sense of order. Because infants and toddlers create constant disorder as they spread toys and materials around, pull things apart, and dump and rearrange everything they can get their hands on, the environment needs to provide a sense of basic order that is a contrast to the constant mess on the floor. Room arrangement should contribute to the sense of order. Using furniture, shelves, and screens to divide play space into small modules just large enough for two or three children (or slightly more for older toddlers) helps them focus and cuts down on noise (visual as well as auditory). Clear pathways should lead to these play spaces, and each space should contain shelves of toys. In addition, if entrances to spaces offer some motor challenge, such as stepping up or crawling through, children spend less time wandering.

Of course, the divided room need occur only below the three-foot level, so the whole room is in view at the adult level. That's an important point to make—there are two environments in the room: below three feet and above three feet. To fully understand the children's environment, you need to get down at their level. When you're down there, you'll discover things like baseboards, of which you are probably totally unaware. It is good to get low and take the children's perspective regularly when planning and maintaining an environment for them.

The environment is never determined once and for all. Planning, arranging, evaluating, and rearranging is an ongoing process as caregivers strive for quality and find what works best for them and for the children.

This chapter has examined the layout of the physical environment as well as three factors that influence the quality of the setting: safety, health, and learning. The last part of the chapter focused on planning a learning environment, looking at a variety of factors including toys and materials. The physical environment is only part of what makes for quality in programs. Equally important is the social environment, which is the subject of the next chapter.

Thought/Activity Questions

1. Look around the environment you are in right now. What messages does it send about the way you are supposed to behave in it? Think about a contrasting environment you have been in recently. What different messages did it send?
2. Think about the place you are most comfortable and feel happy in. What are the characteristics of this place? Can you learn anything from your own experience about how to set up an environment for infants and toddlers?
3. How is the sleeping place in your own life different from the "play space"? Are there any implications here for infant-toddler care?
4. Figures 12.1, 12.2, and 12.3 show center-based program environments. Draw a layout of a home (it could be your own home) and design spaces in it that would accommodate a group of children of varying ages, including infants and toddlers.

Notes

1. "Together in Care: Meeting the Intimacy Needs of Infants and Toddlers in Groups," in *Child Care Video Magazine* (Sacramento, Calif.: Far West Laboratory and California Department of Education, 1992), pp. 7–8.
2. Louis Torelli, "The Developmentally Designed Group Care Setting: A Supportive Environment for Infants, Toddlers and Caregivers," *Zero to Three*, December 1989, pp. 7–10.
3. Elizabeth Prescott, "The Physical Environment—Powerful Regulator of Experience," *Child Care Information Exchange*, Reprint #4, C-44, Redmond, Wash. 98052.
4. Roger G. Barker, *Ecological Psychology: Concepts and Methods for Studying the Environment of Human Behavior* (Stanford, Calif: Stanford University Press, 1968).
5. Dennie Wolf, "An Interview with Jim Greenman," *Child Care Information Exchange*, September 1987, p. 19.
6. Thanks to Maggie Cole for these ideas that she has used with infants and toddlers at Napa Valley College Child Care Center.
7. These ideas come from Molly Sullivan, who used them in her family day-care home in Berkeley, California.
8. Elizabeth Jones and Elizabeth Prescott, *Dimensions of Teaching-Learning Environments, II, Focus on Day Care* (Pasadena, Calif: Pacific Oaks, 1978).
9. Torelli, "The Developmentally Designed Group Care Setting."
10. Jim Greenman, "Designing Infant/Toddler Environments," in *Caring for Infants and Toddlers: What Works, What Doesn't*, vol. 2, edited by Robert Lurie and Roger Neugebauer (Redmond, Wash.: Child Care Information Exchange, 1982).

For Further Reading

American Academy of Pediatrics, Committee on Infectious Diseases, *Report of the Committee on Infectious Diseases* ("Red Book") (Elk Grove Village, Ill.: The American Academy of Pediatrics, 1997).

California Department of Education and the Center for Health Training, *Keeping Kids Healthy: Preventing and Managing Communicable Diseases in Child Care* (1994).

Caring for Our Children: National Health and Safety Performance Standards: Guidelines for Out-of-Home Child Care Programs (American Public Health Association and American Academy of Pediatrics, 1992).

Lorraine DeJong and Barbara Hansen Cottrell, "Designing Infant Child Care Programs to Meet the Needs of Children Born to Teenage Parents," *Young Children* 54(1), January 1999, pp. 37–45.

Amy Laura Dombro, Laura J. Colker, and Diane Trister Dodge, *Creative Curriculum for Infants and Toddlers* (Washington, D.C.: Teaching Strategies, 1997).

Lyn Fasoli and Janet Gonzalez-Mena, "Let's Be Real: Authenticity in Child Care," *Exchange,* March 1997.

Mary Fauvre, "Including Young Children with 'New' Chronic Illnesses in an Early Childhood Education Setting," *Young Children* 43, 1988, pp. 71–78.

Jerry Ferguson, "Creating Growth-Producing Environments for Infants and Toddlers," in Elizabeth Jones, ed., *Supporting the Growth of Infants, Toddlers and Parents* (Pasadena, Calif.: Pacific Oaks, 1991).

George E. Forman and Fleet Hill, *Constructive Play: Applying Piaget in the Preschool* (Menlo Park, Calif.: Addison-Wesley, 1984).

Magda Gerber and Andrea King, "Modifying the Environment to Respond to the Changing Needs of the Child," *Educaring* 6(1), Winter 1985, pp. 1–2.

Jim Greenman, *Caring Spaces, Learning Places: Children's Environments That Work* (Redmond, Wash.: Exchange Press, 1988).

Jim Greenman, "Just Wondering: Building Wonder into the Environment," *Child Care Information Exchange,* January/February 1993, pp. 32–35.

Jim Greenman and Anne Stonehouse, *Prime Times* (St. Paul: Redleaf, 1996).

Fran Hast and Ann Hollyfield, *Infant and Toddler Experiences* (St. Paul: Redleaf, 1999).

Infant/Toddler Caregiving: A Guide to Setting Up Environments (Sacramento: California State Department of Education, 1990).

Elizabeth Jones and Elizabeth Prescott, *Dimensions of Teaching-Learning Environments, II, Focus on Day Care* (Pasadena, Calif.: Pacific Oaks, 1978).

A. S. Kendrick, R. Kaufman, and K. P. Messenger, eds., *Healthy Young Children: A Manual for Programs* (Washington, D.C.: National Association for the Education of Young Children, 1995).

J. Ronald Lally and Jay Stewart, *Infant/Toddler Caregiving: A Guide to Setting Up Environments* (Sacramento, Calif.: Far West Laboratory for Educational Development and California Department of Education, 1990).

L. R. Marotz, M. Z. Cross, and J. M. Rush, *Health, Safety and Nutrition for the Young Child,* 3rd ed. (New York: Delmar, 1993).

V. Moukaddem, "Preventing Infectious Diseases in Your Child Care Setting," *Young Children* 45, 1990, pp. 28–29.

A. R. Olds, "Designing Play Environments for Children under Three," *Topics in Early Childhood Education* 2, 1982, pp. 87–95.

Elizabeth Prescott, "The Physical Environment—Powerful Regulator of Experience," *Child Care Information Exchange,* Reprint #4, C-44, Redmond, Wash. 98052, 1994.

Louis Torelli, "The Developmentally Designed Group Care Setting: A Supportive Environment for Infants, Toddlers and Caregivers," *Zero to Three,* December 1989, pp. 7–10.

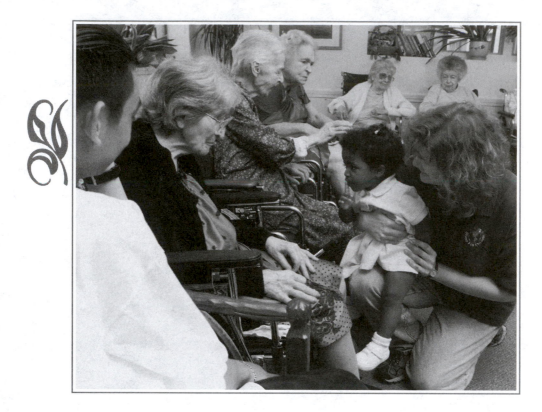

CHAPTER 13

Social Environment

The social environment is harder to talk about than the physical environment because it is far less visible. You can stand and look around the physical environment to evaluate it. But you have to catch behaviors as they happen in order to see the social environment.

A good deal of part 1 and some of part 2 focus on the social environment without calling it that. The environmental chart in appendix B outlines the social environment. This chapter discusses aspects of the social environment that haven't been discussed elsewhere.

SELF-CONCEPT

An important goal of the social environment is that each child in it develop a good self-concept. The self-concept, which relates to attachment, is made up of the child's perceptions of and feelings about him- or herself. Self-concept comes from body image as well as cultural and gender identification. The social environment, the way the child is treated by adults and children, affects self-concept and influences the degree of self-esteem.

Attachment

The prerequisite for high self-esteem in infants and toddlers is attachment. From attachment comes the feeling "I matter to somebody; who I am and what I do is important because somebody cares." All the self-esteem activities in the world won't make a difference if the child's basic attitude is "Nobody cares about me."

"Caring" in the sense of attachment has to happen at home, but it is important in day care, too. It seems as though "caring" is what infant-toddler programs are all about because of all the caregiving focus. But "caring" the feeling is different from "caring" the action (taking care of). You can care for a child, wash his bottom, feed his face, without really caring for him. And you can't *make* yourself care for him (in the feeling sense). You can make yourself respect the child, and that may help the caring feeling come. Respecting the child will help you deal with all of him, not treating him as a bottom or a face, and in turn he may feel better about himself and reveal more of himself to you. That may help the caring feeling come.

What If You Don't Feel Attached?   But what can you do if you are respectful and you still find a child doesn't "matter to you"? First of all, don't blame yourself, and don't work up a good case of guilt. Perhaps you and the child just don't hit it off—you have personality differences; you clash. If you're in a center, it's possible that another caregiver has a different feeling about this child, and that's all that's needed. Someone cares about him. It doesn't have to be you, as long as you continue to be respectful.

If you're the only caregiver of a child you don't care about, that's a real problem, but it's not insolvable. Here are a couple of ideas of what to do that might work.

Observe the child. Step back and really pay attention to her every move. Try to understand her. See if you can view the world from her perspective. Do a "child study" in which you make a series of short observations over a period of time and then put them together and examine them for evidence of growth. Carry a notebook around in your pocket, and every chance you get make notes about what you see this child doing. Be very detailed and specific. Note body posture, quality of movement, facial expressions, and tone of vocalizations. Try hard to be very objective—don't judge; just observe. If you get good at stepping into and out of an "observation mode," you can do it quickly and effectively many times during the course of a day. In addition, at the end of the day, write some anecdotal records—notes about what you remember about the child that day and what you remember about your interactions with her. These reflection records as well as on-the-spot observations will provide you with material for your child study in the course of a few months. Observations alone may help your feeling for this child grow.

Observation can have powerful effects, as proved by an exercise in which participants are asked to examine an orange or other piece of fruit for a short time. Once they "really get to know" their orange, they introduce their orange and all its uniqueness to someone else in the class. Then the leader collects all the oranges in a basket. When the basket is passed around again, each student is able to identify his or her "own" orange. An outcome of this activity for some people is attachment. They have a personal feeling for "their" orange. If five minutes of observation attaches you to a piece of fruit, think of what a few hours spread over several months can do to your feeling for a child.

One student who was required to do an extensive child study chose a child she didn't like very much. She reported that it was the best choice she could have made because after she really got to know this child and began to understand him better, her feeling for him changed.

Studying a child is a very rational approach to take—a left-brain way of approaching the problem. If that idea leaves you cold, here's another idea—a right-brain approach—to help you increase your ability to care about a particular child. Use visualization. Spend some quiet time each day visualizing yourself interacting with this child in a truly caring mode. If she has behaviors that get in your way, try imagining the child without those behaviors. See her not as she *is* but as she *could be*. Here's a sample of how a visualization can work:

You work with a two-and-a-half-year-old who doesn't appeal to you at all. She is very verbal, and she has a loud, piercing voice that becomes even louder when she is angry, which is 90 percent of the time. She is bossy to the other children and reports every little misdeed to any nearby adult. When you ask her to do something, she's very likely to say no. If you try to persuade her, she stands with her feet apart and screams, "You can't make me." All of those behaviors bother you, and the more you try to change them, the worse they get. The days she is absent are a big relief. You notice a big difference not only in you but in the other children.

One day you decide you have to do something about your feelings about this child. You've heard about visualization—a form of meditation. You're dubious, but at this point you'll try anything. It can't hurt.

You take ten minutes before bedtime to sit quietly, in a relaxed position, and clear your mind. As a person who is used to meditating, this part is easy. But then it gets harder.

First you try to visualize the child without the behaviors that bother you so much, but nothing comes. You just can't seem to disconnect her from the way she behaves. So you try a different tack. You decide if you can't even *imagine* her different, you'd better work on yourself first.

So you spend your ten minutes imagining the little girl as she behaves every day, but you visualize yourself not reacting to her. It's hard. At first you are like a statue, standing still and cold. You don't like that image very much. After a short time of cold silence, you notice that your image has become more like a wooden puppet. In your mind's eye, you watch as the child screams, tattles, defies you, and bosses, and you just dangle from your strings with a blank smile on your face. You don't like that image very much either, but you continue to let your visualization lead where it will. You watch in surprise as the wooden puppet changes before your eyes to a strong, sturdy tree. Now you're in a comfortable image (though it seems a little weird to you). You feel good as you respond to the wind of the little girl's voice—your leaves rustle, your branches bend, but it doesn't affect you. She tries harder to affect you. She seems to want to blow you over, but your roots are deep and your trunk is strong. You bend slightly, but you come back upright as soon as she stops. She tries harder. She gives up and walks away. You end the visualization.

For the next few nights you try the same visualization. You're a tree and she's herself. You practice withstanding her onslaught without getting caught up in it. You do nothing different during the day, but for some reason her behavior isn't bothering you so much. You wonder if it is changing or if you just feel it less.

One night after you have been doing this for a few days, ten minutes at a time, a change in your visualization surprises you. The child has been frantically trying to get to you, trying to do damage, but all is in vain. She is kicking your trunk (which you can't feel because of your thick bark) when suddenly she throws her arms around your trunk, slides to the ground, and lies there sobbing pathetically, one little hand clutching at an exposed root. The little girl who rises off the ground is a different child—though she looks the same. Now at last you can imagine her without the behaviors that were so much a part of her before. You change out of your tree shape, melting and twisting, and end up in your own shape. You sit down on the ground and hold her.

The next time your visualization is very different. You can now imagine yourself interacting with her during the day, and the behaviors are gone. Sometimes it's hard to see her, but other times the images come quite easily. You notice that she is very insecure at times, and other times she seems to need attention very badly. At one point you are astounded to take a close look at her face and discover your own!

Meanwhile, during the day you've gained a deeper understanding of her behavior, seeing the scared, uncertain, powerless little girl who's behind the defiant, bossy one. Her behavior hasn't changed much, but yours has. No longer do you react so strongly. No longer do you dislike her so intensely.

Eventually you begin to find ways to help her both gain social skills and feel better about herself. You've learned something about this child—and something about yourself too. You give up the visualization, satisfied that it has done its job.

Of course, visualization doesn't work for everyone, but we all carry around in our heads unconscious images that influence our expectations of others as well as our own behavior toward them. These images can be very powerful, and visualization is one way of clarifying them in order to change them.

Self-Image

Children are influenced not only by the images of them that adults carry around but also by the image they have of themselves. Part of self-concept is one's own perception of oneself that relates to body image and awareness.

Body awareness is a major task of infants and toddlers and grows as their motor skills develop. As they learn what capabilities their bodies have, they develop an image of themselves. You can watch a nine-month-old backing down off a couch he has crawled up on and get an idea of his body awareness. The child with good body awareness knows where he is in space and how far to back before putting his feet over the edge of the couch. He can guess how far it is to the floor, so he is able to slide off and remain in control.

When working with children who have physical disabilities, it is important to take their body awareness and self-image into account. If you focus only on their lack of skills, they'll have some difficulties with self-concept. Pay special attention to whatever abilities they have, emphasizing what they *can do* rather than concentrating on what they can't do.

As children develop competence, their self-concept expands. They take pride in each accomplishment. Thus the thrust for independence and the development of self-help skills relate to body image and the growth of self-concept.

Cultural Identity

Cultural identity is also a part of self-concept. The culture we come from influences every detail of every action of our lives, including how close we stand to people, where we touch them, gestures we make, what we eat, how we talk and think, how we regard time and space—how we look at the world. You bring your culture to your work with infants and toddlers. You are teaching them your culture every day in everything you do. In a program where the children and caregivers are of the same culture, there is real consistency. Those children don't think about culture—it's so much a part of them.

In fact, few of us think about culture until we encounter someone who comes from a different one. This can happen to infants and toddlers quite early when they go into day care. The question is, How does exposure to two cultures affect infants and toddlers? What do they do with a second set of cultural messages? This is no new phenomenon: throughout history members of one culture have been involved in raising the children of another. A modern example, outside of day care programs, is the au pair system popular among some well-off American families. A young woman, the "au pair," comes from another country to live with the family and be a nanny. Her culture may be similar or very different from that of the parents.

One theory is that children who are raised biculturally or multiculturally have a greater understanding and acceptance of differences in people. They may also be more willing to see beyond cultural differences and relate to people as individuals, regardless of their cultural differences. This is the theory behind the push at present for multicultural education. The goal in multicultural education is to help children appreciate their own culture and cultural differences. The advocates of multicultural education see it as a way to fight bias of all kinds and racism in particular.

A Multicultural Infant-Toddler Curriculum   But what is a multicultural curriculum in an infant-toddler center? It is easier to talk about what it is not than what it is. It is not pictures stuck on walls, rotating ethnic foods, or celebration of holidays. Infants and toddlers do not gain much understanding of culture from those devices, though you may choose to include those components in your program for various reasons, including your own enjoyment and satisfaction or that of the parents.

A more meaningful multicultural approach comes from learning from parents how their culture is different from yours. Some of this you may be able to just observe. It helps to ask. By asking, you may open up a dialogue about cultural differences. All of this may turn out to be very interesting and valuable to you.

However, none of this makes a real difference to the infants and toddlers in your care. What does matter when you care for children from a culture different from your own is when you listen to what their parents want for them in their day-to-day care. This means discussion of caregiving practices. It also means potential conflict when your beliefs and values clash with those of the parents. For example, take a parent who does not understand your goals for each child to become independent. She may insist on spoon feeding her child way beyond an age you feel is appropriate. Or take a parent who stresses independence beyond your own goals. She may ask you to allow a toddler to sleep or eat whenever or wherever he or she wants without regard to any kind of schedule. Or a parent may want to keep siblings together even though the age difference makes your environment inappropriate for one or the other. Or a parent may ask you to help her with toileting her child even though the child is far younger than you think appropriate. Or a parent may ask you to dress or not to dress his or her child in a certain way, or in certain kinds of clothes you don't approve of. All of these can be cultural issues.

A true multicultural infant-toddler approach in such cases would be to invite parent input and then figure out what to do with it. Some requests are easy to respond to immediately; others take more talking, clarifying, understanding, and perhaps negotiating. Still others go against your very deeply held values and beliefs, and no amount of talking or negotiating will convince you to comply with the parent's wishes. Sometimes when a serious conflict like this occurs, the parent has other choices for child care, in which case he or she may find someone who is more able to comply. But often the parent has no other choice, so difficulties arise.

One way some caregivers get around these difficulties is to stop discussing the issue, pretend to go along with the parent just to keep peace, and then keep doing what they believe in when the parent leaves. That approach can leave the child in the position of coping with a culturally assaultive environment while in day care. Imagine yourself in a culturally assaultive environment. How would that feel?

It is much better to work continually toward resolving the conflict. It's good practice for all of us to open up and expand our cultural awareness by being persistent in resolving difficult dilemmas that arise when parent beliefs and practices conflict with caregiver beliefs and practices. It may be that you and the parent will come to an agreement that it won't hurt the child if day care is one way and home is another way. Or it may be that together you'll find some middle ground. It may even be that you'll change your practices once you understand the parent's point of view, or she will change hers when she understands your point of view.

Gender Identity

Part of self-concept is gender identity. Most children are aware quite early whether they are a boy or a girl, and their feelings about their gender influence how they perceive themselves.

Throughout this book mention has been made of sex role stereotyping. The information has come mostly in the form of questions designed to heighten your awareness of sex role stereotyping.

Children can grow up with a severely limited view of their capabilities and potentials by being taught narrow sex roles. These teachings start early. The expectations even at birth can be very different for a boy baby than for a girl baby. Those expectations influence a child's self-concept. If you expect boys to grow to be strong, brave, unemotional, and capable, you act differently toward them than you do toward girls. If you expect girls to be sweet, kind, attractive, emotional, and not too smart, they are likely to live up to your expectations.

You can see for yourself how people treat boys differently from the way they treat girls with a simple observation. Just keep track of what adults, especially strangers, say to very young children. They are much more likely to comment to girls on appearance and clothes. Boys are noticed for their deeds and less often for appearance.

Children learn about what is expected of their gender by such simple, innocent remarks. They also learn from the clothes they are given to wear. (It's hard to crawl and climb in a dress.) Toys give messages too. When boys are encouraged to play with tools, construction sets, and doctors' kits, they get one message. When girls are given dolls, play dishes, and makeup kits, they get another message. Children learn about expected gender roles from television, books, and above all, role models. If the family day-care provider waits until her husband gets home to fix the screen door and makes it clear that she never touches tools, she is giving a message. When centers leave their tricycles unrepaired until a man comes on the scene, they too are giving a message.

If current trends continue, the children in infant and toddler programs today will grow up into a world of a variety of job opportunities for both sexes. The days men were restricted from some jobs and women from others are mostly in the past. Yet, if children grow up with a limited view of their capabilities because of the narrow sex roles taught them, their freedom to qualify for these jobs will be limited.

Here are four ideas about how to offer both the boys and the girls you work with a broad view of their gender roles. First, be aware of treating boys and girls differently. Do you offer more support and sympathy to girls when they get hurt and expect boys to "tough it out"? Do you help girls when they need it and wait for boys to figure things out on their own? Do you offer girls dolls and boys blocks, or do you encourage and support both sexes to play with all the toys? Do you touch girls more than boys (or vice versa)? Do you talk to girls more than boys (or vice versa)?

Second, model expanded gender roles. If you're a woman, how often have you tried to fix something, or do you just put it aside, convinced you don't know how? Can you check your own oil? (Learn—it's easy.) If you're a man and you're reading this book, you've already expanded your gender role. Can you think of ways to expand it further?

Third, avoid exposing children to media messages that teach narrow gender roles. We hope the infants and toddlers in your program aren't watching any television, so you don't need to worry about that medium. Find books and pictures that show strong, capable women as well as nurturing men in a variety of occupational roles.

Finally, avoid linking occupations to gender—say "police officer" rather than "policeman," "firefighter" rather than "fireman." These are simple changes, but they make a difference.

Self-Concept and Discipline

The way you guide and control behavior can influence children's ideas of and feelings about themselves. The discussion here will center around ways to discipline that don't tear down self-esteem.

Much of what is appropriate discipline for infants and toddlers comes about naturally through meeting individual needs in a timely fashion and through setting up an environment that is appropriate to their age level. If they can't get to hot stoves, they won't touch them. If they can't reach radio knobs, they won't turn them. If they have no access to steep stairs, you don't have to find ways to prevent them from climbing them. To a great extent, the environment sets the limits.

However, you do have to protect the children from hurting each other, and sometimes you do have to prevent them from ruining toys and furniture by banging, chewing, and throwing. You can do this by firmly but gently physically restraining the child (if a word won't do it) and removing the object or the child if he or she threatens to continue this behavior. If you remain calm and gently persistent, you won't be as apt to trigger rebellion as you would if you issue sharp warnings or commands. You do need persistence because older infants and young toddlers continually test limits. That's how they find out about you and the world they live in. Once they're satisfied you really mean it, the test is over—until the next situation anyway. The way to preserve their good feelings about themselves as well as their sense of power while you enforce the limits is to avoid shaming, belittling, blaming, or criticizing them.

Don't Punish or Scold   Punishment, scolding, and anger have no place in the discipline of infants and toddlers. You may, of course, feel and express anger at times when you are not able to control the behavior of the children you care for. That's normal and doesn't hurt anything. However, recognize that the anger is personal. Don't blame the children for it, and don't use anger to control their behavior. Find other ways to get the effect you want from them. Using anger to get your way will quickly be picked up by the children, and you'll find them trying it on you.

Punishment damages self-esteem. There are other ways to change undesirable behavior that not only leave self-esteem intact but actually enhance self-concept as children learn to control their own behavior and feel good about getting attention for staying within the limits and exhibiting prosocial behavior.

Define Unacceptable Behavior   Before you consider ways of changing behavior, you must first define what is undesirable behavior. The child's age will influence your definition. For example, the screams of a young infant are not undesirable behavior; they are communication and must be attended to. Touching and mouthing objects are not undesirable behaviors in older infants; they have a need to touch and mouth. Experimentation and exploration are not undesirable behaviors in toddlers; that's how they learn about the world.

No One "Right" Way   When considering alternatives to punishment, you have to realize that no one approach works for all the children all the time. What works depends on the child, the situation, and the origins of the behavior. For example, if a certain toddler behavior has in the past been rewarded by adult attention, it has been learned. Therefore, the approach is to "unlearn" it by removing the reward. At the same time, you must be sure to replace the attention the child has been receiving when you remove it from its connection with a particular behavior. Sometimes adults forget that there must be two parts to this approach of removing the reward from undesirable behavior. The children *need* the attention you're denying them. Find other ways to give it to them. Also be sure before you try this approach that you determine whether this behavior is communicating some other unfulfilled need. If that is the case, don't ignore the behavior; regard it as communication, and fulfill the need.

Some behaviors are expressions of feelings. Accept the feelings. Help the child learn to express them in socially acceptable ways. What is considered an acceptable expression of feelings varies with the culture. Some people see screaming in anger as healthy; others find screaming unacceptable.

Changing Behavior in Toddlers   Here is a summary of six approaches to changing undesirable behavior in toddlers:

1. Teach socially acceptable behavior. Modeling is one of your most effective teaching methods. Children naturally pick up your behavior—make sure it is the behavior you want to teach.
2. Ignore the behavior you want to see change. Often it is being done for your benefit. (But of course don't ignore behavior that threatens safety or communicates a need—a hungry, crying baby needs to be fed, not ignored.)
3. Pay attention to behavior that is socially acceptable. Praise children publicly for being gentle with one another, for taking care of toys and equipment. Make a big fuss over desirable behavior (not undesirable behavior).
4. Restructure the situation. Perhaps there are too many choices of things to do, or not enough. Either situation can cause infants and toddlers to act in less than desirable ways. Maybe two children need to be separated for awhile.
5. Prevent harmful behavior from happening. Stop the hitting before it occurs. Catch the biting before the teeth sink in. The strong reaction children get from the children they hurt can be very rewarding. That reward is cut off when the action is not allowed to happen. Such behaviors will decrease if you stay on your toes instead of letting them happen and then dealing with them afterward.
6. Redirect the energy when appropriate. When you must restrict a child, give several other choices of things he or she can do. ("I won't let you throw the block, but you can throw the pillow or the soft ball." "I won't let you bite Maria, but you can bite this washcloth or this plastic ring.")

"Time Out"?   A word about time out. A 1987 California law pertaining to children in child care who are under the age of two reads "Confinement to cribs, high chairs, playpens or other similar furniture or equipment shall not be permitted as a form of discipline or punishment."[1] Time out, which is touted as nonpunitive, is obviously seen as harmful by California lawmakers. Time out has become an alternative to spanking because corporal punishment is illegal in California child care facilities. It is used as a blanket approach by caregivers and teachers who have limited knowledge of other means of discipline, and it ends up being quite punitive, which must be the reason for the California law.

However, time out is not punitive, ineffective, or illegal when it meets the need of a particular child at a particular time. Sometimes toddlers are out of control because of being overstimulated. They need to get out of the situation. Removing an out-of-control toddler to a quieter place for a short time helps him or her regain composure and control. Confining children, even by making them sit in a chair, as a punishment for an infraction of a rule is not the same as helping them gain control when they need to.

Once you perceive that a particular child has this need occasionally, you can help her learn to judge the situation and make the decision to leave on her own. The ultimate goal of discipline, after all, is to turn it over to the individual. Your approaches to discipline should lead eventually to self-discipline—the establishment of inner controls.

Cultural Notes   Feelings for or against the use of time out can relate to cultural differences. What has been said here about time out as an effective practice is based on a particular view of children and what they need. When privacy is a cultural value, careful use of time out makes sense. The person with that value thinks that by giving children time and space alone they can gather themselves back together and regain control. This value fits for those whose cultures stress independence and individuality. Not all cultures see the benefits of stressing those two priorities. For some, belonging in the group is more important than the notion of individuality. From a collectivist orientation, time out is like shunning and is an extreme punishment. No matter how kindly it is done, and with what intentions, cutting the child off from the group is punishment. It's important to be sensitive to differences in perspective.

Another difference in perspective relates to notions of authority. In her book *Other People's Children,* Lisa Delpit discusses the problem of the way some European-Americans speak to children as compared with some African-Americans.[2] The soft-spoken request for a certain behavior is not recognized by some children as a command. They are more used to hearing the command form of the verb (tempered or not): "Sit down, please." "Stop banging your cup." These children may not pay attention to other forms of guiding behavior. A pleasant voice saying "It's not safe to stand up" or "I don't like it when you bang your cup" is ignored. Children who ignore adults whose tone or words don't convey authority can end up being labeled as problems. That isn't fair! Caregivers should be sensitive to children's differing backgrounds and learn to speak their language, even if it's just another form of English. That doesn't mean that those adults can't continue to behave in authentic ways that feel comfortable to them. It does mean that they have to *teach* children in their care that they mean it when they make a soft-spoken statement that sounds indirect. They teach by following up with action when the words alone don't work, which is a good approach to use with anybody's children!

One last point: not all cultures see the goal of discipline as establishing "inner controls." From some perspectives, discipline always comes from an outside authority, whether it's a person or group pressure. Discipline is not something that is inside but is external to the individual.[3] Children who expect to be monitored may feel justified in misbehaving if no one is paying attention. Again, this difference in views of controlling behavior (internal control or external control) may result in a situation where children from diverse backgrounds end up labeled as problems unless caregivers are aware of the difference.

MODELING SELF-ESTEEM BY TAKING CARE OF YOURSELF

It may seem strange to find a section on taking care of yourself in a book that focuses on caring for infants and toddlers. But many caregivers are very poor models for the children they work with. The job demands sacrifice, it is true, and you need to put your own needs last quite often. But the job also demands high self-esteem. Children need to be around adults who see themselves as worthy, who respect and care for themselves. The opposite of the worthy adult is the adult whom everyone tramples on—the children, the parents, and the coworkers.

No one can tell you how to increase your worth in your own eyes, but here is some advice on how to take care of yourself. First, take care of your needs. You have the same range of needs that the children have (that is, physical, intellectual, emotional, and social needs). Don't neglect yourself. Eat right, exercise, pamper your body regularly with a swim, a hot bath, a walk, whatever it enjoys most. Take regular breaks at work, even if that's hard to arrange. Find a way. Stimulate your mind with a good book, a class, a game of chess. People who work with children sometimes feel as if their minds are decaying. Don't let that happen to you. Feel your feelings; don't stuff them. Learn to express them in ways that are healthy for you and the children. Find ways to use anger to help you solve problems or gather needed energy for making changes. Nurture your social life. Build relationships. Build a broad base of support. Don't depend on just one person to support and nurture you—spread that function out to several people. The more choices you have, the less chance you'll be let down. And don't hide your relationships from the children. It's good for the children to be with an adult who relates to other adults.

Second, learn to be assertive. Say no when appropriate. Family day-care providers are especially famous for saying yes, yes, yes, until everyone in their lives is taking advantage of them. Don't let that happen to you.

Third, learn conflict management. Negotiation and mediation skills are important, in working not only with children but also with adults.

Fourth, learn time management. This set of skills helps you immeasurably by teaching you to use the time you have in ways that benefit you most.

Fifth, find ways to explain the importance of your job so that you can be proud of it. Don't apologize for what you do. The first years are the most important ones. The high school teacher or the college professor touches lives minimally and makes little difference compared to you. The people who rear children (that is, you and the parents) are the people responsible for the future of their country.

And finally, play. Adults need to play just as children need to play. You may even be able to find a way to play at work and do your job at the same time. Play renews energy and brings out a creative spirit.

This chapter has covered a lot of territory—from *caring about* each child that you *care for* (and how to work toward that goal if it doesn't happen naturally) to taking *care of* yourself, with stops along the way to look at self-concept from the view of culture, gender, and discipline. The social environment is made up of all these factors and more! The next chapter examines another programmatic issue: adult relationships. Although it is in a chapter by itself, this topic is part of the social environment.

Thought/Activity Questions

1. Try visualization to see a child differently. Pick a child whose behavior bothers you and try the exercise outlined in this chapter.
2. Imagine yourself in a culturally assaultive environment. If you can't imagine such an environment, pick an environment you feel most comfortable in and imagine its opposite. How would it feel to spend a good part of your waking hours in such an environment? What relationship do your own imaginings and experience have to caring for culturally diverse children?
3. Observe adults interacting with infants and toddlers. Can you see any ways they treat the boys and girls differently? Do they tend to comment on girls' appearance and nurturing qualities? Do they tend to comment on boys' strength and capabilities?
4. Imagine yourself working in a toddler program using the principles of this book and the ideas about discipline outlined in this chapter. You are confronted with a hard-to-handle child whose parent thinks she acts that way because you aren't behaving the way her daughter expects an authority to behave. Create a dialogue between you and this parent.

Notes

1. California State Health and Safety Code, Title 22 Child Care Facility Licensing, Subchapter 2. Infant Care Centers. Section 101423.1, Infant Care Discipline.
2. Lisa Delpit, *Other People's Children,* New York: New Press, 1995.
3. In *Black Children: Their Roots, Culture, and Learning Styles,* Janice Hale-Benson discusses how discipline works in the black community. Every adult in the community is expected to firmly correct undesirable behavior even when someone else's child is the one misbehaving. Any misbehavior is not only immediately corrected but reported to the parent as well. In other words, in the black community, there is a social control network that takes responsibility for all the children in that community. Children aren't on their own; they're always being watched by somebody. Hale-Benson says that this approach is different from that in schools, where the teachers don't watch so closely because they expect the children to develop inner controls. Therefore, children who are used to being diligently observed and controlled find themselves more on their own than they're used to. Parents who expect to be notified immediately of any misbehavior may find school a lax place where there seem

to be fewer external pressures to keep children behaving properly. See Janice E. Hale-Benson, *Black Children: Their Roots, Culture, and Learning Styles* (Baltimore: Johns Hopkins University Press, 1986), p. 85.

For Further Reading

Affirming Children's Roots: Cultural and Linguistic Diversity in Early Care and Education (San Francisco: California Tomorrow, 1993).

Amy Laura Dombro, Laura J. Colker, and Diane Trister Dodge, *Creative Curriculum for Infants and Toddlers* (Washington, D.C.: Teaching Strategies, 1997).

Lorraine DeJong and Barbara Hansen Cottrell, "Designing Infant Child Care Programs to Meet the Needs of Children Born to Teenage Parents," *Young Children* 54(1), January 1999, pp. 37–45.

Lyn Fasoli and Janet Gonzalez-Mena, "Let's Be Real: Authenticity in Child Care," *Exchange,* March 1997.

S. Feinman, ed., *Social Referencing and the Social Construction of Reality in Infancy* (New York: Plenum, 1992).

Lilly Wong Fillmore, "A Question for Early-Childhood Programs: English First or Families First?" *Education Week,* June 19, 1991.

Magda Gerber, *Dear Parent: Caring for Infants with Respect* (Los Angeles: Resources for Infant Educarers, 1998).

Janet Gonzalez-Mena, "Observation Involves More Than Just Looking," *Educaring* 15(4), Fall 1994, p. 4.

Janet Gonzalez-Mena and Judith K. Bernhard, "Out-of-Home Care of Infants and Toddlers: A Call for Cultural and Linguistic Continuity," *Interaction* 12(2), Summer 1998.

Janet Gonzalez-Mena and Navaz Bhavnagri, "Diversity and Infant/Toddler Caregiving," *Young Children,* in press.

Jim Greenman and Anne Stonehouse, *Prime Times* (St. Paul, Minn.: Redleaf, 1996).

Stanley I. Greenspan, "Emotional Development in Infants and Toddlers," in *Infant/Toddler Caregiving: A Guide to Social-Emotional Growth and Socialization,* edited by J. R. Lally (Sacramento, Calif: California Department of Education, 1990).

Michael Gurian, *The Wonder of Boys* (New York: Tarcher/Putnam, 1997).

Edward T. Hall, *Beyond Culture* (Garden City, N.Y.: Anchor Press/Doubleday, 1981).

Fran Hast and Ann Hollyfield, *Infant and Toddler Experiences* (St. Paul, Minn.: Redleaf, 1999).

Beverly A. Kovach and Denise A. Da Ros, "Respectful, Individual, and Responsive Caregiving for Infants: The Key to Successful Care in Group Settings," *Young Children* 53(3), 1998, pp. 61–64.

J. Ronald Lally, "The Impact of Child Care Policies and Practices on Infant/Toddler Identity Formation," *Young Children* 51(1), November 1995, pp. 58–67.

J. Ronald Lally, Abbey Griffin, Emily Fenichel, Marilyn Segal, Eleanor Szanton, and Bernice Weissbourd, *Caring for Infants and Toddlers in Groups* (Washington, D.C.: Zero to Three, 1995).

Robin Leavitt, *Power and Emotion in Infant-Toddler Day Care* (New York: State University of New York Press, 1994).

Dorothy Lee, *Valuing the Self* (Englewood Cliffs, N.J.: Prentice-Hall, 1976).

Alicia F. Lieberman, *The Emotional Life of the Toddler* (New York: Free Press, 1993).

Judith Leipzig, "Helping Whole Children Grow: Non-Sexist Childrearing for Infants and Toddlers," in *Alike and Different: Exploring Our Humanity with Young Children,* edited by Bonnie Neugebauer (Redmond, Wash.: Exchange Press, 1987).

Mary Benson McMullen, "Achieving Best Practices in Infant and Toddler Care and Education," *Young Children* 54(4), July 1999, pp. 69–76.

Barbara J. Myers, Heather Carmichael Olson, and Karol Kaltenbach, "Cocaine-Exposed Infants: Myths and Misunderstandings," *Zero to Three* 13(1), June 1992, pp. 1–5.

Carol Brunson Phillips and Renatta M. Cooper, "Cultural Dimensions of Feeding Relationships," *Zero to Three* 12(5), June 1992, pp. 10–13.

William Pollack, *Real Boys: Rescuing Our Sons from the Myths of Boyhood* (New York: Owl Books, 1998).

Martha W. Pratt, "The Importance of Infant/Toddler Interactions," *Young Children* 54(4), July 1999, pp. 26–29.

Judy Reinsberg, "Understanding Young Children's Behavior," *Young Children* 54(4), July 1999, pp. 54–57.

Eleanor Reynolds, *Guiding Young Children: A Child-Centered Approach* (Mountain View, Calif.: Mayfield, 1990).

Mike and Nancy Samuels, *Seeing with the Mind's Eye* (New York: Random House, 1975).

Lyndall Shick, *Understanding Temperament* (Seattle: Parenting Press, 1998).

Evelyn B. Thoman and Sue Browder, *Born Dancing: The Relaxed Parents' Guide to Making Babies Smart with Love* (New York: Harper and Row, 1987).

Jane C. Warrent, Carla Oswald Reed, Susan Manker-Seale, and Lani A. Comp, "CHILDSPACE—Creating an Environment of Respect for Infants and Toddlers and Caregivers of Children," *Zero to Three* 7(4), April 1992, pp. 21–28.

Donna Wittmer and Sandra Petersen, "Social Development and Integration: Facilitating the Prosocial Development of Typical and Exceptional Infants and Toddlers in Group Settings," *Zero to Three* 7(4), April 1992, pp. 14–20.

CHAPTER 14

Adult Relations: Parent and Staff

Even though left until the end, the subject of parent-caregiver relations is very important. Every professional who provides a service to others must develop a relationship with his or her clients. In the field of infant-toddler care, this relationship with the client, that is, the parent(s), is vital because it affects the relationship of the children to the caregiver.

Although the term *parent* occurs in this chapter title and throughout the chapter, it is important to recognize that in many cases it is the *family* to whom the staff or provider must relate. It is worthwhile to understand lines of authority and responsibility within each family.[1]

PARENT-CAREGIVER RELATIONS

Sometimes caregivers forget that their client is the parent(s) and not the child alone. They make their own decisions about what to do for the child without consulting parents as to their goals and desires. They may even have feelings of competition with the parent. If these competitive feelings are strong enough, they result in a "savior complex," when caregivers see their role as rescuing children from their parents. The savior complex is a stage many of us go through when we first find ourselves in charge of someone else's children.

The caregiver as savior is an interesting phenomenon. Not only is she out to save each child in her care from his parents (with a few exceptions, of course), but she plans to save the whole world through what she is doing with children! Stage-one caregivers ride around on their high horses looking down on parents.

Most people move out of that stage when they realize that their charge is only part time and temporary. They may influence children for part of the day while they are in child care, but the parents are the predominant and permanent force in children's lives. It is the parents who give the child a sense of connection with the past and a view of the future. About the same time caregivers come to see the importance of parents in children's lives, they also begin to see individual parents' points of view. Caregivers in this second stage have more understanding about what influences the parents' child-raising practices.

During the second stage, caregivers come to see parents as the client. While still in the glow of the savior complex, caregivers work to change parents—to educate them. The difference between a stage-one and a stage-two caregiver is the perception of who the client is. The savior effect is still in operation as caregivers see themselves as superior substitutes for parents.

The final stage comes when caregivers see themselves as partners—as supplements and supports to parents rather than substitutes. The parent and caregiver *share* in the care of the child. This stage brings on a mutual relationship in which the caregiver and parent communicate openly, even when conflicts arise. In this stage, the caregiver is clear about how important it is to do nothing that weakens children's sense of belonging to their own family.

Being a support, a surrogate, a supplement doesn't make you any less professional. Look at architects. Their job is not to impose ideas on the client but rather to take the client's ideas and needs and, using professional expertise, come up with something that works as well as pleases. Communication is an important part of the process.

The architect's responsibility is considerably less than that of a caregiver. The architect's goal is merely a structure; the caregiver is dealing with human lives.

Communication with Parents

The California state regulations governing licensing of infant-toddler facilities obviously place value on communication between client and professional— between parent and caregiver. They mandate cooperation in planning for infant care in centers. Licensing requires written plans for care developed mutually by caregiver and parent and signed by the parent. The law reads as follows:

> Prior to the infant's first day at the center, the infant care center director or assistant director shall complete a needs and services plan. Such plan shall be completed with the assistance of the infant's parent at the personal interview specified in Section 101219.1. The parent's or guardian's participation in the preparation of the plan shall be verified by the parent's or guardian's signature on the plan. The needs and services plan shall be in writing and shall include the following:

1. The individual feeding plan.
2. The individual toilet learning plan if applicable.
3. Any services needed by the child that are different from those provided by the center's normal program.
4. A plan for subsequent personal interviews with the parent or guardian.

Of course, mandated communication (such as the state of California imposes) is not nearly so successful as communication that occurs because both parties want it to.

Service Plan: Focus on Child

What kinds of information should be discussed in the development of a needs and services plan? Parents should make caregivers aware of their children's habits, special needs, ways of communicating, and daily routines. Such information should include when and how much the child sleeps, how the child goes to sleep, and the child's eating habits, needs, likes and dislikes, bowel function, liquid intake and output, cuddling needs, comfort devices, and so on. These should be talked over when the child enters the program and on a daily basis thereafter. It may be hard to find "talking time," and shift changes may mean the child's caregiver is not present when the parent arrives, but simple written records give the information that may be of great importance to the parent. (Did he just have a snack, or is he crying because he is hungry? How long did he sleep? Can I expect him to go right to sleep when we get home, or did he just wake up from a nap? Did he move his bowels?) Older children can express their needs. Younger children can't, and parents need all the information they can get to help determine just what children need when they get them home.

Although difficult to find time to do it, writing down anecdotes is also useful because some parents appreciate hearing about what went on that day. But be careful about leaving a parent feeling guilty about the child's behavior. It's up to you to guide and control behavior while you are with the child. If you had a hard time that day, don't blame the parent for it. Also when you're relating positive anecdotes, be careful that you don't make parents feel left out because of all the cute things the child did that they missed. If the child took a first step that day, you want to weigh your own excitement with the parents' possible disappointment of not having been there to see it.

Be sure that while you're conveying information you are also listening. You need information too—about what happens in the other part of the child's life. Is she particularly fussy this week because something is going on at home? Is he tired today because he didn't sleep much last night, or might he be coming down with something? Are her bowels loose because of something she ate that didn't agree with her, or might she have picked up an infection? Listening is half of communicating.

Service Plan: Focus on Family

The Parent Services Project (P.S.P.), which was started in California by Ethel Seiderman and is now nationwide, addresses the development of the child and family together. Each participating program has a plan that includes services to the parents, not just a service plan for the child. The idea is to assure the well-being of the parents as a way of caring for their children. One way to promote well-being is to bring parents together in ways that foster community building as parents make connections and develop social networks.

Lisa Lee and others in the national headquarters of the organization train child care professionals to focus on positive attitudes about working with parents and practical activities to serve the family. The program builds on family strengths and resources and regards cultural sensitivity and inclusion an important part of the work. What kinds of activities are written into the service plan? The activities differ from program to program depending on what the families in the particular program need and want. Each P.S.P. program is tailor-made, so no two are exactly alike. A typical sampling might include a menu of adult activities, such as support groups, classes, workshops, leadership opportunities; family fun activities, such as Friday night pizza parties with a rented video for entertainment; field trips on weekends to the beach, to an amusement park, to the zoo; specialized child care such as respite care, sick child care; programs for men, for grandparents, for foster parents; multicultural experiences; mental health activities.

The following is a summary of the principles under which the P.S.P. programs operate. They should be guiding principles for *all* child care programs. The way to ensure the health and well-being of the children is to ensure the health and well-being of their parents. Parents are the child's primary teachers, and they know the child best. The relationship between parents and staff is one of equality and respect. Parents make their own choices about the services they want. Programs and services are voluntary. Programs build on parents' strengths and are ethnically relevant and community-based. Each community sets its own reality based on what is good for it. Social support networks are a crucial element in the happiness, healthiness, and productivity of people. The full set of principles is listed in appendix D.

Communication Blocks

Sometimes it's hard to listen when you are angry with a parent. The source of your anger can be something as simple as a personality conflict or as deep as a basic attitude toward parents who leave their children to go off to work—especially when it seems there is no financial reason to do so. Ironically, some caregivers feel ambivalent about child care and whether or not it is good for children. Some family day-care providers decide it is better for them to stay home with their children than go out to work, so they go into the business of caring for the children of other mothers who leave home to work. If a woman who made this choice sees it as a sacrifice, she may resent a mother who arrives in the morning well dressed, happy, and about to embark on what the caregiver perceives to be a more socially or intellectually stimulating day. This is an unfortunate situation and can cause hard feelings between caregivers and parents. A first step to solving this problem comes when the caregiver faces such feelings squarely, recognizing that anger or annoyance over child or parent behavior really springs from this particular source. What to do about it will become clearer once the feelings are acknowledged.

Sometimes it's hard to listen because a parent is angry. Parental anger is often misplaced—centering on some minor issue instead of the real source. Parents may cover their insecurities, their conflicting feelings, their feelings of guilt and stress with anger. Parents may sense uncomfortable competition— real or not—between themselves and the caregiver. Parents often feel threatened by competent caregivers. They worry that they are losing their children as they see them express affection for the caregiver. Parents who feel insecure about parenting skills may hide that insecurity by acting extra wise or knowledgeable—even pushy. If you listen carefully enough, you may be able to detect the real message behind the words. Just as when children feel insecure you try to bolster their confidence in themselves, point out their strengths and competencies, and steer them toward successes, so you can take the same approach with an insecure parent.

Some parents actually need parenting themselves. They look to you as wise and capable and lean on you for support. You have to decide how much of this need you can fulfill. You can't be everything to everyone, and this parent's needs may be one burden too many for you. Then you have to decide whether you can put the energy into supporting the parent while you help him or her become self-sufficient, whether you have to redirect the parent to someone else, or whether you have to just set a limit and say no. Sometimes you can get parents together with each other, and they will form a mutual support system.

Sometimes it's hard to listen when you feel you're being attacked. You end up defending yourself instead of allowing the other person to really express what is on his or her mind. For example, a parent may say that all her child does is play in your program, and she wishes he were learning something. If you get defensive, show anger, and close down communication, you may never have a chance to create the kind of dialogue in which you can listen to each others' points of view. But if you are able to listen, eventually you'll have a chance to point out all the child is learning through the caregiving and free play.

Opening Up Communication

You can open the communication by letting the parents know you heard them. This can be done as simply as restating their own words, which allows them to correct you or explain further. As you establish a dialogue, you'll be able to get a better picture of what parents want as well as explain your approach and what you believe in.

Besides day-to-day communication, periodic informal conferences can be helpful to gain insights and set long-range goals. It is important to help parents feel secure about such a conference. They may perceive themselves as being in the "hot seat." Some parents arrive at conferences with all the old feelings left from report card sessions in their elementary or high school days. In such situations, you need to do all you can to relax them and make them feel comfortable so you have real communication.

Start by looking at the environment in which you will conduct the conference. If you sit behind a desk with a file folder in front of you and a wall of reference books behind you, that sets a certain tone to the proceedings in which you are an expert, removed from the amateurs—the parents. Any insecurities they arrive with will be magnified in this setting.

Because you are on your own territory, it is especially important that you make the parents feel welcome and at home. If you know educational, psychological, or developmental jargon, try not to use it. That gets harder as you begin to see yourself as a professional. After all, professionals have their own way of talking that sets them apart. But just think how you appreciate the doctor who can explain your symptoms without sending you off to a medical encyclopedia. At the same time, don't talk down to parents. It's hard to communicate openly when one party is being patronizing.

If you have a specific goal for the conference, state it at the beginning. If it is to be just an informal give and take, state that. Don't leave parents wondering why they have been asked to this conference. Use conferences to examine issues between you, explore problems and questions concerning the child, decide on ways to approach behavior that needs changing, exchange information, and develop goals. If the child is present at the conference, don't talk around him or her. Include the child in the conversation (even babies).

Issues of Parents of Special-Needs Children

Recognize that parents of special-needs children may have an extra set of issues that other parents don't have when they come to a conference with you. They may be in denial about their child's condition. Denial is a normal stage in coming to grips with something as serious as giving birth to a baby with special needs. Be gentle and understanding with parents in denial, and be patient about helping them beyond this stage. It may take some time.

Some parents of children with special needs carry a heavy burden of guilt. They may not show this guilt to you, but it may affect your relations with them, especially if they have a sense that you blame them.

Anger may also be present in these parents. Though it may come out at you, it may well have nothing to do with you personally. Approach the parents' anger the way you do children's anger. Allow them to express their feelings without getting defensive or angry back.

Realize that these parents may have had a number of dealings with "experts" before they met you, and they may bring the issues from these experiences to their conference with you. Of course, not all parents of special-needs infants and toddlers will bring anger, guilt, or unresolved issues to their conferences with you. Some will have had positive experiences in working together with "experts" and will be ready to establish a partnership with you, their child's caregiver. But others will come with a load on their back, and if you recognize this fact, you can deal with it.

Sometimes parents and caregivers have disparate needs or differences of opinion that put them in conflict with one another. Just listening isn't enough; what is needed is a problem-solving or conflict resolution approach. When this happens, it is important both to listen and to express your own feelings and position. When you have defined the problem, then brainstorm potential solutions. Try to keep out of a blaming mode and in a problem-solving mode. Here is an example of that process in a not-so-unusual day-care situation:

A mother arrives, obviously in a hurry. She greets the caregiver, grabs a diaper bag from a shelf, and enters the room to pick up her daughter. Her daughter runs toward her, arms outstretched. The mother starts to smile, then takes a look at the knees of her little pink pants, which are bright green with grass stains. A big frown takes over the mother's face. She picks her daughter up a little brusquely. Muttering to herself, she strides over to the nearest caregiver.

"How did this happen?" Her voice sounds strained. The caregiver looks concerned and seems to be weighing her words before she responds.

"We were outside this morning—it must have happened then. I'm sorry. I can see that you're pretty upset about it."

"You bet I am!" the mother spits back at her.

"It's going to be hard to get out," the caregiver says understandingly.

"Yes, it is." There is a pause in the conversation. The caregiver waits, still attentive to the mother. She seems to be waiting to see if the mother wants to say more. Then she adds, "You must be pretty mad at us."

At that the mother explodes. The words rush out on top of one another, first about her anger and then about how she is going to meet her fiancé's mother, and it's important that her daughter look her very best. She talks about how insecure she feels around the new family that she's about to become a part of. When she's finished, she looks a lot better. The frown is gone, replaced by a slightly nervous look.

"Do you have time to sit down for a minute?" the caregiver asks kindly.

"Not really," replies the mother, sitting down anyway. She's holding her daughter with tenderness now, and the child plays with her hair.

"I'm just wondering how we could keep this from happening next time," says the caregiver tentatively.

"You could keep her inside," says the mother immediately.

"I hate to do that," says the caregiver. "She loves to be outside."

"Yes, I know," admits the mother.

"Besides," continues the caregiver, "there are times when we are all outside, and there's no one inside to watch her."

"Well," says the mother hesitantly, "I suppose I could send her in jeans—but she looks so cute in her little outfits. . . . When I'm going someplace after work, like today, I want her to look nice." She thinks for a minute. "I guess it makes more sense to dress her up when I pick her up than to expect her to keep an outfit nice all day."

"It would sure make us feel better to have her in jeans instead of trying to keep her from getting her clothes dirty."

"Yes, I guess I can understand that. Well," she says, standing up, "I really do have to go. Thanks for listening to me."

This problem was resolved quickly and easily by the caregiver listening and not getting defensive and angry herself. This particular problem of clothes is not always solved so easily. Some parents do not want their children to be away from home in anything but good clothes. They won't be persuaded so easily that it's better for everybody if the child arrives in play clothes with sturdy knees. Sometimes this reflects a cultural attitude about "school" and has to do with the family wishing to retain a certain image. A cross-cultural conflict like that would take a lot more talking, brainstorming, and problem solving.

Communicating with parents whose culture is different from yours may be very difficult; yet it is important that you accept the parents' ways of doing things as much as possible and try to carry out their wishes. That is easy to do when the ways and the wishes don't tread on your theories of what is good for children. It's much harder when what the parents want is in conflict with what you think is right. The problem is that theories are culturally bound—there is no one right answer, no one truth. I forget that now and then when I get carried away telling people what is good for babies. I have to remember to listen to their ideas rather than just sell mine. The danger in writing a book like this is that it is culturally bound; even the experience and research behind it is culturally bound. For that reason, when you are deciding what is good for babies and toddlers, you have to take culture into consideration.

And while you're looking at culture, you also have to look at generation as a determiner of perspective. The generation gap is real. If you're a grandmother and the parents of the children in your care are much younger, they may well have a different way of looking at what's good for children, even if they are of the same culture you are. The experience differential doesn't explain all the differences; you have to consider the times in which the person grew up. Or if you're twenty and many of the parents are twice your age, you have to recognize that they may have a different view. One isn't right and the other wrong; they are just different.

A gender difference may create a communication gap. The way a father perceives his child may be different from the way a mother does. Male caregivers' responses, reactions, and understandings of children may be different, because of their gender, from those of female caregivers.

Whether communication comes easily or not because of age, gender, or cultural differences or just individual differences, there are some ways that you can facilitate it. Here are some tips for opening and maintaining lines of communication with parents:

- Regard communication as a two-way process. If you're having problems with a child's behavior, the parent probably is too. Make it easy to exchange information.
- Develop your listening skills. Learn to listen for the feelings behind the words, and discover ways to encourage parents to express those feelings without offending you.
- Develop a problem-solving attitude, and learn techniques of communication, mediation, and negotiation to use during conflict management and resolution.
- Keep records so you can report specifics.
- Make time available when it is clear that a parent needs to talk. It helps to have a comfortable place to sit.
- Try to talk to each parent every day at arrival and pickup, even if you're busy.
- Try to make parents feel welcome whenever they are around—even if they pop in and disturb your program. In some teen parent programs on high school campuses, mothers come by between classes. It is hard on some of the children for a while because they to have to learn to handle the more frequent hellos and good-byes. But it is important for the staff to be understanding about these parents' needs even though it makes their job harder.

PARENT EDUCATION

Your job is not only infant and toddler education but parent education as well. Education involves not just knowledge, but knowledge along with attitudes and skills. If you build a relationship, parents will be influenced by you in all these areas. But if you set yourself up as an expert and try to teach them directly, you're bound to run into trouble. Knowledge alone doesn't change attitudes. They change over time with exposure to different people's values, ideas, methods, and attitudes. Most parents leave a program knowing more and feeling different from when they first enrolled, even if they never attend any kind of formal lecture on parenting or child development. Over time they will pick up knowledge of child development by watching other children and seeing what is common behavior, by reading what you make available, and by asking questions and getting into discussions with you. You may set up discussion groups or even have parent meetings with guest speakers to augment this knowledge building that happens naturally when parents spend any time around a center—even just short drop-off and pickup sessions.

Parents of Children with Special Needs

Parents of special-needs children may need to learn different things than other parents. If these parents have not been exposed to other children before they come to your program, at first they may learn more than they want to know about normal development. It can come as a great shock to some parents to compare their children for the first time to children who don't have special needs. Be extra sensitive to their feelings.

Most parents are eager to learn more if they don't feel threatened or pushed. An invitation to observe or participate either occasionally or regularly is welcomed by many parents and is a further means to parent education. In a family day-care home, a father regularly stayed an extra half hour in the afternoon when he had time. He would sit and play the piano and interact with the children who approached him. He not only contributed to the program but he gained knowledge just by being there.

Skill building comes gradually too. Parents come to you with varying degrees of parenting skills. Most will gain more by being exposed to professional caregivers. However, a danger lurks when caregivers present themselves as models for parents. The parent role is different from your role as a professional caregiver, though it may look very similar at times. You don't have the parent's involvement or commitment. You don't have the shared history, nor will you be part of the child's future. You don't have the intensity of interest that brings about passionate exchanges. If the child "behaves just fine" with you and becomes a tyrant when the parent arrives, don't brag or feel superior. The explanation for the contrast is more likely to relate to the normal parent-child relationship and strong attachment than to your seemingly superior competence.

Children need competent caregivers, but they also need totally human, emotional, and connected parents. What you see as poor handling of a situation is more likely a parental handling rather than a professional handling. The two are different—though each should have many elements of the other. Parents operate (and should operate) from the gut level, reacting emotionally rather than responding reasonably. Of course, parents should also use their heads, should be objective now and then, and should build some of the competencies you have (which will happen to some extent through observing you). They should also gather information about child development and caregiving so they can *think* about what they are doing. But they should still parent mostly from gut reactions rather than from thought-out approaches. Parents should be far more human than competent. Caregivers should also be human and step out of their usual role now and then and interact intensely and passionately with children; but they should mostly be fairly objective and thoughtful in goals and reactions.

If you are both a parent and a caregiver, you can probably understand when you think about those times you handled things differently as a parent of your own child than you would have as the caregiver of someone else's. Perhaps at the time you felt guilty. But if you look at role differences, you can be glad that you are a normal parent. Your children deserve a real parent, not a professional caregiver. And other people's children deserve professional caregivers, not more parents.

That doesn't mean a professional caregiver should be cold and detached. If you've read this far in this book, you know that the message throughout has been to be real, to get connected, to feel your feelings. The point is balance. The balance swings more to feelings and spontaneity in the parenting role and more to thoughtfulness, objectivity, and planning in the caregiver role.

Relating to the Parents of a Child Who Isn't Doing Well

Sometimes, in spite of all your efforts in the parent relations and parent education department, you may have a child in your care who isn't doing well. He or she may be disrupting your whole program, taking a large portion of your time so that you have to worry about neglecting the other children. If you're in a center, the first step is to talk to other staff members (and the director). If you're in a family day-care home, you may not have such a clearly defined problem-solving support group with which to discuss issues like this, but it is important that you find somebody—another day-care provider perhaps.

You'll also want to talk to the parent(s)—not to place blame, but to get additional perspectives on the problem and further ideas for strategies to find ways to meet this child's needs. Teamwork and cooperation at home and in the program may work.

Or nothing may work. After trying and assessing various strategies, you may find that the child's behavior is still causing considerable turmoil. You'll probably also come to the conclusion that the situation isn't good for you, the other children, *or* the child. It is hard to realize that you can't meet every child's needs to the fullest extent. You may resist the idea that you can't be everything this particular family needs.

The next step is a referral. Perhaps some outside source can be of assistance to this family. Often that works. With specialized help the situation becomes tolerable, and you find you can meet the child's needs. But sometimes you have to realize that you've done all you can for a particular child, and it's time to ask the family to find care elsewhere. This is an extremely painful process for all concerned, but sometimes a necessary one.

CAREGIVER RELATIONS

Staff relations are of extreme importance in a job as demanding as day care. In a family day-care home, you don't have staff relations; instead the issue is family relations, which is somewhat different. We'll deal with this subject briefly before discussing center staffs.

The Family Child Care Provider

Getting support is valuable if you are a family day-care provider. But if the rest of your family is resentful, it may be hard to get their support. One family day-care provider sat down and wrote out a contract with her family—husband and two preteen children—before she went into business. She felt it was important to be clear about the use of the house, which belonged to all four, and about what was or was not expected of each family member regarding the children in care. This contract was not something she forced them into; it was an agreement that they built together, considering everyone's ideas and feelings. In this family, the children were old enough to understand the contract, their rights, and their obligations. The contract saved the family a good deal of conflict.

In many day-care families, conflict is the name of the game. If the children are younger, it's hard for them to understand why they have to share room, toys, even "mommy." Usually the agreements are less clear than a written and negotiated contract. As a result, a good deal of resentment, tension, and friction can arise. Some friction is, of course, normal but may be unexpected when a provider first goes into business. But in most families the advantages outweigh the disadvantages, and the friction falls into place with the other ordinary family conflicts.

Family day-care providers should also look for support outside their own families. It is hard because you're tied to your home all day every weekday, but if you look, you can find other family day-care providers to talk to. The provider who worked out the contract with her family found another family day-care provider in her own neighborhood through attending local support meetings. The two meet regularly at the park with their children (it is a short walk), so they have adult company as well as an outing for the children. No one can listen with more understanding to a family day-care provider than another family day-care provider. Find someone to talk to if you haven't already.

Center Staff

In a center setting, staff relations are different because you work together and are not related to one another. It's a strange situation to be around adults all day but seldom focus on them. That can create problems because you have little time to sit down and talk things out. Most day-care staffs have staggered schedules, so the only time all the staff is there together is during the busiest time of the day, when the adults have little time to relate to each other. Some staffs working with older children are able to get together during nap time, but that won't work for most infant center staffs. In many centers, even breaks are staggered so that no two staff members are off the floor at the same time.

If day care were like other fields, there would be built-in time for staff meetings, for staff training, even provisions for staff renewal. But for most programs on a tight budget, those are unaffordable luxuries.

Obviously, staff members can seldom get off and talk to each other without the children around. And they need to talk to establish relationships, to settle conflicts, to share information on children and families, to set goals, to evaluate, and to share resources. Most of all they need adult contact to alleviate the isolation that adults who spend many hours a day with children commonly feel.

If you are new to the field and in a training program where you learn to focus almost exclusively on the children, you may be surprised to come into a center and see adults sitting around talking to each other while the children play. You may be quite critical if your training has made it sacrilege to focus on anything but the children when you are working (except on break). But over time, you may come to realize that those talks are important to staff members who work all day every day with very young children. And they are important to the children. How else are children to see adults relating to adults if their daily contact consists only of adults who focus on them and ignore the other adults present? Children need to see adults exhibit a wider range of behavior than what they see when the adults relate only to them.

In a three-hour program, it is still preferable to see adults concentrate mostly on the children, but that expectation is neither realistic nor desirable in all-day care. Of course, it isn't good policy to focus on adult relationships to the exclusion of the children and to the point of neglecting their needs. But if each child gets plenty of "wants nothing" quality time, when the caregiver is available to him or her during free play, as well as "wants something" quality time during caregiving activities when the focus is on the individual child, the adult can relate to other adults while the children are present without neglecting the children.

This chapter has been about adult relations and their importance to the children in day care. Children need to see their caregivers as full human beings, and they can't if they don't see them in relation to other adults—their parents as well as other staff members.

Thought/Activity Questions

1. If you are a caregiver, which caregiver stage of development are you in at present? Are you saving children from their parents, educating the parents to be as good as

you are, or seeing parents as partners? Can you think of someone who is in a different stage from you? How do your perceptions, behaviors, and attitudes contrast with one another?

2. If a baby took the first step while in your care, would you tell the parent? What considerations would go into your decision?

3. Suppose you are a caregiver and a parent is very angry about something you did with her child. How would you handle this situation?

4. Suppose you work with someone from a culture different from your own who has very different ideas about child rearing and caregiving. What steps would you take to open up communication between the two of you?

Note

1. A teenage parent may rely on her mother or at least need to consult with her mother. A wife may need her husband's approval to make decisions. Sometimes the grandmother, rather than the parents, makes decisions concerning her grandchildren. Some families have joint decision making. It's of no use to discuss a problem with a mother if she has no authority to make any decision. The family structures in some cultures leave someone other than the mother or even the father as the ultimate decision maker.

For Further Reading

T. Berry Brazelton, *Working and Caring* (Reading, Mass.: Addison-Wesley, 1987).

California State Health and Safety Code, Title 22 Child Care Facility Licensing Subchapter 2. Infant Care Centers. Section 101423.1, Infant Care Discipline.

Ellen Galinsky, "Parents and Teacher-Caregivers: Sources of Tension, Sources of Support," *Young Children,* March 1988, pp. 4–12.

Magda Gerber, *Dear Parent: Caring for Infants with Respect* (Los Angeles: Resources for Infant Educarers, 1998).

Janet Gonzalez-Mena, "Cross Cultural Conferences," *Exchange,* July 1997.

Janet Gonzalez-Mena, "Dialogue to Understanding across Cultures," *Exchange,* July 1999, pp. 6–8.

Janet Gonzalez-Mena, "Do You Have Cultural Tunnel Vision?" *Child Care Information Exchange,* July 1991, pp. 29–31.

Janet Gonzalez-Mena, "Mrs. Godzilla Takes On the Child Development Experts: Perspectives on Parent Education," *Child Care Information Exchange,* September 1987, pp. 25–26.

Janet Gonzalez-Mena, *Multicultural Issues in Child Care* (Mountain View, Calif.: Mayfield, 2001.)

Janet Gonzalez-Mena, "Raising a 'Gifted' Infant," *Educaring* 8(2), Spring 1993, pp. 4–5.

Janet Gonzalez-Mena, "Understanding the Parent's Perspective: Independence or Interdependence?" *Exchange,* September 1997.

Janet Gonzalez-Mena and Navaz Bhavnagri, "Diversity and Infant/Toddler Caregiving," *Young Children,* in press.

Ann Gordon and Kathryn Williams Browne, *Guiding Young Children in a Diverse Society* (Boston: Allyn and Bacon, 1996).

Joel Gordon, "Child Care Professionalism and the Family," *Child Care Information Exchange,* July 1986, pp. 19–23.

Joel Gordon, "Separation Anxiety: How to Ask a Family to Leave Your Center," *Child Care Information Exchange,* January 1988, pp. 13–15.

Jim Greenman and Anne Stonehouse, *Prime Times* (St. Paul: Redleaf, 1996).

Elizabeth Jones, ed., *Supporting the Growth of Infants, Toddlers and Parents* (Pasadena, Calif.: Pacific Oaks, 1991).

Elizabeth Jones, *Teaching Adults: An Active Learning Approach* (Washington, D.C.: National Association for the Education of Young Children, 1986).

Margot Kaplan-Sanoff and Kathleen Fitzgerald Rice, "Working with Addicted Women in Recovery and Their Children: Lessons Learned in Boston City Hospital's Women and Infants Clinic," *Zero to Three,* 13(1), August/September 1992, pp. 17–23.

Mary Lane and Sheila Signer, *Infant/Toddler Caregiving: A Guide to Creating Partnerships with Parents* (Sacramento: California State Department of Education, 1990).

Dora Pulido Tobaissen and Janet Gonzalez-Mena, *A Place to Begin: Working with Parents on Issues of Diversity* (Oakland, Calif.: California Tomorrow, 1998).

Conclusion

Caregiving as a profession needs a boost up the status ladder. Caregiving is an *important* profession. People in whose hands the lives of our children and future lie need to be recognized for what they do.

"I'm not a baby-sitter" is the plaintive cry heard over and over from caregivers as they explain time and again that they're professionals in the early childhood education field. This is not a message the general public is ready to hear. The U.S. Department of Labor ranks the status of child care workers on the same level as parking lot attendants. It doesn't really matter who takes care of your car while you are gone, but it matters a great deal who takes care of your child. If that fact weren't immediately obvious, it is also backed up by research. According to the classic National Day Care Study, the training of the adults is what determines the quality of the program.[1] The way they relate to and interact with the children is of primary importance in outcome.

More than one group is working on improving the quality of child care and the status of its workers through professionalization. Some states require training and certification of child care workers, though requirements vary greatly from state to state. At best they mandate only minimum standards.

The largest professional group working nationally to improve the quality of care and the status of workers is the National Association for the Education of Young Children (NAEYC). The Child Development Associate (CDA) credentialing process, supported by NAEYC, has resulted in a number of child care workers nationally, including those who work with infants and toddlers, being trained and credentialed through a field-based assessment of their competencies. NAEYC has also developed an assessment process for programs that allows programs to become voluntarily accredited. The accreditation process sets high standards—above the minimum state licensing regulations.

NAEYC has taken the initiative to produce an outline of developmentally appropriate practices—guidelines to help programs and individuals understand the particular needs of each age group and respond accordingly in growth-promoting ways.[2]

NAEYC has also developed a code of ethics and continues to examine them. A code of ethics is a must for a profession, which by its very definition regulates itself and its members.

These are changing times for the field of early childhood education in general and for child care in particular. Just what the future will bring is not clear. What is clear is that the responsibility for the next generation lies not with parents alone, but with all of us. In Hawaii, there is a concept called "ohana," which means the community taking responsibility for children in an extended family kind of way. It's time for North America to incorporate the Hawaiian concept of ohana. We cannot afford to leave parents feeling isolated, alone, and burdened in their responsibility for their children.

Parents need options to choose from in order to meet their child care needs. They should have available to them a variety of quality programs, both centers and homes, staffed with well-trained personnel who earn decent salaries and enjoy reasonable benefits. Backing up these programs should be the support services so vital to keeping America's families strong—access to pediatricians, social workers, physical therapists, speech therapists, neurologists, and child and family psychotherapists.

Infant-toddler care, one of the newer stars in the child care constellation, is currently in great demand. It is vital that as we give the need for infant-toddler care the attention it demands, we direct that attention toward *quality*, the essential ingredient upon which depends healthy development. The approach in this book is dedicated to quality infant-toddler caregiving.

Notes

1. R. Ruopp, J. Travers, F. Glantz, and C. Coelen, *Children at the Center.* Final report of the National Day Care Study, vol. 1 (Washington, D.C.: Office of Human Development, Department of Health, Education and Welfare, 1979).
2. Sue Bredekamp, ed., *Developmentally Appropriate Practice in Early Childhood Programs Serving Children from Birth through Age 8.* (Washington, D.C.: National Association for the Education of Young Children, 1997).

For Further Reading

J. Ronald Lally, "The Impact of Child Care Policies and Practices on Infant/Toddler Identity Formation," *Young Children* 51(1), November 1995, pp. 58–67.

APPENDIX A

Quality in Infant-Toddler Programs: A Checklist

1. Look for evidence of a *safe* environment:
   - ☐ no obvious safety hazards, such as electric cords, open sockets, broken equipment, toys with small parts, cleaning supplies within children's reach, unsecured doorways
   - ☐ no hidden safety hazards, such as toxic paint or toys stuffed with toxic materials
   - ☐ fire and disaster plan that includes how adults will get babies outside
   - ☐ emergency numbers posted by telephone
   - ☐ parents' emergency cards on file indicating what to do when the parents can't be reached in an emergency
   - ☐ safe ratios maintained at all times (California law reads no more than four infants [children under two] to one adult.)
   - ☐ children allowed optimum risk-taking opportunities ("Optimum" means failure involves learning but not injury.)
   - ☐ interaction allowed but children protected from hurting materials or one another

2. Look for evidence of a *healthy* environment:
   - ☐ sanitary diaper changing process
   - ☐ consistent hand washing after diapering and before eating
   - ☐ proper food preparation and storage
   - ☐ staff recognizes symptoms of common illnesses
   - ☐ health policies that indicate when children are to be excluded from the program because of illness
   - ☐ health records, maintained on all children, showing evidence that their immunizations are up to date

- ☐ regular washing of sheets and toys
- ☐ staff knowledge of infant and toddler nutritional needs
- ☐ food allergies posted prominently

3. Look for evidence of a *learning* environment:
   - ☐ optimum amount of age-appropriate toys, materials, and equipment available for children to choose from
   - ☐ caregivers consider caregiving times as "learning times"
   - ☐ free play valued above exercises, adult-directed play activities, group times
   - ☐ environment includes plenty of softness, some seclusion, provisions for high mobility
   - ☐ environment developmentally appropriate for all children present any given day

4. Look for evidence that the staff's goal is to advance physical and intellectual competence:
   - ☐ staff's ability to explain how the environment, the free play, the caregiving activities, and the staff's relationship with the children make up the curriculum
   - ☐ staff's ability to explain how the curriculum promotes development of fine and gross motor skills and cognitive skills, including problem solving and communication skills

5. Look for evidence that the program supports social and emotional development and that staff members provide positive guidance and discipline:
   - ☐ staff members encourage children to develop a sense of themselves through body awareness, by using their name, and through promoting cultural identification
   - ☐ staff members recognize and accept children's feelings and encourage appropriate expression
   - ☐ staff members control and guide behavior without using either physical or verbal punishment
   - ☐ staff members encourage creative social problem solving when children experience conflict with another child
   - ☐ staff members teach respect by showing respect

6. Look for evidence that the program strives to establish positive and productive relationships with families:
   - ☐ regular and ongoing communication with parents at pickup and dropoff times emphasizing an *exchange* of information
   - ☐ friendly atmosphere
   - ☐ conferences and parent meetings
   - ☐ mutual problem-solving approach to conflicts

7. Look for evidence that the program is well run, purposeful, and responds to participants' needs:
   - ☐ good record keeping
   - ☐ attention to infants' individual needs
   - ☐ attention to parents' needs
   - ☐ responsible program management

8. Look for evidence that the staff is professional:
   - ☐ well trained
   - ☐ respect confidentiality

APPENDIX B

Environmental Chart

This chart shows how to set up both the physical and the social environments to promote development. Remember that rates of development vary a great deal among normal children. These age guides may not fit individual children, but the chart as a whole does reflect the *sequence of development*.

Level I: The Beginning of Life

Area of Development	Physical Environment	Social Environment
PHYSICAL *Large Muscles* Infants' primary task is head control • lifts head briefly • can turn head to clear nose for breathing • most arm and leg movements are reflexive and are not under infants' conscious control	**APPROPRIATE TOYS AND EQUIPMENT** • crib or bassinet, a place to feel secure while sleeping • mat, rug, or blanket in a safe space to lie unencumbered: room to move around • few toys needed yet because environment is stimulating enough	**ADULT ROLE** • use sensitive observation to determine infants' needs • provide a feeling of security when necessary (wrap infants in a blanket and place in a small enclosed space) • let infants experience wide open space, like the floor, at times

Level I: The Beginning of Life (continued)

Area of Development	Physical Environment	Social Environment
PHYSICAL *Small Muscles* • cannot control hands—often keep them clenched • grasp whatever is put into hands because of reflexive action • stare at objects, especially faces; begin to coordinate eyes	APPROPRIATE TOYS AND EQUIPMENT • faces are interesting and so is a bright-colored scarf • don't put rattles or toys into hands because they can't let go of them	ADULT ROLE • provide peace and quiet and a minimal amount of stimulation—people infants associate with (caregiver and other children) provide enough stimulation • put infants in a safe spot where they can be part of the center but not overstimulated • call infants by name • encourage infants to focus on caregiving tasks
EMOTIONAL/SOCIAL *Feelings and Self-Awareness* • infants show only satisfaction or dissatisfaction • infants do not differentiate self from the rest of the world	• infants need to be where safe and secure and needs can be easily met • large pen provides safety from more mobile toddlers (should be large enough to hold both adults and children)	• respond to infants' messages and try to determine real needs (remember that dissatisfaction is not always due to hunger) • provide for attachment needs by having a consistent caregiver • hold during feeding • provide for infant-to-infant contact • minimum adult interference: infants should be free to develop at their own rates
Social • may smile • make eye contact • are soothed by faces • respond to being held		
INTELLECTUAL • can coordinate eyes and follow objects or faces as they move • respond to faces or objects they see • suck and gum objects that come near the mouth	• infants need an interesting yet safe environment with a limited variety of soft, washable, colorful toys to be looked at or sucked on (be sure there are no small parts to come off and be swallowed) • allow space for infants to move freely (though they can't yet go anywhere)	• give them faces to look at (especially that of the primary caregiver) and opportunities to see, touch, and gum objects • don't force anything on them

- display reflexes that are the beginnings of the sensory skills, which in turn provide the basis for the development of intellectual skills

LANGUAGE
- listen
- cry
- respond to voices

- don't prop in infant seat or other restrictive device

- at this level people are more important for language development than is physical environment
- set up environment so that infants' needs are easily met and they don't have to wait for long periods of time

- place on their back so they can have a broader view, both ears can hear, and they can use their hands
- listen to infants
- try to interpret their cries
- talk to infants, especially during caregiving times; tell them what will happen; give time for a response; tell them what is happening as it happens

Level II: Month 3

Area of Development	Physical Environment	Social Environment
PHYSICAL *Large Muscles* • beginning to lose reflexes and have voluntary control of arms and legs • can lift head and control it better when held in upright position	APPROPRIATE TOYS AND EQUIPMENT • large playpen—big enough for caregivers and several infants • variety of washable objects within reach of infants for them to look at and stretch for • rug or mat for infants to lie on • avoid restrictive devices	ADULT ROLE • sit with children periodically and watch attentively • respond when called for • don't continually distract with unnecessary noise or talk; entertainment isn't necessary • allow infants freedom to explore through looking, sucking, stretching, and reaching
Small Muscles • grasp reflex no longer takes over hands all the time • reach for objects with both arms, but with hands fisted • swipe and miss	• same as above	• same as above
EMOTIONAL/SOCIAL *Feelings and Self-Awareness* • show wider variety of feelings and use voice to express them • begin to see hands and feet belong to them and begin to explore them, as well as face, eyes, and mouth, with hands • begin to recognize primary caregiver • respond differently to different people • coo and babble when talked to	• people are more important than objects	• provide for attachment needs because infants need to develop a primary relationship • recognize and respect infants' feelings: talk about what infants seem to be expressing, especially during caregiving

INTELLECTUAL

- respond to what they see
- attend longer than at first
- look from one object to another
- can hold object on their own and manipulate to some extent
- give signs of remembering
- when they hear a noise they look for the source
- look and suck at the same time, but have to stop sucking to listen

- some interesting toys and objects for infants at this level of development include bright scarves, soft balls, rattles, squeeze toys, plastic keys, and large plastic beads

- encourage exploration and curiosity by providing a variety of objects of different textures, shapes, and sizes
- allow children freedom and peace to explore by putting them on their back in a safe area large enough for them to move freely
- provide for interaction with other infants

LANGUAGE

- listen attentively
- coo, whimper, gurgle, and make a variety of other sounds
- cry less often
- "talk" to themselves as well as to others, particularly primary caregiver

- people are still more important than equipment or objects for language development
- some toys to give auditory experiences—let them try making noise with bells, rattles, and squeaky toys

- talk to infants, especially during caregiving routines—prepare them ahead of time for what is going to happen
- respond to babbling and cooing: play sound games with infants

Level III: Month 6

Area of Development	Physical Environment	Social Environment
PHYSICAL *Large Muscles* • have control of head • turn from back to stomach and stomach to back • may move from place to place by rolling • may creep or inch forward or backward • may almost get to sitting while rolling over *Small Muscles* • reach with one arm and can grasp at will • hold objects and manipulate them • can grasp with thumb and forefinger but not well yet • change objects from one hand to the other	APPROPRIATE TOYS AND EQUIPMENT • need more open space and freedom than before • need a variety of textures under their body—hard floor, rugs, grass, wooden deck, etc. • need a variety of interesting objects to move and reach toward	ADULT ROLE • place objects far enough from them so that infants must work to get them • provide plenty of room and motivation for moving around as well as manipulating and grasping objects • provide for interaction with other infants • keep infants in positions they can get in by themselves
EMOTIONAL/SOCIAL *Feelings and Self-Awareness* • display a wider variety of feelings • becoming aware of body parts • see difference between self and rest of the world • respond to name • have taste preferences • may want to start self-feeding	• space large enough for exploration and social interactions will promote relationships	• talk to infants, especially during caregiving; place special emphasis on naming body parts • call children by name • encourage children to take over self-help skills as they are able

Social

- may respond with fear to strangers
- call to primary caregiver for help
- enjoy games with people (peek-a-boo)

INTELLECTUAL

- visually alert a good part of waking hours
- recognize familiar objects
- can see and reach for objects they want
- can pick up and manipulate objects
- look for dropped objects
- can use several senses at once
- a memory is developing

- infants continue to enjoy all the toys and objects listed in Level II under Intellectual Development
- can now appreciate a wider variety of objects at once
- place objects around a safe area so that infants have reason to move around and reach for them

- provide for attachment needs and let children use primary caregiver to provide security in presence of stranger
- play games like peek-a-boo
- allow children freedom to explore
- change or rearrange objects in the environment periodically
- provide for interaction with other infants

LANGUAGE

- respond to different voice tones and inflections
- more control over sounds produced
- use a variety of sounds to express feelings
- imitate tones and inflections

- cloth or cardboard books

- respond to children's communication
- talk to children, especially during caregiving routines
- during playtimes, comment on what children are doing if appropriate (be careful not to interrupt so the words get in the way of the experience)

Level IV: Month 9

Area of Development	Physical Environment	Social Environment
PHYSICAL	**APPROPRIATE TOYS AND EQUIPMENT**	**ADULT ROLE**
Large Muscles	• infants need more room to explore—a greater variety of objects, textures, experiences, toys	• watch for children who stand up but can't sit back down; help when they indicate they are stuck
• crawl	• plastic or wooden cars and trucks, play or real telephones, blocks, dolls, balls of different sizes, nesting toys	• be sensible about helping children who get stuck: don't rescue, but promote problem solving
• may crawl stiff legged		
• may crawl while holding object in hand		
• pull to stand on furniture		
• may stand alone	• pillows and low platforms (or steps) can be added to the environment to provide a variety of levels for children to explore	• provide open spaces and safe climbing opportunities
• may or may not be able to get back down from standing		• allow children to explore with little adult interference
• get into sitting position	• rails or low furniture needed for standing or cruising	• encourage infants to use manipulative skills, such as pulling off socks, opening doors, taking apart nesting toys
• may move along holding onto furniture		
Small Muscles		
• can pick up small objects easily with thumb and forefinger		
• explore and manipulate with forefinger		
• growing in eye-hand coordination		
EMOTIONAL/SOCIAL		
Feelings and Self-Awareness		• provide enough of a schedule for infants to come to anticipate the sequence of events
• clearly attached to primary caregiver and may fear separation		• allow opportunities for uninterrupted concentration
• reject things they don't want		
Social		• encourage problem solving
• feed selves biscuit	• need the tools for self-help, such as cup and spoon	• don't help until they're really stuck
• drink from cup holding handle		• allow them to discover the consequences of their behavior whenever it is safe to do so
• usually a willing performer if asked		
• becoming sensitive to and interested in the moods and activities of others		
• tease		
• anticipate events		

INTELLECTUAL

- remember games and toys from previous days
- anticipate people's return
- can concentrate and not get interrupted
- pull cover off toy they have seen hidden
- enjoy taking things out of container and putting them back
- solve simple manipulative problems
- interested in discovering the consequences of their behavior

- the objects and toys listed under Physical Development are also appropriate for promoting intellectual development
- also provide interesting and safe objects from the adult world: pots, pans, wooden spoons, and junk such as discarded boxes, both big and little (infants appreciate real objects as much as toys)

- provide the opportunity for infants to become self-assertive
- help children interpret the effect of their actions on others
- give plenty of opportunities for children to develop self-help skills
- help children express separation fears, accept them, and help them deal with them
- provide for attachment to primary caregiver
- provide good models for children (adults who express honest feelings, neither minimized nor exaggerated)

LANGUAGE

- pay attention to conversations
- may respond to words other than own name
- may carry out simple commands
- use words such as "mama" and "dada"
- have intonation
- may repeat a sequence of sounds
- yell

- appreciate a greater variety of picture books

- include infants in conversations
- don't talk about them if they're present unless you include them (especially important at this stage)
- promote interactions with other infants
- respond to infants' sounds
- encourage use of words
- ask questions infants can respond to

Level V: Year 1

Area of Development	Physical Environment	Social Environment
PHYSICAL *Large Muscles* • can stand without holding on • may walk but probably prefer to crawl • climb up and down stairs • may climb out of crib *Small Muscles* • may use both hands at the same time for different things • use thumb well • show preference for one hand • may undress self or untie shoes	**APPROPRIATE TOYS AND EQUIPMENT** • need lots of space both indoors and outdoors to enjoy crawling and practice walking • need lots of objects to manipulate, explore, experiment with, and carry around	**ADULT ROLE** • provide for safety and plenty of movement • don't push children to walk: allow them to decide when they are finished with crawling
EMOTIONAL/SOCIAL *Feelings and Self-Awareness* • show wide variety of emotions and respond to those of others • fear strangers and new places • show affection • show moods and preferences • may know difference between their possessions and others'	• provide an environment that encourages and facilitates self-help skills	• provide for self-help skills • acknowledge infants' possessions and help protect them • give approval • set reasonable limits • accept uncooperative behavior as a sign of self-assertion • give choices • give and return affection • accept and help infants deal with fears and frustrations
Social • feed self • help dress self • obey commands • seek approval but are not always cooperative	• provide needed tools and equipment for self-help skills	• encourage self-help skills

INTELLECTUAL

- good at finding hidden objects
- increased memory
- solve problems
- use trial-and-error method effectively
- explore new approaches to problems
- think about actions before doing them (sometimes)
- imitate people who are not present

- children at this level enjoy most of the toys and household objects already mentioned but use them in more sophisticated ways
- also enjoy large beads to string, large Lego blocks, small building blocks, stacking cones, wooden snap trains, etc.

- promote active problem solving
- provide for interaction with other children
- set up environment so children see new and more complex ways to use toys and equipment

LANGUAGE

- know words stand for objects
- begin to sound like they speak the language of their parents (use same sounds and intonations)
- use gestures to express self
- may say two to eight words

- toy telephones, dolls, and books promote language development at this level
- any toy can become a reason to talk as children play
- music promotes language development

- promote interaction among children; children learn to talk from adults, but they practice as they play with other children
- give simple instructions
- play games with children
- sing songs and do finger plays
- encourage expression of feelings
- fill in missing words and expand utterance for children when responding

Level VI: Month 18

Area of Development	Physical Environment	Social Environment
PHYSICAL *Large Muscles* • walk fast and well • seldom fall • run, but awkwardly • walk up stairs holding a hand *Small Muscles* • can use crayon to scribble as well as imitate marks • better control at self-feeding	**APPROPRIATE TOYS AND EQUIPMENT** • need room to walk and run • enjoy taking walks if adult isn't too goal oriented • enjoy plenty of sensory experiences such as water play and sand	**ADULT ROLE** • keep the environment full and interesting; may need to change arrangement periodically and introduce new toys • promote interactions among children • allow for enough physical exercise
EMOTIONAL/SOCIAL • imitate adults in dramatic play • interested in helping with chores • interested in dressing process; can undress to some extent • may be beginning to get some bladder and bowel control	• provide the tools for dramatic play, such as dress-up clothes, dolls, housekeeping equipment, dishes	• allow children to help as they are able • set limits and gently but firmly enforce them • encourage self-help skills • help children with their interaction and talk them through aggressive situations
INTELLECTUAL • can begin to solve problems in their head • rapid increase of language development • beginning of ability to fantasize and role-play	• provide a variety of toys available on low shelves for children to choose: small people, animals, doll houses, containers filled with small objects, measuring cups, spoons, etc.	• provide a number of choices • help children work on a problem uninterrupted • encourage use of language
LANGUAGE • may use words to gain attention • can use words to indicate wants • may know ten words • enjoy picture books	• books with clear, simple pictures	• provide a variety of experiences and help children put language to them • ask questions and encourage children to ask them too • read aloud

Level VII: Month 24

Area of Development	Physical Environment	Social Environment
PHYSICAL *Large Muscles* • run headlong, have trouble stopping and turning • walk up and down stairs (may hold on) • throw a ball • kick a ball forward *Small Muscles* • put on some easy clothing • hold spoon, fork, cup, but may still spill • can use a paintbrush but don't control drips • can turn the pages of a book	APPROPRIATE TOYS AND EQUIPMENT • low climbers and slides • large balls, both lightweight and heavier • low three- and four-wheeled, steerable, well-balanced vehicles both with pedals and without • swings children can get into and out of themselves • hills, ramps, low stairs • space to run • large, lightweight blocks • wooden puzzles with two to four large pieces • pegboards • stacking toys • big beads to string • construction sets (easy to put together) • play dough • rhythm instruments • texture matching games • feely boxes • sand and water and toys to play with in them • dolls to dress and mostly *undress* • books • felt pens, crayons, finger paint	ADULT ROLE • encourage freedom to move in any way they like (within limits, of course) • allow for plenty of physical and sensory experiences • encourage children to find new ways to combine and use familiar toys and equipment • offer choices • allow loving chases or loving wrestles • play circle games and sing songs with movements (but not with the whole group as a circle time compulsory activity) • encourage small muscle use by offering a wide variety of choices • offer a number of sensory activities • allow children to use toys and materials in creative ways (within limits, of course) • allow children to combine materials and toys in unique ways (within limits, of course) • facilitate problem solving when children get stuck

Level VII: Month 24 (continued)

Area of Development	Physical Environment	Social Environment
EMOTIONAL/SOCIAL • may understand personal property concepts ("That's mine—that's Daddy's") • may tend to hoard possessions—may resist sharing • assert independence ("Me do it!") • take pride in accomplishments • may say "no" even to things they want	• provide space for personal possessions (cubbies or boxes) • provide duplicates of favorite toys so sharing isn't such an issue • provide plenty of things to do so sharing isn't such an issue • hand puppets sometimes allow children to express their feelings • art, music, and dramatic play experiences (listed under Small Muscles) allow children to express their feelings • large muscle experiences also allow children to express their feelings	• respect children's need to hold on to their possessions • model sharing rather than require it • allow children to try things by themselves, even when you know you can do it better or faster • help them have accomplishments they can take pride in
INTELLECTUAL • can identify parts of a doll—hair, ears, etc. • can fit forms into a form board • can solve many problems on their own • can work simple puzzles	• provide books, puzzles, records, in addition to toys listed above, that allow choices and provide opportunities for concept development and for problem solving	• provide a variety of choices of materials to use and ways to spend time • give freedom to use materials in creative ways • encourage problem solving • allow exploration

LANGUAGE

- use personal pronouns (I, me, you), but not always correctly
- refer to themselves by name
- use two- and three-word sentences
- may know as many as fifty to two-hundred words
- talk about what they are doing

- provide a good variety of books (children can use them carefully now)
- pictures at child's eye level around the room, changed often, give children something to talk about
- allow and set up "happenings," experiences that give children something to talk about
- provide for music experiences

- encourage conversation both between children and between child and adult
- help children speculate ("I wonder what would happen if . . .")
- go places and talk about what you do and see
- encourage verbalization of feelings and wants
- help children begin to talk out differences instead of relying on hitting, kicking, and other negative physical behaviors

Level VIII: Month 36

Area of Development	Physical Environment	Social Environment
PHYSICAL *Large Muscles* • walk, run with control, climb well, throw a ball with aim • jump in place • balance on one foot for a second or two • may pedal tricycle	APPROPRIATE TOYS AND EQUIPMENT Need all the toys and equipment listed for the twenty-four-month-old, but larger versions that provide more challenges. The thirty-six-month-old can begin to use the equipment designed for preschoolers and is probably ready to move on from the toddler program • may enjoy some large wooden blocks, balance boards, planks, boxes, ladders for building	ADULT ROLE • offer choices • can move gross motor equipment outside for this age group and expect them to be slightly more restrained inside • be careful about encouraging gross motor experiences in boys more than in girls (they should get equal encouragement; indeed, girls should get extra encouragement if they are reluctant)
Small Muscles • put on shoes but don't tie laces • put on clothing except for buttoning • feed self alone and well • scribbles with more control • can draw or copy a circle • can use paintbrush and control drips • use construction toys imaginatively • exercise bowel and bladder control	• unit blocks and accessories to go with them • construction sets with more and smaller pieces • small-wheeled vehicles to go with blocks • sensory table • puzzles • objects to sort • flannel board and figures • small beads to string • wide range of art materials, including paint, collage, scissors, glue, crayons, felt pens, chalk • dolls and accessories • doll house • extensive dramatic play equipment • puppets	• allow plenty of choices • encourage children to use toys and materials in creative ways • find ways that older children can become involved in small-muscle, manipulative activities without being interrupted by younger children who want to dump rather than build • keep small parts from younger children, who might put them in their mouths • encourage fine motor activities in both boys and girls (if boys are less interested, find materials that entice them)

EMOTIONAL/SOCIAL

- may show regard for people or possessions
- play with sustained interest
- play and interact with another child
- willing to use toilet
- can conform to group for short periods

- provide space for personal possessions
- provide plenty of materials to allow children to share feelings and to role-play, such as dramatic play equipment, dress-up clothes, puppets, dolls, small figures, musical instruments and experiences, art materials
- books that children can identify with also help them express their feelings
- have toilet readily available

- begin to encourage sharing and cooperative play
- help children get involved and stay involved in play activities by preventing interruptions by other children
- can expect children to participate in short active group times, such as circle time
- encourage interaction among children

INTELLECTUAL

- may count to two or three
- may draw face or very simple figure
- can work simple puzzles
- more sophisticated problem solving
- calls self "I" and other people "you"
- knows he is a boy or she is a girl
- know most of the parts of the body
- compare sizes

- the variety of construction materials, manipulative toys, dramatic play, and art materials listed above all contribute to intellectual development
- objects to sort
- plenty of puzzles
- parquetry blocks
- simple games such as lotto
- simple, hands-on science displays and experiments

- provide plenty of choices
- encourage peer interaction during problem solving
- encourage absorption, involvement with materials, activities, and people
- encourage an inquiring attitude
- encourage creative thinking
- encourage children to think about past experiences as well as future ones
- encourage development of number concepts in a natural context

Level VIII: Month 36 (continued)

Area of Development	Physical Environment	Social Environment
LANGUAGE • use plurals • converse in short sentences, answer questions, give information, use language to convey simple ideas • name pictures and label actions • may have nine-hundred-word vocabulary • articulation fairly clear	• setting up the environment for gross motor, fine motor, social, emotional, and intellectual experiences should provide plenty for the children to talk about • add to variety and complexity of books and pictures provided for two-year-olds • music experience • simple hands-on science displays and experiments	• encourage comparisons of size, weight, etc., of objects in a natural context • read books, tell stories, sing songs • embed language in all experiences • encourage questioning • encourage conversations • encourage speculation • encourage verbal conflict resolution • encourage verbalization of feelings • help children listen to one another • play language games such as lotto

APPENDIX C

Curriculum and Lesson Planning: A Responsive Approach

J. Ronald Lally, Ed.D., August 1997

In the United States of America we have related to infant and toddler development in a peculiar way. We have practiced curriculum extremes. One camp feels that all infants and toddlers need are safe environments and tender loving care and that intellectual activity is unnecessary, while the other believes that infants needed to be intellectually stimulated by adult-directed developmentally appropriate activities in order for them to grow cognitively. In many other nations this is not the approach taken toward infant learning. It is understood that tender loving care is necessary, but that intellectual development must be based on an understanding of each child's innate motivation and interest in learning. In these countries curriculum focuses not on one pole or the other but on how to create a climate that supports child-initiated learning. In Italy and Germany, for example, caregivers study the children in their care and keep detailed records of children's interests and skills so that they can facilitate children's learning. They are trained to search for how to use the children's natural interests and curiosity to lead to appropriate early lessons. A good portion of their lesson planning for infants involves training caregivers to understand each infant and toddler's development and how to relate to it. It would serve us well if we learned from their approach.

American child care managers need to come to grips with the fact that much of what they are requiring of their caregivers with regard to lesson plans is inappropriate. Anticipating that the caregivers will need to adapt their actions to the momentary needs and interests of each child should be an essential part of any lesson plan. Lesson planning for infants, if done correctly, should first explore ways to help caregivers get in tune with each infant they serve and learn from the infant what he or she needs, thinks, and feels. Second, they should include strategies to broaden the caregiver's relationship with each individual child. Third, they should include a number of possible approaches for relating to a child's unique thoughts and feelings, meeting his or her needs, and matching interest with activity. All components of lesson planning must include adaptation of the plan and subsequent caregiver action to match the infant's response.

Another critical planning component is the context of learning. Much of what infants need is not the planning of specific lessons but a wise adult who can create a rich setting for learning. Learning environments and policies of care—the climate for learning—are more important to infant development than specific lessons. Research has shown us that much of what needs to happen with infants is not specific lessons but the preparation of their caregivers to capitalize on natural learning opportunities.

A RESPONSIVE CURRICULUM

For the past twelve years the *Program for Infant Toddler Caregivers* has developed video and print materials to assist center and family day-care providers implement high-quality infant and toddler care. We have developed strategies that help caregivers read and respond to the intellectual, social, and emotional messages of the infants in their care and have recommended policies that help programs focus on the importance of the relationships between the caregiver and child, and the caregiver and family, as the foundation of good care. Our materials and approach have been used to train many trainers throughout the country, who in turn have trained thousands of caregivers. It has recently come to our attention that help is needed in selecting curriculum and in developing lesson plans. It is imperative that activities, environments, and interaction styles are responsive to the needs of infants and toddlers, respect the competencies infants and toddlers bring to each interaction, and reflect the young child's need for relationship-based experiences.

From all we know about how infants best learn we have concluded that they must have a hand in the selection of what they learn. Our approach to curriculum therefore includes the infant as an active partner in the process of curriculum selection. In this way it is a curriculum that is responsive and respectful of what the infant brings to and wants from each experience. This type of curriculum is different from most. It needs to be well planned yet remain dynamic enough to move and flow with changing infant interests. It needs to anticipate developmental stages, but it also needs to allow for individual variations in learning style. It also must be broad enough in scope to respond to all developmental domains simultaneously. For example, just because you think you are teaching about object permanence it doesn't mean that is what the child is learning. He or she may be learning about their prescribed role in learning relationships.

In a responsive curriculum a good portion of lesson planning has to do with preparing caregivers and environments so that lessons can be learned. Implementation of a responsive curriculum involves training caregivers to understand and relate to infant and toddler development generally and also specifically. Much of lesson planning explores ways to help caregivers get in tune with each infant they serve and learn from the infant what he or she needs, thinks, and feels. When this is accomplished, often lessons being learned become quite obvious. Yet even "in tune" caregivers need to plan and re-plan how to form a relationship with and best meet each individual child's needs and relate to that child's unique thoughts and feelings. In a responsive curriculum often the most critical curriculum components are not lessons but the planning of settings that allow learning to take place. If the curriculum isn't planned so that environments, materials, group size, and management policies don't maximize the child's sense of security in care and in connection with the caregivers, promote a safe and interesting place to learn, and optimize connections with the child's family, very little positive learning will take place regardless of what lessons are planned.

CURRICULUM PLANNING: A PLACE TO BEGIN

Because infants and toddlers have unique needs, their care must be constructed specifically to meet those needs. Good infant-toddler care is not baby-sitting and is not preschool. It is a special kind of care that looks like no other. For curriculum to be designed well and carried out appropriately, lesson plans, environments, routines, staffing, group size, relationships with families, and supervision and training must have as their starting point the following ten factors that differentiate infant-toddler care from the care of older children.

1. Infants and toddlers experience life more holistically than any other age group. Social, emotional, intellectual, language, and physical lessons are not separated by the infant. Adults who are most helpful to the young child interact in ways that understand that the child is learning from the whole experience, not just that part of the experience to which the adult gives attention.
2. Between birth and age three a child goes through three distinct developmental stages, and the type of care given needs to change as the stage changes and also takes into consideration transitions between stages.
3. The infant is dependent on close, caring, ongoing relationships as the source of positive, physical, social, emotional, and intellectual growth. Infants develop best when they are assured of having a trusted caregiver or caregivers who can read their cues and respond to their needs. Infant-toddlers care policy must be organized to ensure that these relationships exist and prosper. Policies that encourage and nurture these secure relationships are the backbone of quality care.

4. An infant or toddler learns most of how he or she thinks and feels by imitating and incorporating the behaviors of those around him or her. For this reason it is particularly important that caregivers be carefully selected and well trained.

5. Each infant is born curious and motivated to learn and actively participates in learning each day. Caregivers need specific training in infant learning to understand how to read and respond to infant behavior and to delight in the types of learning in which the infants are engaged. They also need training in how to construct environments and activities that keep motivation, experimentation, and curiosity alive and how to facilitate the infant learning process.

6. All children come into the world temperamentally different from each other, and because of these differences they need to be treated differently by their caregivers.

7. Parents and caregivers of infants and toddlers often experience a heightened sense of emotionality related to the care of the infants and toddlers. Strategies for dealing with conflicts that can emerge from this "protective urge" must be considered as part of care.

8. Much of the first two years of life are spent in the creation of a child's first "sense of self" or the building of a first identity. Because this is such a crucial part of children's makeup—how they first see themselves, how they think they should function, how they expect others to function in relation to them—early care must ensure that in addition to carefully selected and trained caregivers, links with family, home culture, and home language are a central part of program policy. If care becomes a substitute for, rather than a support of, family, children will often incorporate a less-than-positive sense of who they are and where they come from because of their infant care experience.

9. The development of language is particularly crucial during the infant-toddler period. Good care provides many opportunities for infants to engage in meaningful and context-based dialogue with their caregivers and to have the child's communications acknowledged and encouraged.

10. Infants and toddlers are strongly influenced by the environments and routines they are subjected to each day. This is particularly true for very young infants who cannot physically move themselves from a noxious to a more pleasant environment. Physical environment, group size, daily schedules, lesson plans, and the conduct of routines must foster the establishment of small intimate groups in which relationships with trusted caregivers can be established and have a chance to grow and become the base for social, emotional, and intellectual learning in a safe and interesting environment.

APPENDIX D

Guiding Principles of the Parent Services Project

THE PARENT SERVICES PROJECT PHILOSOPHY

PSP recognizes that the well-being and sense of significance of parents are of central importance to the development of the child. Parents who possess a sense of fulfillment will enrich their children's lives, take more active roles in their communities, and strengthen their families, adding to the overall quality of life.

Partnership

The relationship between families and staff is one of equality and respect, resulting in the creation of a mutually beneficial partnership. Success comes from promoting the excellence of all partners.

Empowerment

Families are their own best advocates. They are decision makers on a collaborative team. Parents who are confident and competent empower their children to achieve success and foster their well-being.

Family Strengths

Families are assets—not barriers to overcome or work around. They are a vital resource to themselves and to one another. Programs build on these family strengths. Seeking services is considered a sign of strength.

Cultural Competence

Respect is possible when each family's culture is valued and recognized. Programs are community-based and are culturally and socially relevant to the families they serve.

Participant Driven

Program services are best determined by participants. Parents make choices to participate in activities that reflect their own needs and interests.

Social Support

Support is important to all families. Social support networks reduce social isolation and promote the well-being of the child, the family, and the community. Programs are a bridge between families and other services.

References

GENERAL

California State Department of Education. *Visions for Infant/Toddler Care: Guidelines for Professional Caregiving.* Sacramento: California State Department of Education, 1988.

Gerber, M. "Caring for Infants with Respect: The RIE Approach." *Zero to Three,* February 1984, pp. 1–3.

Godwin, A., and L. Schrag, eds. *Setting Up for Infant Care: Guidelines for Centers and Family Day Care Homes.* Washington, D.C.: National Association for the Education of Young Children, 1988.

Greenspan, S. I., and G. H. Pollock, eds. *The Course of Life,* vol. 1 of *Infancy.* Madison, Conn.: International Universities Press, 1989.

Hale-Benson, J. E. *Black Children: Their Roots, Culture, and Learning Styles.* Baltimore: Johns Hopkins University Press, 1986.

Kagan, J. *The Nature of the Child.* New York: Basic Books, 1984.

Widerstrom, A. "Educating Young Handicapped Children." *Childhood Education* 63(2), December 1986, pp. 78–83.

CHAPTER 1

Acredolo, L., and S. Goodwyn. *How to Talk with Your Babies before They Can Talk.* Lincolnwood, Ill.: Contemporary Books, 1996.

Bruner, J. S. "The Organization of Action and the Nature of Adult-Infant Transaction." In *The Analysis of Action,* edited by M. von Cranach and R. Harve. Cambridge: Cambridge University Press, 1982.

Ferraro, P. "Supporting Competence in Children." *Educaring* 8(2), Spring 1993, pp. 1–3.

Garcia, R. *Home Centered Care: Designing a Family Day Care Program, a Guide for Caregivers and Parents.* San Francisco: Children's Council of San Francisco, 1985.

Gerber, M. "Respecting Infants: The Loczy Model of Infant Care." In *Supporting the Growth of Infants, Toddlers and Parents,* edited by E. Jones. Pasadena, Calif.: Pacific Oaks, 1979.

Gerber, M. *Resources for Infant Educarers.* Los Angeles: Resources for Infant Educarers, 1991.

Klass, C. S. "Childrearing Interactions within Developmental Home- or Center-Based Early Education." *Young Children,* March 1987, pp. 9–13.

Nguyen, T. D. "Honey, the Baby Is Wet!" *Educaring* 16(2), Winter-Spring 1995, pp. 10–12.

Pinto, C. "Is Faster Better?" *Educaring* 16(2), Winter-Spring 1995, pp. 4–6.

Solter, A. "Listening to Infants." *Educaring* 15(1), Winter 1994, pp. 1–4.

Sterling Honig, A. "Quality Infant/ Toddler Caregiving: Are There Magic Recipes?" *Young Children,* May 1989, pp. 4–10.

Vygotsky, L. S. *Mind in Society: The Development of Higher Psychological Processes.* Cambridge: Harvard University Press, 1978.

CHAPTER 2

Bower, T. G. R. *Development in Infancy.* San Francisco: W. H. Freeman, 1982.

Flyer, J. "Profound, I Say!" *Educaring* 15(2), Spring 1994, pp. 1–4.

Gerber, M. "Conflict Resolution with Infants." *Educaring* 4(4), Fall 1983, p. 3.

Gibran, K. *The Prophet.* New York: Alfred A. Knopf, 1965.

Goffin, S. G., with C. Tull, "Problem Solving: Encouraging Active Learning." *Young Children,* March 1985, pp. 28–32.

Gonzalez-Mena, J. "Praise with a Purpose Is Sneaky and Manipulative." *Educaring* 14(4), Fall 1993, pp. 1–4.

Gonzalez-Mena, J. "Toddlers, What to Expect." *Young Children,* November 1986, pp. 47–51.

Greenberg, P. "Do You Take Care of Toddlers?" *Young Children,* January 1991, pp. 52–53.

Grey, K. "Not in Praise of Praise." *Child Care Information Exchange* 104, July/ August 1995, pp. 56–59.

Honig, A. S. "Quality Infant/Toddler Caregiving: Are There Magic Recipes?" *Young Children,* May 1989, pp. 4–10.

Levine, S. "Stimulation in Infancy." *Scientific American,* May 1960, pp. 436, 624.

Maslow, A. H. *Toward a Psychology of Being,* 2nd ed. New York: Van Nostrand, 1968.

Paretto, H. P., Jr., N. S. Dunn, and D. R. Hoge. "Low-Cost Communication Devices for Children with Disabilities and Their Family Members." *Young*

Children 50(6), September 1995, pp. 75–81.

Reinsberg, J. "Reflections on Quality Infant Care." *Young Children* 50(6), September 1995, pp. 23–25.

Widerstrom, A. H. "Educating Young Handicapped Children." *Childhood Education* 63(2), December 1986, pp. 78–83.

CHAPTER 3

Beal, S. M., and C. F. Finch. "An Overview of Retrospective Case Control Slides Investigating the Relationship between Prone Sleep Positions and SIDS." *Journal of Pediatrics and Child Health* 27, 1993, pp. 334–339.

Cortez, J., ed. *Infant-Toddler Caregiving: A Guide to Culturally Sensitive Care.* Sacramento: California Department of Education, 1991.

Educaring, published quarterly by Resources for Infant Educarers.

Garcia, R. *Home Centered Care: Designing a Family Day Care Program, a Guide for Caregivers and Parents.* San Francisco: Children's Council of San Francisco, 1985.

Gerber, M. "Respecting Infants: The Loczy Model of Infant Care." In *Supporting the Growth of Infants, Toddlers and Parents,* edited by E. Jones. Pasadena, Calif.: Pacific Oaks, 1979.

Gerber, M. *Resources for Infant Educarers.* Los Angeles: Resources for Infant Educarers, 1991.

Gonzalez-Mena, J. *Infant-Toddler Caregiving: A Guide to Routines.* Sacramento: California Department of Education, 1990.

Gonzalez-Mena, J. *Multicultural Issues in Child Care.* Mountain View, Calif.: Mayfield, 1996.

Gonzalez-Mena, J., and A. Stonehouse. "In the Child's Best Interests." *Child Care Information Exchange,* November/December 1995, pp. 17–20.

Honig, A. S. "Quality Infant/Toddler Caregiving: Are There Magic Recipes?" *Young Children,* May 1989, pp. 4–10.

Josephs, Z. "Reducing the Risk of SIDS." *Educaring* 14(4), Fall 1993, p. 5.

Lally, J. R. "The Impact of Child Care Policies and Practices on Infant/Toddler Identity Formation," *Young Children* 51(1), November 1995, pp. 58–67.

Mangione, P., ed. *Infant-Toddler Caregiving: A Guide to Culturally Sensitive Care.* Sacramento, Calif.: Far West Laboratory and California Department of Education, 1995.

Phillips, C. B., and R. M. Cooper. "Cultural Dimensions of Feeding Relationships." *Zero to Three* 7(5), June 1992, pp. 10–13.

Provence, S. "Feeding Problem." *Zero to Three* 7(5), June 1992, pp. 18–19.

Satter, E. "The Feeding Relationship." *Zero to Three* 7(5), June 1992, pp. 1–9.

Widerstrom, A. H. "Educating Young Handicapped Children." *Childhood Education* 63(2), December 1986, pp. 78–83.

CHAPTER 4

Chang, H. *Affirming Children's Roots: Cultural and Linguistic Diversity in Early Care and Education.* San Francisco: California Tomorrow, 1993.

Clark, A. L., ed. *Culture and Childrearing.* Philadelphia: F. A. Davis, 1981.

Feeney, S., and M. Magarick. "Choosing Good Toys for Young Children." *Young Children,* November 1984, pp. 21–25.

Gerber, M. "Good Play Objects for Babies." *Educaring* 7(3), Spring 1986, pp. 4–6.

Gonzalez-Mena, J. *A Caregiver's Guide to Routines in Infant-Toddler Care.* Sacramento, Calif.: Child Development Division, Center for Child and Family Studies, Far West Laboratory for Edu-

cational Research and Development, California Department of Education, 1990.

Gonzalez-Mena, J., "Cultural Sensitivity in Routine Caregiving Tasks." In *Infant/Caregiving: A Guide to Culturally Sensitive Care,* edited by Peter Mangione. Sacramento, Calif.: Far West Laboratory and California Department of Education, 1995.

Monighan-Nourot, P., B. Scales, J. Van Horn, and M. Almy. *Looking at Children's Play: A Bridge between Theory and Practice.* New York: Teachers College Press, 1987.

Morelli, G., B. Roqoff, and D. Oppenheim. "Cultural Variation in Infants' Sleeping Arrangements: Questi Independence." *Developmental Psychology* 28(4), 1992.

Phillips, C. B., and R. M. Cooper. "Cultural Dimensions of Feeding Relationships." *Zero to Three* 12(5), June 1992, 10–13.

Tardos, A. "Facilitating the Play of Children at Loczy." *Educaring* 6(3), Summer 1985, pp. 1–7.

Tonge, M. J. "Hanging Out with Babies at Play: Vignettes from Participant-Observer." In *Supporting the Growth of Infants, Toddlers and Parents,* edited by E. Jones. Pasadena, Calif.: Pacific Oaks, 1991.

Van Horn, J., P. Nourot, B. Scales, and K. Alward. *Play at the Center of the Curriculum.* Columbus, Ohio; Merrill, 1993.

Williams, C. K., and C. Kamii. "How Do Children Learn by Handling Objects?" *Young Children,* November 1986, pp. 23–26.

CHAPTER 5

Ainsworth, M. D., and B. A. Wittig. "Attachment and Exploratory Behavior of One-Year-Olds in a Stranger Situation." In *Determinants of Infant Behavior,* vol. 4, edited by B. M. Foss. New York: Barnes and Noble, 1969.

Beginnings Workshop: "Working with Parents of Children with Differing Abilities." *Child Care Information Exchange* 88, November 1992.

Bowlby, J. *Attachment and Loss,* vol. 1 of *Attachment.* London: Hogarth, 1969.

Brazelton, T. B., and B. Cramer. *The Earliest Relationships.* New York: Addison-Wesley, 1990.

Caldwell, B. M., C. Wright, A. S. Honig, and J. Tannenbaum. "Infant Care and Attachment." *American Journal of Orthopsychiatry* 40, 1970, pp. 397–412.

Harlow, H. "The Nature of Love." *American Psychology* 13, 1958, pp. 59–86.

Kagan, J., R. B. Kearsley, and P. R. Zelazo. "The Effects of Infant Day Care on Psychological Development." *Education Quarterly* 1(1), February 1977, pp. 143–158.

Karen, R. "Becoming Attached." *Atlantic* 265, February 1990, pp. 35–70.

Klaus, M., and Kennell, J., *Parent-Infant Bonding.* New York: Mosby, 1982.

Lally, J. R., "The Impact of Child Care Policies and Practices on Infant/Toddler Identity Formation." *Young Children* 51(1), November 1995, 58–67.

Lamb, M. *The Father's Role: Cross-Cultural Perspectives.* Hillside, N.J.: Erlbaum, 1987.

McCracken, J. "So Many Goodbyes." Brochure #573, National Association for the Education of Young Children, Washington, D.C., 1986.

Portnoy, F. C., and C. H. Simmons. "Day Care and Attachment." *Child Development* 49, 1978, pp. 239–242.

Rubenstein, J. "Caregiving and Infant Behavior in Day Care and in Homes." *Developmental Psychology* 15(1), 1979, pp. 1–24.

Stern, D. *The Interpersonal World of the Infant.* New York: Basic Books, 1985.

Thomas, E., and S. Browder. *Born Dancing: How Intuitive Parents Understand Their Baby's Unspoken Language and Natural Rhythms.* New York: Harper & Row, 1988.

CHAPTER 6

Abbott, C. F., and S. Gold. "Conferring with Parents When You're Concerned That Their Child Needs Special Services." *Young Children,* May 1991, pp. 10–15.

Bower, T. G. R. *A Primer of Infant Development.* San Francisco: W. H. Freeman, 1977.

Bower, T. G. R. *Development in Infancy,* 2nd ed. San Francisco: W. H. Freeman, 1982.

Bornstein, M., and M. Lamb. *Development in Infancy: An Introduction,* 3rd ed. New York: McGraw-Hill, 1992.

Patton, J. R. *Exceptional Children in Focus,* 5th ed. New York: Merrill, 1991.

Samples, R. *The Metamorphic Mind.* Menlo Park, Calif.: Addison-Wesley, 1976.

Sherman, T. "Categorization of Skills in Infants." *Child Development* 56, 1985, pp. 1561–1573.

Stern, D. *Diary of a Baby.* New York: Basic Books, 1990.

Warren, D. H. *Blindness and Early Childhood Development,* 2nd ed. New York: American Foundation for the Blind, 1984.

Weiss, W., J. Salomon, and P. Zelazo, eds. *Newborn Attention: Biological Constraints and the Influence of Experience.* Norwood, N.J.: Ablex, 1991.

CHAPTER 7

Blenk, A., with D. L. Fine. *Making School Inclusion Work: A Guide to Everyday Practices.* Cambridge, Mass.: Brookline, 1995.

Chandler, P. A. *A Place for Me: Including Children with Special Needs in Early Care and Education Settings.* Washington, D.C.: National Association for the Education of Young Children, 1994.

Bower, T. G. R. *Development in Infancy,* 2nd ed. San Francisco: W. H. Freeman, 1982.

Fallen, N. H., and W. Ilmansky. *Young Children with Special Needs.* Columbus, Ohio: Merrill, 1985.

Hayslip, W., and L. Vincent. "Opening Doors to Activities That Include ALL Children." *Child Care Information Exchange* 105, September/October 1995, 43–46.

Krog, S. *The Intergrated Early Childhood Curriculum.* New York: McGraw-Hill, 1990, pp. 6–41.

Pikler, E. "Data on Gross Motor Development of the Infant." *Early Child Development and Care* 1, 1972, pp. 297–310.

Sullivan, M. *Feeling Strong, Feeling Free: Movement Exploration for Young Children.* Washington, D.C.: National Association for the Education of Young Children, 1982.

Tardos, A. "The Pikler/Loczy Philosophy." *Educaring* 7(2), Spring 1986, pp. 1–7.

CHAPTER 8

Beginnings Workshop: "Make-Believe Play." In *Child Care Information Exchange* 99, September 1994.

Berk, L. "Vygotsky's Theory: The Importance of Make-Believe Play." *Young Children* 50(1), November 1994, 30–39.

Bower, T. G. R. *Development in Infancy.* San Francisco: W. H. Freeman, 1982.

Bredekamp, S., ed. *Developmentally Appropriate Practice in Early Childhood Programs Serving Children Birth through Age 8.* Washington, D.C.: National Association for the Education of Young Children, 1986.

Brooks, P. H., and C. McCauley. "Cognitive Research in Mental Retardation." *American Journal of Mental Deficiency* 88, 1984, pp. 479–486.

Flavell, J. H. "On Cognitive Development." *Child Development* 53, 1982, pp. 1–10.

Gowen, J. "The Early Development of Symbolic Play." *Young Children* 50(3), March 1995, 75–84.

Hughes, F., J. Elicker, and L. Veen. "A Program of Play for Infants and Caregivers." *Young Children* 50(2), January 1995, 52–58.

Gross, T. F. *Cognitive Development.* Monterey, Calif.: Brooks/Cole, 1985.

Kamii, C., and R. DeVries. *Physical Knowledge in Preschool Education.* Englewood Cliffs, N.J.: Prentice-Hall, 1978.

Marzolla, J. *Supertot: Creative Learning Activities for Children One to Three and Sympathetic Advice for Their Parents.* New York: Harper & Row, 1977.

Phillips, J. L., Jr. *The Origins of Intellect: Piaget's Theory.* San Francisco: W. H. Freeman, 1969.

Pugmire-Stoy, M. C. *Spontaneous Play in Early Childhood.* Albany, N.Y.: Delmar, 1992.

Schickendanz, J., K. Hansen, and R. Forsyth. *Understanding Children.* Mountain View, Calif.: Mayfield, 1990, pp. 175–203.

CHAPTER 9

Barclay, K., C. Benelli, and A. Curtis. "Literacy Begins at Birth: What Caregivers Can Learn from Parents of Children Who Read Early." *Young Children* 50(4), May 1995, 24–28.

Bower, T. G. R. *A Primer of Infant Development.* San Francisco: W. H. Freeman, 1974.

Brown, R. *A First Language: The Early Years.* Cambridge: Harvard University Press, 1973.

Cazden, C. B., ed. *Language in Early Childhood Education.* Washington, D.C.: National Association for the Education of Young Children, 1981.

Cook, R., A. Tessier, and V. Armbruster. *Adapting Early Childhood Curriculum for Children with Special Needs,* 2nd ed. Columbus, Ohio: Merrill, 1987.

Gerber, M. "Babies Understanding Words." *Educaring* 3(4), Fall 1982, pp. 5–6.

Gleason, B., ed. *The Development of Language,* 3rd ed. New York: MacMillian, 1993.

Hakuta, K. *Mirror of Language: The Debate on Bilingualism.* New York: Basic Books, 1986.

Hallahan, D., and J. Kauffman. *Exceptional Children: Introduction to Special Education,* 5th ed. Englewood Cliffs, N.J.: Prentice-Hall, 1991, pp. 217–261.

Hearne, B. *Choosing Books for Children.* New York: Bantam Doubleday Dell, 1990.

Heath, S. B. *Ways with Words: Language, Life, and Work in Communities and Classrooms.* Cambridge: Cambridge University Press, 1983.

Honig, A. "Singing with Infants and Toddlers," *Young Children* 50(5), July 1995, 72–78.

Lally, J. R., P. L. Mangione, and C. L. Young-Holt, eds. *Infant/Toddler Caregiving: A Guide to Language Development and Communication.* Sacramento, Calif.: Far West Laboratory for Educational Development and California Department of Education, 1992.

Richman, R., Jr., and C. Patterson. "Cultural and Educational Variations in Maternal Responsiveness." *Developmental Psychology* 28, 1992, pp. 614–621.

Salkind, N. *Child Development,* part 2, 6th ed. Fort Worth, Tex.: Holt, Rinehart and Winston, 1990.

Stiames, G., and H. Rubin, eds. *Stuttering: Then and Now.* Columbus, Ohio: Merrill 1986.

CHAPTER 10

Abbott, C. F., and S. Gold. "Conferring with Parents When You're Concerned That Their Child Needs Special Services." *Young Children,* May 1991, pp. 10–15.

Belsky, J., and D. Eggebeen. "Early and Extensive Maternal Employment and Young Children's Socioemotional Development." *Journal of Marriage and the Family* 53, 1991, pp. 1083–1110.

Brooks, J. *The Process of Parenting,* 3rd ed. Mountain View, Calif.: Mayfield, 1991.

Egeland, B., and E. A. Farber. "Infant-Mother Attachment: Factors Related to Its Development and Changes over Time." *Child Development* 55, 1984, pp. 753–771.

Eisenberg, N., and R. Fabes. "Emotion and Its Regulation in Early Development." In *New Directions for Child Development.* San Francisco: Jossey Bass, 1992.

Gerber, M. "Helping Baby Feel Secure, Self-Confident, and Relaxed." *Educaring* 1(4), Fall 1980, p. 4.

Hallahan, D., and J. Kauffman. *Exceptional Children: Introduction to Special Education,* 5th ed. Englewood Cliffs, N.J.: Prentice-Hall, 1991, pp. 176–178.

Izard, C. E. *The Psychology of Emotions.* New York: Plenum, 1991.

Kagan, J. *The Nature of the Child.* New York: Basic Books, 1984.

Kagan, J. *Galen's Prophecy. Temperament in Human Nature.* New York: HarperCollins, 1994.

Kauffman, J. *Characteristics of Children's Behavior Disorders,* 3rd ed. Columbus, Ohio: Merrill, 1985.

Kuebli, J. "Young Children's Understanding of Everyday Emotions." *Young Children* 49(3), March 1994, pp. 36–47.

Leboyer, F. *Birth without Violence.* New York: Random House, 1978.

Lee, D. *Valuing the Self.* Englewood Cliffs, N.J.: Prentice-Hall, 1976.

Maslow, A. *Toward a Psychology of Being,* 2nd ed. New York: Van Nostrand, 1968.

McCarrol, T. *Morning Glory Babies: Children with AIDS and the Celebration of*

Life. New York: St. Martin's Press, 1988.

Sternad, R. "Separation." *Educating* 1(3), Summer 1980, pp. 1–2.

Thomas, A., and S. Chess. *Temperament and Development.* New York: Brunner/Mazel, 1977.

Thomas, A., S. Chess, and H. Birch. "The Origin of Personality." *Scientific American* 223, 1970, pp. 102–109.

Thomas, A., S. Chess, and S. J. Korn. "The Reality of Difficult Temperament." *Merrill-Palmer Quarterly* 28, 1982, pp. 1–20.

von Franz, M. L. "The Process of Individuation." In *Man and His Symbols,* edited by C. G. Jung and others. New York: Doubleday, 1964.

CHAPTER 11

Bower, T. G. R. *Development in Infancy,* 2nd. ed. San Francisco: W. H. Freeman, 1982.

Carter, M. "Building Self-Esteem: Training Teachers of Infants and Toddlers." *Child Care Information Exchange* 92, July/August 1993, pp. 59–61.

Crockenberg, S. "How Children Learn to Resolve Conflicts in Families." *Zero to Three,* April 1992.

Curry, N., and C. Johnson. *Beyond Self Esteem: Developing a Genuine Sense of Human Values.* Washington, D.C.: National Association for the Education of Young Children, 1990.

Erikson, E. *Childhood and Society,* 2nd. ed. New York: W. W. Norton, 1963.

Freiberg, K., ed. *Educating Exceptional Children,* 7th ed. Guilford, Conn.: Dushkin Publishing Group, 1994.

Gibran, K. *The Prophet.* New York: Alfred A. Knopf, 1965.

Gordon, A., and K. Browne. *Guiding Young Children in a Diverse Society.* Boston: Allyn and Bacon, 1986.

Greenberg, P. *Character Development: Encouraging Self Esteem and Self-Discipline in Infants, Toddlers, and Two-Year-Olds.* Washington, D.C.: National Association for the Education of Young Children, 1990.

Honig, A. S. "Compliance, Control and Discipline." *Young Children,* January 1985, pp. 50–58.

Lally, J. R. "The Impact of Child Care Policies and Practices on Infant/Toddler Identity Formation." *Young Children* 51(1), January 1995, 58–68.

Meyerhoff, M. "Of Baseball and Babies: Are You Unconsciously Discouraging Father Involvement in Infant Care?" *Young Children* 49(4), May 1994, pp. 17–19.

Miller, C. S. "Building Self-Control, Discipline for Young Children." *Young Children,* November 1984, pp. 15–19.

Reynolds, E. *Guiding Young Children: A Child-Centered Approach.* Mountain View, Calif.: Mayfield, 1990.

Roopnarine, J. L., and A. S. Honig. "The Unpopular Child." *Young Children,* September 1985, p. 61.

CHAPTER 12

Caring for Our Children: National Health and Safety Performance Standards: Guidelines for Out of Home Child Care Programs. American Public Health Association and American Academy of Pediatrics, 1992.

Fauvre, M. "Including Young Children with 'New' Chronic Illnesses in an Early Childhood Education Setting." *Young Children* 43, 1988, pp. 71–78.

Ferguson, J. "Creating Growth-Producing Environments for Infants and Toddlers." In *Supporting the Growth of Infants, Toddlers, and Parents,* edited by E. Jones. Pasadena, Calif.: Pacific Oaks, 1979.

Forman, G. E., and F. Hill. *Constructive Play: Applying Piaget in the Preschool.* Menlo Park, Calif.: Addison-Wesley, 1984.

Gerber, M.. and A. King. "Modifying the Environment to Respond to the Changing Needs of the Child." *Educaring* 6(1), Winter 1985, pp. 1–2.

Greenman, J. *Caring Spaces, Learning Places: Children's Environments That Work.* Redmond, Wash.: Exchange Press, 1988.

Greenman, J. "Just Wondering: Building Wonder into the Environment." *Child Care Information Exchange,* January/February 1993, pp. 32–35.

Greenman, J. "Designing Infant/Toddler Environments" and "Furnishing the Infant/Toddler Environment." In *Caring for Infants and Toddlers: What Works, What Doesn't,* vol. 2, edited by Robert Lurie and Roger Neugebauer. Redmond, Wash.: Child Care Information Exchange, 1982.

Infant/Toddler Caregiving: A Guide to Setting Up Environments. Sacramento: California State Department of Education, 1990.

Jones, E., and E. Prescott. *Dimensions of Teaching-Learning Environments, II: Focus on Day Care.* Pasadena, Calif.: Pacific Oaks, 1978.

Kendrick, A. S., ed. *Healthy Young Children: A Manual for Programs.* Washington, D.C.: National Association for the Education of Young Children, 1988.

Lally, J. R., and J. Stewart. *Infant/Toddler Caregiving: A Guide to Setting Up Environments.* Sacramento, Calif.: Far West Laboratory for Educational Development and California Department of Education, 1990.

Lewis, K. D., B. Bennett, and N. H. Schmeder. "The Care of Infants Menaced by Cocaine Abuse." *Maternal Child Nursing* 14(5), October 1989, pp. 324–329.

Marotz, L. R., M. Z. Cross, and J. M. Rush. *Health, Safety, and Nutrition for the Young Child,* 3rd ed. New York: Delmar, 1993.

Moukaddem, V. "Preventing Infectious Diseases in Your Child Care Setting." *Young Children* 45, 1990, pp. 28–29.

Olds, A. R. "Designing Play Environments for Children under Three." *Top-*ics in Early Childhood Special Education 2, 1982, pp. 87–95.

Prescott, E. "The Physical Environment—Powerful Regulator of Experience." *Child Care Information Exchange,* Reprint #4, C-44. Redmond, Wash. 98052.

Torelli, L. "The Developmentally Designed Group Care Setting: A Supportive Environment for Infants, Toddlers, and Caregivers." *Zero to Three,* December 1989, pp. 7–10.

West, K., ed. *Family Day-to-Day Care.* Mound, Minn.: Quality Child Care, 1979.

Visions for Infant/Toddler Care: Guidelines for Professional Caregiving. Sacramento, Calif.: Far West Laboratory for Educational Development and California Department of Education.

Widerstrom, A. H. "Educating Young Handicapped Children." *Childhood Education* 63(2), December 1986, pp. 78–83.

Wolf, D. "An Interview with Jim Greenman." *Child Care Information Exchange,* September 1987, p. 19.

CHAPTER 13

Affirming Children's Roots: Cultural and Linguistic Diversity in Early Care and Education. San Francisco: California Tomorrow, 1993.

Clark, J. I. *Self Esteem: A Family Affair.* Minneapolis: Winston Press, 1978.

Fillmore, L. W. "A Question for Early-Childhood Programs: English First or Families First." *Education Week,* June 19, 1991.

Feinman, S., ed. *Social Referencing and the Social Construction of Reality in Infancy.* New York: Plenum, 1992.

Gonzalez-Mena, J. "Observation Involves More Than Just Looking," *Educaring* 5(4), Fall 1994, p. 4.

Greenspan, S. I. "Emotional Development in Infants and Toddlers." In *Infant/Toddler Caregiving: A Guide to*

Social-Emotional Growth and Socialization, edited by J. Lally. Sacramento: California Department of Education, 1990.

Hall, E. T. *Beyond Culture*. Garden City, N.Y.: Anchor Press/Doubleday, 1981.

Jones, E. *Teaching Adults: An Active Learning Approach*. Washington, D.C.: National Association for the Education of Young Children, 1986.

Lally, J. R. "The Impact of Child Care Policies and Practices on Infant/Toddler Identity Formation." *Young Children* 51(1), November 1995, pp. 58–67.

Lee, D. *Freedom and Culture*. Englewood Cliffs, N.J.: Prentice-Hall, 1959.

Lee, D. *Valuing the Self*. Englewood Cliffs, N.J.: Prentice-Hall, 1976.

Leipzig, J. "Helping Whole Children Grow: Non-Sexist Childrearing for Infants and Toddlers." In *Alike and Different: Exploring Our Humanity with Young Children,* edited by Bonnie Neugebauer. Redmond, Wash.: Exchange Press, 1987.

Lieberman, A. F. *The Emotional Life of the Toddler*. New York: Free Press, 1993.

Myers, B. J., H. Carmichael Olson, and K. Kaltenbach. "Cocaine-Exposed Infants: Myths and Misunderstandings." *Zero to Three* 13(1), June 1992, pp. 1–5.

Phillips, C. B., and R. M. Cooper. "Cultural Dimensions of Feeding Relationships." *Zero to Three* 12(5), June 1992, pp. 10–13.

Reynolds, E. *Guiding Young Children: A Child-Centered Approach*. Mountain View, Calif.: Mayfield, 1990.

Samuels, M., and N. Samuels. *Seeing with the Mind's Eye*. New York: Random House, 1975.

Samuels, M., and N. Samuels. *The Well Baby Book*. New York: Summit Books, 1979.

Thoman, E. B., and S. Browder. *Born Dancing: The Relaxed Parents' Guide to Making Babies Smart with Love*. New York: Harper & Row, 1987.

Warrent, J. C., C. Oswald Reed, S. Manker-Seale, and L. A. Comp. "CHILD-SPACE—Creating an Environment of Respect for Infants and Toddlers and Caregivers of Children." *Zero to Three* 7(4), April 1992, pp. 21–28.

Wittmer, D., and S. Petersen. "Social Development and Integration: Facilitating the Prosocial Development of Typical and Exceptional Infants and Toddlers in Group Settings." *Zero to Three* 7(4), April 1992, pp. 14–20.

CHAPTER 14

Bjorklund, G., and C. Burger. "Making Conferences Work for Parents, Teachers, and Children." *Young Children,* January 1987, pp. 26–31.

Brazelton, T. B. *Working and Caring*. Reading, Mass.: Addison-Wesley, 1987.

California State Health and Safety Code, Title 22 Child Care Facility Licensing Subchapter 2. Infant Care Centers. Section 101423.1, Infant Care Discipline.

Galinsky, E. "Parents and Teacher-Caregivers: Sources of Tension, Sources of Support." *Young Children,* March 1988, pp. 4–12.

Gonzalez-Mena, J. "Mrs. Godzilla Takes on the Child Development Experts: Perspectives on Parent Education." *Child Care Information and Exchange,* September 1987, pp. 25–26.

Gonzalez-Mena, J. "Do You Have Cultural Tunnel Vision?" *Child Care Information and Exchange,* July 1991, pp. 29–31.

Gonzalez-Mena, J. *Multicultural Issues in Child Care*. Mountain View, Calif.: Mayfield, 1996.

Gonzalez-Mena, J. "Raising a 'Gifted' Infant." *Educaring* 8(2), Spring 1993, pp. 4–5.

Gordon, A., and K. Williams Browne. *Guiding Young Children in a Diverse Society*. Boston: Allyn and Bacon, 1996.

Gordon, J. "Child Care Professionalism and the Family." *Child Care Information Exchange,* July 1986, pp. 19–23.

Gordon, J. "Separation Anxiety: How to Ask a Family to Leave Your Center." *Child Care Information Exchange,* January 1988, pp. 13–15.

Jones, E. *Teaching Adults: An Active Learning Approach.* Washington, D.C.: National Association for the Education of Young Children, 1986.

Jones, E., ed. *Supporting the Growth of Infants, Toddlers, and Parents.* Pasadena, Calif.: Pacific Oaks, 1990.

Kaplan-Sanoff, M., and K. Fitzgerald Rice. "Working with Addicted Women in Recovery and Their Children: Lessons Learned in Boston City Hospitals Women and Infants Clinic." *Zero to Three* 13(1), August/September 1992, pp. 17–23.

Lane, M., and S. Signer. *Infant/Toddler Caregiving: A Guide to Creating Partnerships with Parents.* Sacramento: California State Department of Education, 1990.

O'Connell, J. C. "Children of Working Mothers: What the Research Tells Us." *Young Children,* January 1983, pp. 63–70.

CONCLUSION

Gunzenhauser, N., and B. Caldwell, eds. *Group Care for Young Children.* Johnson and Johnson Baby Products Company pediatric roundtable series, no. 12, 1986.

Lurie, R., and R. Neugebauer, eds. *Caring for Infants and Toddlers: What Works, What Doesn't,* vol. 2. Redmond, Wash.: Child Care Information Exchange, 1982.

Ruopp, R., J. Travers, F. Glantz, and C. Coelen. *Children at the Center.* Final report of the National Day Care Study, vol. 1. Washington, D.C.: Office of Human Development, Department of Health, Education and Welfare, 1979.

Index